WITHDRAWN

Strategic Communications Management

Making Public Relations Work

Jon White

Laura Mazur

E·I·U

The Economist
Intelligence Unit

ADDISON ___ HING COMPANY

Harlo ___ ırk, California • New York
Don N ___ gapore
Tokyo ___ / • Seoul • Taipei

D0301100

Cover designed by Viva Design Ltd, Henley-on-Thames incorporating photograph by Kerry Lawrence
Text designed by Valerie O'Donnell.
Line diagrams drawn by Margaret Macknelly Design, Tadley.
Typeset by Meridian Phototypesetting Limited, Pangbourne.
Printed and bound by Antony Rowe Ltd, Eastbourne

First printed 1993. Reprinted 1995 and 1996.

ISBN 0-201-59376-9

British Library Cataloguing in Publication Data
A catalogue record for this book is available from the British Library.

Library of Congress Cataloging in Publication Data
White, Jon.
    Strategic communications management : making public relations
work / Jon White, Laura Mazur.
        p.   cm. -- (The EIU series)
    Includes bibliographical references and index.
    ISBN 0-201-59376-9
    1. Public relations--Corporations. 2. Communication in
management. 3. Corporate image. 4. Public relations--Corporations-
-Case studies. I. Mazur, Laura. II. Title. III. Series.
HD59.W45 1995   94-37011
659.2--dc20   CIP

Preface

There is a growing body of evidence that companies fail to make good use of communication as they pursue their strategic objectives. The evidence comes partly from the incidents which occur from time to time that show managers are inadequately prepared to communicate in ways that will protect their strategic interests at times of corporate takeover battles, in environmental or industrial mishaps, or during conflict between management and interest groups such as unions or community activists. It also comes from a number of recent studies, carried out by organizations as diverse as The Conference Board in the USA and Europe, the Royal Society of Arts in the UK and the International Association of Business Communicators, which have shown the more effective use that can and should be made of communication to achieve business and other objectives.

This book, the result of a collaboration between a member of the faculty of the City University Business School, London, who has specialized in public relations and public affairs management, and a writer on the uses of communications for corporate and marketing purposes, draws on these studies and other research to argue that communication can be managed strategically to greater effect.

It sets out to show how public relations in its widest sense is now an essential element in management practice. It differs from other books on these topics by the breadth and depth of its research base. It refers to relevant studies on topics such as environmental management, business culture and ethics and public relations management. It is also based on interviews with practitioners and users dealing with current concerns in public relations and communication management.

Public relations, public affairs and corporate communication specialists are, we believe, essentially consultants, working in companies or other organizations, or in agencies outside those organizations, who should provide advice and services aimed at solving a specific category of management problems or exploiting opportunities. This is not a commonly accepted view, but is one that we believe embodies the future of the practices discussed in this book.

Consultants working in these specialist areas will over the next few years need to develop an easy familiarity with a wide range of research findings – the body of knowledge which will underlie their practice. This book is a signpost to some of the work already completed. Like any good signpost, it is intended to provide a clear pointer to the material it draws upon and the future of public relations.

What this book sets out to do is to examine and analyse in some detail common public relations issues faced by companies. It shows that what have been described as the 'soft' areas of management like communication are being recognized as an important source of competitive edge – as important, indeed, as getting costs down and becoming leaner and fitter. More organizations are realizing that developing a defined and coherent public relations strategy as part of the overall strategic plan is vital to the long-term success of the business.

As the case studies illustrate, the approach to communications has to be consistent across borders. Companies must not only behave well as corporate citizens but be seen to behave well. Their global reputation for how they do business and how their activities affect the environment is under intense scrutiny from the world's media. Their public relations profile can have a significant effect on their ability to sell their products, recruit staff and expand in new markets.

Key features of the book include:

- What exactly public relations is – an area frequently misunderstood and misused.
- What concrete contribution good communication can make to strategic planning and decision-making.
- Different options for managing public relations both internally and externally.
- The role public relations/communication should play alongside other corporate functions like marketing, investor relations and internal communications.
- An analysis of the impact on companies of demands to be both more 'green' and more ethical in their behaviour.

We hope that managers, students of management and current practitioners will find the book of value as a key to this wealth of material which is now available to illuminate what we regard as a specialized area of management consultancy. One of the features of this practice is that it is evolving rapidly thanks to technology, changes in the workplace and the work market. This provides not only interest and excitement, but also some major challenges to all companies. We hope to capture some of the interest and excitement, while examining those challenges that modern management faces.

Structure

The book is based on a number of sources: several management reports researched and written between 1990 and 1992, plus additional material and research gathered by the authors over the last few years. While some of the company executives quoted in case studies may have moved jobs (those that are known to have moved are described as 'former') and corporate structures may have altered, the purpose of this book is not to describe current events but to examine deeper, underlying trends to provide pointers for the future. While a number of the case studies are drawn from European companies, they highlight management themes applicable to any complex market.

The book is organized into four parts. Part One, Public Relations and Communications Management, looks at the main elements in getting to grips with managing public relations, including its contribution to strategic planning and decision-making, options for management, and budgeting, control and evaluation. Part Two, Special Areas of Practice, focuses on the main areas comprising public relations, including media relations, marketing and internal communications, public affairs and crisis management. Part Three, Managing Relationships, considers some of the features of relations with customers and suppliers, investors, the community and pressure groups. Part Four, Issues in the Practice, examines the framework of ethical and legal issues in which companies increasingly have to operate and the future of public relations for both providers and users.

Each chapter concludes with a summary for ease of reference, and a bibliography of pertinent publications is listed at the end.

Jon White
Laura Mazur
London, October 1994

References

Economist Intelligence Unit (1990). *Managing the Environment*. London: Economist Intelligence Unit.

Economist Intelligence Unit (1991). *Building a Pan-European Image*. London: Economist Intelligence Unit.

Economist Intelligence Unit (1991). *The Greening of Global Investment*. London: Economist Intelligence Unit.

Economist Intelligence Unit (1992). *Why You Need Public Relations*. London: Economist Intelligence Unit.

Contents

Executive summary

(1) Public relations has been poorly regarded in the corporate world and outside. Its role has been seen mainly as a presentational one. But the complexities of a changing global business environment fuelled by a growing demand that companies not only operate responsibly but be seen to do so make it crucial for companies to begin to put public relations on a higher platform and treat it in its most literal sense of fostering consistent relationships with their publics.

(2) The function of public relations should be to have a dialogue with all the different corporate audiences. These can include not only the media and shareholders, but employees, the community, governments at various levels and in whichever countries there are operations, customers, suppliers and employees.

(3) The precise nature of public relations' contribution to organizations and their management is a topic of current debate. For some, the practice is seen as being part of marketing and is viewed mainly as a marketing support activity. Others see the practice as involving more than contributing to the success of marketing activities and assign it a key role in strategic management, helping organizations to understand their environments, to establish objectives in relation to groups important to the achievement of strategic goals and communicating that strategic direction to their members – employees – and to external groups.

(4) Each company has to define its public relations strategy in the way best suited to its needs. However, there are several common issues to be faced:

- where public relations sits compared with other functions
- the role public relations plays in supporting marketing
- programme management and evaluation
- choosing and using external consultants
- dealing with the European market.

(5) One of the biggest challenges facing public relations practitioners today is managing programmes across borders consistently and effectively. This is particularly complex when it comes to Europe, not only because of the multicultural aspect, but also because different markets are at different stages of development.

(6) There is both a long-term and a short-term aspect to evaluating the effectiveness of public relations. Long-term evaluations mean measuring over time what can be small but significant shifts, while short-term evaluations can be carried out for specific campaigns. It is still a relatively new area, however. Increased pressure to find more formal ways of measuring effectiveness will probably arise from the Total Quality Movement, with its emphasis on research, setting benchmarks and then measuring achievements and results.

(7) Modern communications demands a rethinking of how to deal with a hungry and amazingly diverse collection of journalists who themselves have different audiences to satisfy and different proprietors with which to deal.

(8) Public relations is making its mark in areas such as marketing, investor relations, internal communications and public affairs.

(9) Crises place organizations experiencing them into the public spotlight and call management competence into question. They impose a need for companies to communicate quickly, accurately and skilfully with a number of important groups, such as employees, shareholders and the media.

(10) Environmental concern is the latest in a wave of social issues that have swept across industry: civil rights, equal opportunities for women, armaments, nuclear power have all been leading issues in their time. Environmental pressures take social concerns to a new height. Single issues are no longer enough. A reorientation of the purpose of business seems inevitable – not just the targeting of individual companies over single issues, but a reappraisal of industrial processes, undermining some of the time-honoured systems.

PART ONE

Public relations and communications management

1

Public relations management

The importance of public relations

Public relations has been poorly regarded in the corporate world and outside. Despite substantial and increasing expenditure on public relations, the practice is often misunderstood and misused. Its role has been seen mainly as a presentational one. But the complexities of a changing global business environment fuelled by a growing demand that companies not only operate responsibly but be seen to do so make it crucial for companies to begin to put public relations on a higher platform and treat it in its most literal sense of fostering consistent relationships with their publics.

It also makes good business sense: competitive leadership in an age of declining product differentiation is gained not only from quality of performance in terms of products and overall behaviour, but also from the perception of the company's different audiences that it is indeed so. After all, companies no longer have to justify their actions only to shareholders, but to employees, customers, the general public and governments. They face a growing demand to have consistently high standards wherever they operate, particularly in environmental matters, and to behave generally as good corporate citizens, before being forced to do so by more stringent regulations.

Persuading governments where they operate that they are indeed acting responsibly means using public relations to build up effective links, particularly where governments themselves are embracing its use.

What makes using public relations thoughtfully to achieve overall consistency an area fraught with potential pitfalls is the sheer scale of the task: the globalization of communications means that any deviation from proclaimed values will be found out by a media that is both more international and increasingly interested in how companies act.

Public relations, carried out properly, is not about presentation, image and reputation alone. Energy spent contriving to present an upbeat image rarely works backward into corporate reality. Instead, the opposite seems to be true: reality seeps out into image. Unpalatable truths can be hidden or smothered for a time, but not for very long; reality has a nasty habit of popping up in unexpected and unprotected places.

The function of public relations should be to have a dialogue with all the different corporate audiences. These can include not only the media and shareholders, but also employees, the community, governments at various levels and in whichever countries there are operations, customers, suppliers and employees.

It has, in some ways, been a practice ahead of its time. Only now, in studies such as the Royal Society of Arts 'Tomorrow's Company' study currently examining questions regarding the management of the company of the future, is it coming to be recognized that sustained competitive performance will only come from inclusion of, and communication with, important stakeholder groups. In a number of cultures, including that of the UK, there is resistance to the idea of inclusion, for example of employees, in decisions which affect their future well-being. In such cultures, it will be less easy to practise public relations as dialogue. Nevertheless, there is evidence that practising public relations in this way is associated with superior business performance.

Strategic management of communications

New levels of expertise are increasingly required to manage all external and internal communications. Factors driving this demand include:

(1) a business environment that is not only becoming fiercely competitive but is also one in which national boundaries are fast disappearing;

(2) a need to streamline organizations not just to reduce costs but also to make the carrying out of strategic objectives both more consistent and more effective internationally;

(3) technological advances which make communications on a global scale virtually transparent.

This is strikingly evident in Europe, where the slow but inevitable progress towards a single market provides exciting if daunting new opportunities for corporate growth, economies of scale, improved productivity, greater profitability, professional mobility, reduced price variability and wider consumer choice.

The trend towards a more thoughtful approach to communications is already well advanced in the USA. According to a survey[1] of top US companies carried out by The Conference Board in 1993, a growing number of senior managers view communication as strategic, and a strategy that can confer competitive advantage. Recent challenges for senior communications personnel highlight this changing attitude:

(1) *Organizational change*: restructuring, streamlining, refocusing, rehabilitating, positioning new management, globalizing.
(2) *Legislative and regulatory concerns*: particularly with regard to creating a strong environmental focus.
(3) *Financial pitfalls*: proxy battles, Chapter 11 problems, sending the message that the company can deliver on financial goals.
(4) *Departmental priorities*: managing internal expectations, establishing credibility with operating units, making the department's culture more proactive and strategic.

These views are backed up by a survey[2] of senior public relations executives in large US and European corporations carried out in 1993 by public relations group Fleishman-Hillard. Its main conclusion was that the public relations function will undergo significant change by the year 2000. Just over 45% believed that public relations will become:

- strategic
- international in scope
- involved in investor/government/media relations
- involved with other operating groups within the company.

Both American and European companies agree that the four following issues will have a major impact on their companies throughout the decade: global competition, technological innovation, environmental concerns and regulatory matters. The Americans, not surprisingly, listed health-care costs in their top five, compared with their European counterparts who identified corporate expansion as a major issue.

Table 1.1 shows the top 10 areas of concern mentioned by the survey respondents.

Table 1.1   The top 10 areas of concern.

Rank	USA (80 respondents)	Europe (113 respondents)
1	Global competition: 74%	Technological innovation 62%
2	Environmental issues: 68%	Environmental issues: 58%
3	Health-care costs: 68%	Global competition: 58%
4	Technical innovation: 55%	Regulatory issues: 49%
5	Regulatory issues: 48%	Corporate expansion: 30%
6	Retirement benefit costs: 28%	Downsizing/layoffs: 23%
7	Labour relations: 16%	Executive compensation: 18%
8	Product liability costs: 15%	Labour relations: 17%
9	Corporate expansion: 15%	Product liability: 16%
10	Women in management: 13%	Health-care costs: 12%

Taking a more ethical stance

Public relations should be an approach more than a technique; a framework that ensures consistency and maintains transparency, not a means to hide uncomfortable facts. This is not to say that demonstrating 'ethical' behaviour always equals commercial success. But if the trends in the USA are indicative, it will become an important element for survival.

A recent four-nation poll reported in *The Guardian* newspaper[3] found that in the USA morality has emerged on to the public agenda as a serious social concern. The USA already has a thriving watchdog industry, with report cards on company behaviour produced regularly in areas such as disclosure of information, equal opportunities, environmental behaviour, community involvement and political affiliation. This is slowly beginning to have an impact on how people view products and services. And although there is less of a tradition in Europe for corporate 'openness', internationalization of business will call for consistency of performance on a global scale (see Chapters 9 and 12).

Working within a closely monitored ethical framework both internally and with all outside external relations will thus make good business sense. Some of it will be forced on companies by increasingly stringent legislation spanning areas from treatment of the workforce through to advertising and packaging. But at detergents to chemicals group Henkel,

Box 1.1 Fleishman-Hillard

In its survey of European and US companies, public relations consultancy Fleishman-Hillard found that companies consider there is a great deal of room for improvement in communicating with what they regard as priority audiences for communication. The first table shows just who they think their main audiences are; the second highlights how effective the respondent companies actually rate themselves in communicating with these groups.

Priority audiences for top management

% Top priority

Rank	US (80 respondents)	Europe (113 respondents)
1	Shareholders: 53%	Shareholders: 48%
2.	Securities analysts: 51%	Employees: 35%
3	Employees: 49%	Securities analysts: 29%
4	Government officials/ agencies: 23%	Business media: 21%
5	Business media: 18%	Government officials/ agencies: 19%
6	Vendors/suppliers: 11%	Vendors/suppliers: 11%
7	General media: 6%	General media: 7%
8	General public: 6%	General public: 6%
9	Activist groups: 3%	Activist groups: 0%

Effectiveness of communication efforts with key audiences

% Very effective

Rank	US (80 respondents)	Europe (113 respondents)
1	Shareholders: 43%	Shareholders: 35%
2	Securities analysts: 41%	Securities analysts: 30%
3	Employees: 30%	Business media: 24%
4	Business media: 29%	Employees: 15%
5	Government officials/ agencies: 20%	Government officials/ agencies: 12%
6	Vendors/suppliers: 16%	Vendors/suppliers: 12%
7	General media: 10%	General media: 6%
8	General public: 6%	General public: 6%
9	Activist groups: 0%	Activist groups: 1%

director of corporate communications Werner Baier argued that: 'You should always change attitudes before you are forced to do so from outside.'

But he avoided the word 'ethics' itself:

'I think it is completely necessary to have values but I prefer not to talk about ethics but about our responsibilities. If you talk about ethics some people mentally shy away because they think – look, what we have to do is business, we have to make good products, be good sales people so let's not talk about ethics. They are willing to share in showing responsibility. So I don't use the word ethics in order to avoid some hurdles in their mentality. I show that it is common sense.'

And it has to be driven from the top. As Sir David Plastow, former chairman of Vickers, argued, consistency of communications, driven by the person at the very top of the company, is crucial. He lamented the fact that this is so little recognized:

'The worst thing about public relations is the lack of commitment by very senior people in understanding it and being objective about it. They think it is something you can just turn on and off again. The underlying requirement is for consistency and direction and to regard it as just as important in corporate terms as finance and human resources. You have to be honest, for goodness sake. Even in the minds of big industrialists you turn on public affairs when you want to put a shine on the job. That is very dangerous and surprisingly prevalent.'

A 1991 report by consultancy Dragon International examining whether consumers really do care about corporate reputation underlined the growing interest in corporate behaviour on a broad scale. Compiled from data in both the UK and overseas, its main component was a qualitative research study of mass market consumers commissioned by Dragon and undertaken by Diagnostics Social and Market research.

Among its findings were:

(1) While consumers do not expect companies to solve the world's problems, they react favourably to companies which do act positively. Interestingly, they do not believe companies should be altruistic, understanding that they are driven by commercial motives. And they are suspicious of companies which profess to be acting for non-commercial reasons.

(2) Consumers increasingly use a diverse range of factors to judge companies. Product quality, safety and innovation are still very important, as can be the company's nationality or the fact that it is a major employer. But, says the survey, these factors are increasingly being taken as given, and consumers are beginning to value companies according to other attributes like environmental behaviour, community involvement or how they treat their employees.

(3)   Consumers are getting more interested in business, fuelled by enhanced coverage of companies in the shape of privatizations, contested takeover and business personalities.

(4)   Companies which understand and embrace these findings and sharpen their reputation in areas like the environment, employee welfare, fair trading, community involvement and ethical marketing could see competitive benefits. As the survey notes, although these benefits may be incremental, in an increasingly competitive market improvement at the margin can be critical.

While issues such as the treatment of employees, dealings with local communities and the stance on equal opportunities are all crucial components of the corporate reputation, it is perhaps a company's environmental behaviour that can generate large amounts of concern and attention. The image–reality gap can play havoc with a company's reputation. The better companies are realizing that ecological issues will affect everything they do over the next decade, from the products themselves to the processes that make them. And not only do they have to get themselves in environmental shape, they also have to be seen to do so. That demands an understanding of the growing list of environmental regulations and legislation coming out of organizations such as the European Commission, as well as building bridges with increasingly high-profile pressure groups. It also means companies should monitor carefully the life cycles of products from 'cradle to grave' to gauge their environmental efficiency, as well as developing consistent and coherent positionings that reflect environmental realities, not false hopes or promises.

Case 1.1   Henkel, 1992

German detergents to chemicals group Henkel is one of the most international of German companies. Of its 42,000 employees, half work outside Germany in the 60 countries where the company is located. Roughly three-quarters of its sales originate from outside its home base. Henkel has to communicate to its publics, on an international basis, that it is not only an environmentally aware company, but also one that has changed dramatically in the last decade. Although 120 years old, in the last 10 years it has acquired more than 40 companies and sold about 20. That has meant not only bringing the corporate identity in line with the reality, but also trying to deal with being a multicultural group, making

continues

continued

all the different parts understand the importance of consistency of corporate values.

The role communications played, both internally and externally, was crucial. In the communications department at the Dusseldorf head-quarters, for instance, there was a section that dealt with Henkel's 12,000 visitors a year, among whom number consumer associations, students and ecological groups. That process began when Henkel first started to invite housewives to its factories to talk about things like its products' performances. It had since become both a wider and more focused programme. As Werner Baier, Henkel's director of corporate communications, said, 'It is far better to communicate and prove what we do. In this way we can lead a group around and actually show them.'

Henkel's sales came roughly half from consumer products such as detergents and half from chemicals. While Henkel had not moved into 'green' products, judging it too small a niche, what it had done was to establish an international ecological management team: 'We are not talking about a green range, but how can we in all product groups improve and meet ecological needs and issues,' said Baier.

German companies in particular have faced an onslaught of rules and regulations and Baier had some reservations about the pace at which they were being made:

> 'Sometimes our politicians can be too opportunistic. So if public opinion – or what is thought to be public opinion – says something about an issue, they tend to create laws and regulations which are sometimes not the best because they have come too fast and without evaluation of the conse-quences. So you get laws which absorb a lot of energy in the company. That doesn't mean we want to put the brakes on. We want to accelerate the process but you need to talk seriously about what will happen if you push button 1, 2 or 3.'

Baier's role in this, as in all the major corporate concerns, was pivotal. He reported directly to the chief executive.

> 'It doesn't make sense to report to anyone but the chief executive officer. I am working for all parts of the group and that means reporting to someone with more limited responsi-bility would mean I would not be seen as competent to speak for the whole company. The other reason is information. The fastest and best way for me to get all the information is to sit in the middle of all the processes.'

Baier's position was at the third level, following the chairman at the top and the management board at level two. The third level also included heads of departments such as finance and research.

Baier would get deeply involved in very basic areas such as new product development. For example, he was part of a team set up with

continues

continued

the senior marketing directors of Henkel in Western Europe to investigate the future strategy for the detergents business in the light of environmental trends. It would discuss everything from production to raw materials to packaging. Baier commented:

'Why am I there? In this company it is clear that the communications person has the right to contribute and take part in these issues because it is far better to be involved in defining the steps to take than to hear about them afterwards and be asked to communicate them. This is one of the most important differences between here and what I have seen in other companies.'

That pivotal role did not, however, mean that Baier would have a high profile as a Henkel spokesman. The company philosophy was that the managers who ran the different parts of the company should answer for their operations: 'In my opinion it is a matter of credibility to have the people in charge engage in the discussion, whether internal or external. My role is to help them avoid mistakes, help them to be well-perceived. But they have to understand that part of their skills as managers means being able to communicate.' To this end, Baier contributed to the personnel department's development programmes to help hone leadership skills among Henkel managers.

Henkel's international spread by no means allowed Henkel to pay lip service to the tough German environmental rules abroad while obeying them at home. Being seen as a good environmental citizen meant that its approach had to be the same in any country where it operated, from India to the USA. Otherwise, as Baier explained, its hypocrisy would be soon found out: 'Environmental groups tap into us worldwide. We can't let them discover double standards.'

While the public relations people throughout the subsidiaries were on a dotted line to Baier, he admitted he had to be very diplomatic in dealing with the more recently acquired companies which had strongly defined cultures of their own. With them Baier operated on what he called 'a very long line. We try and convince them to share our values in areas like ecological issues, social responsibility and so on by openly communicating what and how we are doing.'

What is public relations?

The first step towards establishing effective communications management is to define terms. Public relations, or PR, can be used as a term of abuse, implying that a gloss is being put on events. In many ways that is the fault of both users and practitioners, since both can encourage that attitude.

But public relations in its true sense is a fundamental part of managing almost any organization. The problem is its scope. Public relations is an umbrella term which can cover a wide range of areas, including:

- corporate communications
- issues management
- product publicity
- investor relations
- financial communications
- lobbying
- public affairs
- media relations
- community affairs
- crisis management
- events management
- sponsorship
- a range of services which feed into all these.

Apart from its sheer breadth, an additional complicating factor is that the very nature of communications is changing. The once clear-cut lines dividing the different slices of the marketing cake, for example, have blurred, as more companies push towards centralized and integrated communications, strategically orchestrated and coordinated from within. Thus there are few neat charts or tables as there are with so many other areas. If, for instance, an advertising campaign receives a lot of publicity, is that a measurable part of public relations or not? What about sponsorship?

Moreover, the titles used to denote those involved in public relations have proliferated to a confusing degree: director of corporate affairs, publicity director, corporate communications manager, public affairs counsellor, press officer – the list goes on (see Chapter 3).

The true goal of public relations, or strategic communications, or whatever it is called, is to influence the behaviour of groups of people in relation to each other. Influence should be exerted through dialogue – not monologue – with all the different corporate audiences, with public relations becoming a respected function in its own right, acting as a strategic resource and helping to implement corporate strategy.

Box 1.2 Background of public relations

The history of public relations as a recognized area of business is said to have its origins in the USA at the turn of the century. One of the people credited as a founder of public relations is Edward Bernays. Interviewed just before his 100th birthday in 1991, he had a century's-eye view of it. And that view was as pronounced as ever:

> 'It is about how does one fit, adjust, and relate an actuality, an idea, an object, a corporation, a country, a religion with the public upon which it is dependent. Every institution and certainly every human being, if he isn't living in a jungle, are dependent on other people.'

When Bernays wrote what is considered the first book on public relations back in 1923, he used the term public *opinion* rather than *relations* because Walter Lippman, a respected American commentator, had produced a well-received book on the forces shaping public opinion. Nevertheless, for Bernays, that was too abstract:

> 'He never discussed it in terms of how to deal with public opinion. So I said my book will be about crystallizing public opinion – how to go about it. The book was both accepted and rejected in the sense that a number of people saw it as a new idea that would be useful to the world and others saw it as a euphemism for press agentry.'

He had also begun to recognize the growing force of public opinion, and the fact that organizations were becoming increasingly dependent on public reaction and support:

> 'What I learned from reading psychology when it came in the late 1920s/early 1930s was that the proverb – actions speak louder than words – was so true. Before you ever use words you have to find out what people respond to. I found out that there are only four ways of affecting people. One is authority. The second is reason. The third is persuasion and the fourth is tradition.'

It is perhaps not surprising that psychology played a major role in Bernays' thinking in the early 1920s: his mother was Sigmund Freud's sister and his father's sister was Freud's wife. Over the years Bernays had worked with corporations, governments (including a number of world leaders, although he refused to work with less savoury leaders like Hitler and Franco), celebrities (he was Enrico Caruso's publicity manager) and numerous other institutions, as well as spending a lot of time teaching. Throughout his long career he had put great emphasis on the word 'social' when he talked about public relations: 'Public relations is a vocation in which the individual practitioner advises clients on the

continues

continued

social attitudes and actions to take to win the support of the public upon whom the viability of the client or employer depends.' But it cannot be classified as a profession: 'If it were a profession, I would say that the word social might not have to be used because a profession kicks out people who are anti-social.'

According to Bernays, 'By definition a profession is a vocation which has the following qualifications: number one, it demands that the individual who calls himself a professional has graduated from a university in that field, number two, has passed an exam from the State, number three, has taken a "Hippocratic Oath" as to behaviour and ethics and finally, has agreed to give up using the name of the profession if he is kicked out. But I can be a dope or a crook and still call myself a counsellor on public relations.'

Bernays believed it was in the late 1960s and early 1970s that 'PR' began to attract an increasingly negative image, one with which it was still, on the whole, saddled, although deep inroads had been made by the growing prestige of senior in-house communications employees and their counterparts in agencies. He was still active in trying to put public relations on a more formal footing by getting practitioners licensed and registered by each state. But so far his efforts had failed; he attributed that failure to both ignorance and fear among practitioners of any legislation that would interfere with freedom of speech.

International challenges for public relations and communication management: the example of Europe

Europe presents a particularly difficult challenge in terms of public relations. It also illustrates the difficulties of establishing a coherent communications policy across borders. If issues travel in Europe, so does news and so does opinion. It is unrealistic to assume that a Swedish company's plant closure in France's Haute Savoie will not be reported in the Italian as well as the Swedish media, and that a product withdrawal in the UK will not be picked up in France, where the same product is on the market. Journalists know and read their counterparts in other European countries. Editors have access to information from the USA and Japan, as well as from other countries in Europe.

Decision-makers do not confine their reading to their national press. Regular news summaries are prepared from all over the world for government ministers, regulatory officials, bankers and corporate executives in every European country. If a Brussels-based company executive criticized European customs and living conditions in an interview with a large circulation New York daily, his comments would reach competitors and potential customers in Europe the same day.

In the European financial sector, analysts began in the mid-1980s to look at companies in terms of their ability to compete successfully in the single market. And banks have been taking an active part in cross-border mergers that will accelerate the trend. Financial information is provided more and more on a pan-European basis by companies of non-European parentage, and a growing number of US-based companies are breaking down their European earnings, by line of business, for the benefit of analysts and shareholders on both sides of the Atlantic.

As for Eastern Europe, consultation and advice cross borders constantly from Western Europe. If a company's products have a reputation for quality in the European Union (EU), that reputation carries over to markets and consumers in Eastern Europe. An issue alive in Western Europe will not die in Eastern Europe. If low-fat food products and environmentally friendly washing powders sell well in Western Europe, they will sell well in Eastern Europe too.

Developments in Eastern Europe dramatically support the contention that information and ideas cross borders. And as Larry Snoddon, president of Burson-Marsteller Europe, told a Conference Board seminar on 'Communications Strategies for a United Europe', in 1990, ideas drive business as never before. 'More than finance or natural resources, communications are the key enabler of business strategy today,' Snoddon insisted.

If this is true, then communications in Europe must be designed to implement business strategies for Europe, and this means that both strategies and communications will have to be multicultural. It also means that they cannot be imposed from a central point (for example corporate headquarters) and will have to be carefully planned, with a calculated mix of centralization and decentralization.

At another conference in London in November 1993, 'Communications for a Changing Europe', *Time Magazine* presented the results of its survey[4] into the images of companies across Europe. It listed 38 reasons why having a positive corporate image across Europe can work for the organization:

Image factors:
(1)   increase familiarity which boosts favourability;
(2)   make your corporate reputation work harder for you;
(3)   challenge misconceptions;
(4)   express what your company is uniquely equipped to do best;
(5)   create agreement with corporate positions in controversies;

(6) develop association with positive traits such as high quality products, innovativeness, honesty, competent management;
(7) position the company as aggressive and forward looking;
(8) demonstrate leadership of new product development and research;
(9) provide a human face to large corporations;
(10) unify various divisions under one image;
(11) announce a name change or corporate repositioning.

Selling points:
(12) provide the edge when selling similar products;
(13) sell across a family of products;
(14) open doors for salespeople;
(15) build customer trust;
(16) establish reliability of service;
(17) generate awareness that the company is responsive to consumers' and customers' needs;
(18) help keep customers sold, reinforce purchase decision.

Business advantages:
(19) gain recognition by suppliers as a preferred customer;
(20) encourage distributors, dealers and agents to handle your business;
(21) enhance joint ventures through broader exposure – create more successful partnerships;
(22) ease site expansion into new areas.

Financial benefits:
(23) broaden company's base in financial markets, gain access to new capital sources;
(24) influence company's share value;
(25) expand market for company's stock;
(26) expedite financial transactions through more familiarity with the company;
(27) sell financial security worldwide;
(28) bring out the long-term investment value of your company.

Broader influences:
(29) improve government relations, build political muscle;
(30) reach non-traditional audiences such as governments and professionals with policy issues;
(31) explain company's goals clearly for public understanding;
(32) counteract public hostility because of ignorance or misinformation;
(33) balance inadequate access to the media;
(34) fill the need for explanation for complex issues;
(35) establish company concern with the environment;
(36) educate the company's position with social issues;

(37) explain necessary restructuring which may appear abrupt and/or senseless in one country;

(38) prepare for crises.

Box 1.3   Siegel & Gale

The challenge of developing what US-based identity consultants Siegel & Gale call 'corporate voice' – an organization's distinct personality and culture – has become a daunting challenge for what Adrian Day, a senior consultant at Siegel & Gale's UK arm, described as today's sprawling mega-corporations. He noted: 'The larger and more decentralized the company, the more difficult it is to instil a distinctive voice across the interdepartmental, international and interpersonal boundaries.'

However, as Day told a conference in London 'Communications for a Changing Europe', in November 1993, there are a number of companies that have had the strategic vision to develop a clear and penetrating corporate voice, which both drives and reinforces their position, including Apple Computers, Braun Electronics, Virgin and The Body Shop.

In 1992 the consultancy commissioned market researchers, Mori, to conduct a research study to see if those companies whom it had identified as having a clearly defined voice really did have a more distinctive, compelling personality. Among the findings were the following:

- Even though BA spent around £7.5 million on advertising compared with the fraction of that spent by Virgin, 45% of the respondents felt that Virgin had a distinctive personality compared with only 26% for BA.
- The Body Shop has in the past spent virtually nothing on advertising compared with its main competitor, Boots, which spends many millions annually. Yet 38% of those surveyed felt The Body Shop had a more distinctive voice against 24% for Boots. And just over 23% believed they had heard of The Body Shop through advertising.

According to Day, the survey confirmed that communications on its own cannot create a distinctive character – it has to be based on what makes the company unique in the marketplace. It also showed that companies that have successfully developed a distinctive corporate voice had recognized that 'paid-for' communications are not always the most effective message conduits.

The central role of public relations

Public relations is thus an important part of the overall management task, that will make its contribution to strategy development and implementation, and to promotion and protection of organizational interests in the important relationships discussed in this chapter. Ideally, it should be based on dialogue, on an exchange of information regarding interests, so that interests can be clarified and reconciled. Relationships exist across national borders, and – even in one country – are now influenced by international developments. The task of managing public relations activities is itself complex, and the remainder of this book will be taken up with an exploration of how the practice may be managed, with special areas and with issues in the practice. The next chapter looks in more detail at how public relations makes its contribution to strategic planning and management decision-making.

Summary

(1) The role of public relations has usually been seen mainly as a presentational one. But the complexities of a changing global business environment fuelled by a growing demand that companies must not only operate responsibly but also be seen to do so make it crucial for companies to begin to put public relations on a higher platform and treat it in its most literal sense of fostering consistent relationships with their publics.

(2) It also makes good business sense: competitive leadership in an age of declining product differentiation is gained not only from quality of performance in terms of products and overall behaviour, but also from the perception of the company's different audiences that it is indeed so.

(3) Public relations, carried out properly, is not about presentation, image and reputation alone. Energy spent contriving to present an upbeat image rarely works backward into corporate reality.

(4) The function of public relations should be to have a dialogue with all the different corporate audiences. These can include not only the

media and shareholders, but also employees, the community, governments at various levels and in whichever countries there are operations, customers, suppliers and employees.

(5) New levels of expertise are increasingly required to manage all external and internal communications. Factors driving this demand include:

- a business environment that is not only becoming fiercely competitive but is also one in which national boundaries are fast disappearing;
- a need to streamline organizations not just to reduce costs but also to make the carrying out of strategic objectives both more consistent and more effective internationally;
- technological advances which make communications on a global scale virtually transparent.

(6) This is strikingly evident in Europe, where the slow but inevitable progress towards a single market provides exciting if daunting new opportunities for corporate growth, economies of scale, improved productivity, greater profitability, professional mobility, reduced price variability and wider consumer choice.

(7) Public relations should be an approach more than a technique; a framework that ensures consistency and maintains transparency, not a means to hide uncomfortable facts.

(8) While issues such as the treatment of employees, dealings with local communities and the stance on equal opportunities are all crucial components of the corporate reputation, it is perhaps a company's environmental behaviour that can generate large amounts of concern and attention.

(9) The first step towards establishing effective communications management is to define terms. Public relations is an umbrella term which can cover a wide range of areas, including corporate communications, issues management, product publicity, investor relations, financial communications, lobbying, public affairs, media relations, community affairs, crisis management, events management, sponsorship and a range of services which feed into all these.

(10) Europe presents a particularly difficult challenge in terms of public relations. It also illustrates the difficulties of establishing a coherent communications policy across borders. Communications in Europe must be designed to implement business strategies for Europe, and this means that both strategies and communications will have to be multicultural.

Notes

(1) *Managing Corporate Communications in a Competitive Climate*. New York: The Conference Board, 1993.
(2) *Public Relations 2000*. London: Fleishman-Hillard, 1993.
(3) *The Guardian*, 2 April 1994.
(4) EuroImages II, *Time Magazine*, London, 1993.

2

Public relations: contribution to strategic planning and management decision-making

Contributing to effectiveness

⌐The precise nature of public relations' contribution to organizations and their management is a topic of current debate. For eminent writers on marketing topics such as the US expert Philip Kotler, the practice is seen as being part of marketing and it is viewed mainly as a marketing support activity. Others see the practice as involving more than contributing to the success of marketing activities and assign it a key role in strategic management, helping organizations to understand their environments, to establish objectives in relation to groups important to the achievement of strategic goals, and communicating that strategic direction to their members – employees – and to external groups.

In 1987 the Research Foundation of the International Association of Business Communicators began a major study of aspects of public relations management, asking the question: What contribution does public relations make to an organization's effectiveness? The study, conducted under the title of Excellence in Public Relations and Communication Management, defined public relations as the management of communication between an organization and its publics. ⌐The study set out to examine how and why communication makes companies more effective, how the public relations/communications function should be managed to produce excellent communications, and just what impact that will have on the bottom line.⌐

As Vicki Staveacre, International Association of Business Communications (IABC) UK president-elect, told a conference in London, 'Communications for a Changing Europe', in November 1993, the study has helped identify the key elements of excellent communication:

(1) Excellent communication can make an organization more successful. To do this, it must be developed and managed strategically, and must support the strategic objectives.
(2) It nurtures relationships with key publics, both internal and external publics and stakeholders who provide the greatest threats to and opportunities for the company.
(3) It makes a direct contribution to the bottom line by preventing the costs of conflict with key publics in terms of strikes, litigation and boycotts.
(4) It can also help the company make money by enhancing relationships with customers, shareholders and regulators.

According to Staveacre,

'Excellent communication relies on two-way dialogue between the organization and its publics. It is no longer enough for companies to use one-way communication to inform or try to persuade people to believe what it wants them to believe. Key publics must be able to communicate with the organization and be heard. So excellent communication requires research to take into account the interests and views of all internal and external audiences, and seek to create understanding and dialogue.'

To examine what is actually happening, the study undertook an in-depth survey of communication practices in more than 300 companies in the USA, UK and Canada. Just over 200 chief executive officers (CEOs), 280 heads of public relations, and about 3200 employees were surveyed to establish how communication was managed and its perceived value to the company.

The survey found that CEOs indeed valued communication highly, estimating that it gives a 184% return on investment: for every dollar spent, they felt they received back almost two. However, the heads of communications themselves underestimated the value and rate of return which their chief executives would attribute to communication. It also discovered that the top executive and the 'dominant coalition' understood the strategic role of communication, and wanted to involve the communications function in strategic decision-making for the organization.

However, as Staveacre pointed out, it appears that the greatest barrier in making this happen is the knowledge level, or at least what senior management perceive to be the knowledge level, of the top communicator. She commented:

'The study showed that while most departments were capable of one-way communication, they had little experience in more sophisticated two-way models of communication which took into account the interests and views of all internal and external audiences; they tended to practice press agentry – the dissemination of favourable information about the organization because they mistakenly believed it was what CEOs want and, even more disturbingly, because it is what they know how to do.'

She added that too many senior public relations practitioners still perceived themselves to be technicians or communicators concentrating on the technical, rather than the policy aspects of the function.

The study has thus discovered that the key characteristics of excellence in public relations and communications management are:

(1) that these practices are strategic, not historical; excellent communication programmes are created for strategic purposes. They are not just an evolution of what has been done in the past, and they are aimed at groups which are important to the organization in strategic terms;

(2) they are concerned with impact, not process, and aim to influence audience attitudes, opinions or behaviours rather than simply to put processes into motion such as news release production;

(3) excellent public relations uses both formal and informal research to understand its audiences and monitor effectiveness.

Case 2.1   *Cargill, 1992*

Cargill is large, global and involved in activities that lie at the very heart of daily life. It is a commodity trader, taking everything from concentrated orange juice to steel, grain and rubber and moving it around the world. It takes some of those materials on for further processing, like turning corn into glucose. It also works in the financial markets, including trading futures and risk management. Based in Minnesota, it employs 57,000 people in more than 50 countries, 13,000 in Europe, and has been privately owned throughout its 128-year-old history.

Although Cargill is private, it does not have the luxury of secrecy. Nor does it profess to want it. It has a lot of communicating to do both

continues

continued

internally and externally, particularly as the European market grows more cohesive. In 1991 the company began making moves into more value added areas and considered possible partnerships and alliances with other companies in the food industry.

Joan Wasylik joined Cargill in June 1990 to be its first corporate communications manager, to strengthen the function which already included a director of public affairs. Her brief was to come in and find out what Cargill needed in Europe in terms of activities such as media relations and trade shows as well as from employee communications. 'It has expanded as a result of having been [in Europe] because there is so much that one can work with. There hasn't been a lot that needed to be corrected because there is a lot that needs to be created,' explained Wasylik.

It is not that Cargill was 'uncommunicative' in Europe before, she explained. But, apart from keeping in close contact with various governmental agricultural organizations and staying on top of trade negotiations, the main focus was on dealing with customers, trade shows, corporate literature and speeches. Wasylik's job was to convince managers who might be slightly sceptical about the need for 'public relations' that she could help the bottom line with a highly targeted effort.

The contrast with a public company, of course, is that Cargill did not need to speak to its shareholders. But it did want to address its employees, its customers, governments where it operates, potential partners and the general public, particularly since it was in the sensitive area of agriculture. But Wasylik felt that heightening the media profile had to be done carefully and where it was appropriate:

> 'To go out there and do an interview with a paper when there is nothing we really have to say serves no point if we don't have news to talk about that is of interest to them. There are other things we need to pay attention to. Maybe that is something that is important for public relations to demonstrate: that we are not just here to get you into the press. We are not here to keep you out of the press either. What we are here to see is what you need to accomplish the corporate strategy you have.'

She saw evidence that the managers were beginning to realize that public relations is of value. But, she stressed, public relations has to earn this regard:

> 'You have to demonstrate your value and then others in the company begin to come through your door. You have a couple of case studies that you can stand up, then you can stand in front of senior management and say this is where I think we should go. You have to show you can make a difference to the company's ability to make a profit, and to be seen as a resource by the other managers.'

The strategic contribution of public relations

The IABC study of excellence in public relations practice emphasizes the strategic contribution of the practice. This has to be nurtured, demanded and managed. Strategy is essentially concerned with the long-term direction and scope of any organization.[1] It is arrived at through a process of analysis and decision-making, to which many in the organization will and should contribute. Once developed, it will need to be communicated so that it can be implemented. Public relations has a number of contributions to make to strategy development and implementation, which are overlooked when the practice is seen as mainly concerned with representation or external communication.

Any company exists in the context of number of relationships, with customers, suppliers, competitors and so on. These groups make up the social environment for the company's operations and pursuit of its objectives. Planning and decision-making will be better to the extent that decision-makers are informed with complete and current information about the environment.

Public relations' value in the process of strategy development is that it is a source of intelligence regarding that social environment. This intelligence needs to be fed into the groups or individuals responsible for strategy development. But, while this contribution of public relations has been recognized for some time, it is not always capitalized upon by companies. A study by W.J. Keegan reported on in *The Administrative Science Quarterly* in 1974 of the information sources drawn on by senior management found that 'public relations people are good sources of competitive information because they hear so much. Even if they are not directly involved, they are on the grapevine.'

In technical terms, public relations practitioners 'span' organizational boundaries, carrying information to groups outside and inside the company. In the opposite direction, they bring information in, and this information provides intelligence – but only if it is interpreted and used.

Large organizations generally gather large amounts of information regarding their environments. UK examples would include the large clearing banks, companies involved in providing other kinds of financial services, and telecommunications companies. However, much of this information is not collated in one central collection point, or interpreted sufficiently. Public relations staff, because of their contacts with many sources of information, internal and external, may be in a position to provide these central collation and interpretation functions.

The value of this work may be lost, however, if there are no means for the results to be communicated directly to those involved in developing strategy. There is thus the possibility that the company could be taken by surprise by unforeseen outside developments. Strategy development can be diminished if what is important information is missing.

The contribution that public relations can make to strategy development requires nurturing. This can happen in a number of ways:

(1)   Management must recognize that this is a contribution that public relations can make, by broadening their own conception of public relations beyond communication and representation.

(2)   They must also accept that the contribution that public relations may make is an uncomfortable one which may threaten existing approaches but produce constructive results.

(3)   Practical arrangements need to be made for public relations staff to play their part in strategy development. This means that reporting relationships must be in place for public relations to report findings from contacts. It also means that public relations staff must be given a recognized status in the strategy development process.

Studies of the way in which so-called 'boundary spanning' individuals decide on what they should attend to in the organization's environment have found that they do so on the basis of:

- instructions given to them
- their own skills
- contacts
- their personalities and personal energy.

It is important that, in working with public relations advisers, senior managers are clear about the contribution they expect these advisers to make. If they expect a comprehensive analysis of the external environment from the practitioner's perspective, then this needs to be made explicit. Experienced practitioners will earn their credibility by providing this kind of analysis, whether asked for it or not, but it is more likely to be used, and to be effective, if it has been asked for by senior management.

Managing the process of gathering information from the company's environment and from internal groups will also involve research and a systematic approach to sources of information. Accordingly, a substantial public relations office or programme should have a research component, either as an activity carried out by specialized research staff, or by practitioners themselves, provided they are skilled in and comfortable with the use of research techniques.

There are obvious cost implications of an insistence on research, but the benefits of research include better decision-making, sound programme development and management, and the avoidance of serious mistakes and psychological comfort for decision-makers.

Arrangements also have to be made for the regular provision of this information, in a suitable form, to those having responsibility for the development strategy. A typical report found now in larger organizations, such as the UK's Post Office, provides summaries of media coverage, where these are used to track trends in media coverage and identify issues of concern as these appear in the public media. Media content analysis provides a rich source of intelligence, although this method of research is currently used more often as an attempt to measure the effectiveness of public relations activities rather than as a source of strategic intelligence.

Then there is the communication of strategy. Public relations' contribution to this is often overlooked, not least by writers on strategic management themselves. Writers on strategy – an example is found in the book referred to earlier, in note 1 – stress the importance of communication in transmitting and sharing information about key business values and directions. They are, however, much less explicit about how communication is to be made to happen. The question here is one of responsibility for communication, and public relations staff provide one possible source of expertise in communication which can be used for internal as well as external purposes.

The role of public relations in internal communication will be discussed in more detail in Chapter 8, but its internal role comes from its concern with relationships with important groups, such as employees. Public relations is involved in the flow of information to employees, and this will lead to cooperation with senior management and staff involved in human resource and line management in managing the flow of information about strategic direction to staff. Practically, this may include work in training, briefing techniques, or the development of material to support senior management as they explain strategy throughout the company.

The contribution of public relations to decision-making

In addition to its contribution to strategy development, public relations also aids senior management decision-making – when senior practitioners are in a position within the organization, or in a relationship to the senior management group, which enables them to do this, because of their ability to interpret the environment to those who have to make decisions.

Where those environments generate a variety of problems or uncertainties, staff who are able to interpret and make sense of the surroundings will become influential in decision-making. Some management writers, in fact, maintain that control in organizations has passed to those interpreters. A study by the European Centre for Public Affairs at Templeton College, Oxford, found that in companies that had to survive in difficult environments, such as oil or chemical companies, public affairs has indeed become influential in management decision-making.

Studies of decision-making have shown that some of the most difficult problems faced by management create an uncertainty about how to proceed. It is, in some cases, difficult to even begin to conceptualize the problem, let alone begin to develop a solution. Here the perspective of public relations can help: practitioners are used to complexity, and to trying to interpret social situations. They can make a contribution to management decision-making under conditions of greater uncertainty – if they are allowed to, and if they have the ability to do this.

Practitioner qualifications are dealt with later, but the public relations perspective when fully developed sees the organization 'as though from the outside'. Decision analysts talk of levels of decision-making. At the most senior levels of organizations, decisions need to be supported by information derived from lower levels. Outside and above the company, as with strategic planning there is a need for information about the organization and its operational environment.

What this means is that the public relations practitioner, in order to develop the perspective that will make his or her contribution valuable, must be thoroughly informed about the organization and outside views of it. This is a demanding requirement, one which requires skills in social analysis, as well as realistic knowledge of business operations. This perspective must develop – and be sustained – regardless of whether the practitioner is working internally, in-house, or as an outside consultant.

Where the practitioner is working in-house, there is a possibility that, over time, he or she will become too identified with company values and objectives, and will lose the perspective on which their contribution depends. Some years ago, R. Mason, writing in the *Harvard Business Review*[2] on the role of the public relations director, said that

> 'their usefulness to the corporation hinges on their ability to maintain a degree of detachment from the motives that drive other members of management... the PR director must view corporate policies with a multiple vision to an extent that is never done by any other staff officer... loyalty to the corporation is never an excuse for failure to observe it from every point of view, including the most hostile, actual or potential.'

The Public Relations Society of America's journal[3] picked up on a similar point in 1987. Practitioners must guard against developing an 'internal myopia', where the practitioner can only 'see' within the short-range boundaries of the organization.

Public relations as an aid to clarification of objectives and plans

Where practitioners are able to develop the kind of perspective described, they can make a substantial contribution to strategic planning and decision-making. They can also help senior management groups make sense of the organizational mission, objectives and plans.

At first sight, this seems an extravagant claim to make, and one which takes public relations beyond what many – including practitioners themselves – would regard as its mandate. However, public relations is concerned with the presentation of the organization to important groups. In order for the company to present itself consistently:

- it must be clear about its mission, direction, values and objectives;
- it must be certain that what it says is consistent with what it actually believes or does.

In helping the company to think about what it can say about itself, public relations can help it clarify what it is actually about. Thinking about what can be said helps to make sense of how it works in reality. This can provide a valuable check on the quality of management decisions and actions – if this capability is used for this purpose.

In practice, this aspect of public relations practice is worked through in many discussions between public relations staff and senior management, which produces ideas or statements of purpose which can be edited. The final results of this work are seen in mission statements, company publications, corporate identity programmes, and key phrases which recur in executive speeches. But while these are parts of an organization's presentation of itself, they cannot stand without underlying support. Chief executives who stand on a platform to make a speech claiming that their organization's main assets are its people will find that those words will return to haunt them if, later, the company mistreats its employees during a programme of enforced redundancies, for instance.

Box 2.1   The role of corporate identity

Companies have to close the gap between what they say and the way they behave, according to Philip Mann, a principal at Bamber Forsyth, consultants in identity management. Fierce competition, an explosion of choice, instant communication, and the fact that companies can no longer use quality or technological innovation alone as differentiators mean they need to add new kinds of value to the corporate offer. In particular, the company's personality and identity are becoming an increasingly significant factor in product, service and investment selection. As Mann said:

> 'Perhaps the biggest fundamental change is that companies are beginning to recognize that they are the corporate brand, and that the chief executive is the corporate brand manager. So the same marketing techniques used for products and services need to be brought to bear in the corporation. Corporate communications is thus appearing higher on the corporate agenda than before.'

The problem has been that few chief executives are trained for this role. Mann noted:

> 'One of the bad effects of the 1980s was that it created a decade of senior management who only knew about managing in good times. They didn't really know about managing in bad times. So they make knee-jerk reactions to changing conditions.'

That includes trying to use a new corporate identity as a solution to ambitions or problems or to try and change behaviour throughout the organization. But changing visuals without addressing the fundamental principles of behaviour is pointless: 'You have to address both and make sure that corporate communications are harnessed to get those strands across.'

Getting it right can be a real source of competitive advantage, but only if how the company looks – its image – matches its behaviour – its reputation. Taking the focus away from creating an identity to managing what the company has effectively means a shift away from visual issues to communications issues, demanding the convergence of marketing, design and communications skills both in-house and with outside consultants. Figures 2.1 to 2.3 illustrate how the approach to corporate identity has had to change.

continues

continued

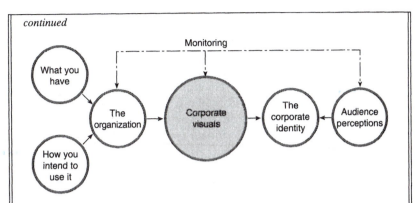

Figure 2.1 How corporate identity has changed: era 1 – 'badging'. (*Source*: Bamber Forsyth)

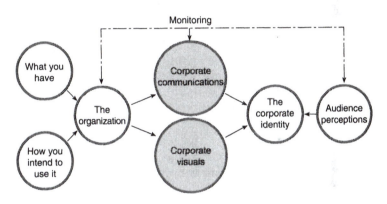

Figure 2.2 How corporate identity has changed: era 2 – visuals plus communication. (*Source*: Bamber Forsyth)

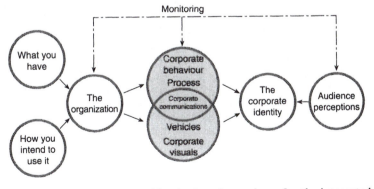

Figure 2.3 How corporate identity has changed: era 3 – the integrated approach. (*Source*: Bamber Forsyth)

Reporting relationships

The International Association of Business Communicators (IABC) study of Excellence in Public Relations and Communication Management mentioned earlier found that effective practitioners are those who are part of the dominant coalition in any organization – the group of people who are able to give direction to the organization. The next chapter looks at the need for senior public relations staff to have a direct reporting relationship to the most senior level of management, and at the place of public relations in the organizational structure.

Studies such as the European Centre for Public Affairs study[4] of public affairs management emphasize the need for senior staff in this area of management to have credibility with senior management. According to Reginald Watts, deputy chairman of Citigate in London, too few public relations people are able to achieve board level status. Headhunters quoted in an article he wrote for *PR Week*[5] suggest that 'most chairmen do not see PR as a suitable business background when they appoint new non-executive directors'. Another headhunter suggested that appointment of a public relations practitioner to a top business post would 'send out the wrong signals'.

Watts sees part of the reason for public relations practitioners' failure to win ready acceptance at senior management level lies with the training and preparation practitioners have. They are, at present, insufficiently prepared for business and management careers, and against the other senior managers competing for board or senior management group positions seem to lack qualifications and stature. More will be said about the training and preparation of practitioners in Chapter 4, in a discussion of the human resources available to public relations practice.

Summary

(1) The precise nature of public relations' contribution to organizations and their management is a topic of current debate. For some, the practice is seen as being part of marketing and is viewed mainly as a marketing support activity. Others see the practice as involving more than contributing to the success of marketing activities and assign it a key role in strategic management, helping organizations to understand their environments, to establish objectives in relation

to groups important to the achievement of strategic goals, and communicating that strategic direction to their members – employees – and to external groups.

(2) A major study by the International Association of Business Communicators has helped identify the key elements of excellent communication:

- Excellent communication can make an organization more successful. To achieve this, it must be developed and managed strategically, and it must support the strategic objectives.
- It nurtures relationships with key publics, both internal and external publics and stakeholders who provide the greatest threats to and opportunities for the company.
- It makes a direct contribution to the bottom line by preventing the costs of conflict with key publics in terms of strikes, litigation and boycotts.
- It can also help the company make money by enhancing relationships with customers, shareholders and regulators.

(3) Public relations has a number of contributions to make to strategy development and implementation, which are overlooked when the practice is seen as mainly concerned with representation or external communication.

(4) Public relations' value in the process of strategy development is that it is a source of intelligence regarding the company's operating environment. This intelligence needs to be fed into the groups or individuals responsible for strategy development. But, while this contribution of public relations has been recognized for some time, it is not always capitalized upon by companies.

(5) The contribution that public relations can make to strategy development requires nurturing. This can happen in a number of ways:

- Management must recognize that this is a contribution that public relations can make, by broadening their own conception of public relations beyond communication and representation.
- They must also accept that the contribution that public relations may make is an uncomfortable one which may threaten existing approaches but produce constructive results.
- Practical arrangements need to be made for public relations staff to play their part in strategy development. This means that reporting relationships must be in place for public relations to report findings from contacts. It also means that public relations staff must be given a recognized status in the strategy development process.

(6)   In addition to its contribution to strategy development, public relations also aids senior management decision-making – when senior practitioners are in a position within the organization, or in a relationship to the senior management group, which enables them to do this, because of their ability to interpret the environment to those who have to make decisions.

(7)   What this means is that the public relations practitioner, in order to develop the perspective that will make his or her contribution valuable, must be thoroughly informed about the organization and outside views of it. This is a demanding requirement, one which requires skills in social analysis, as well as realistic knowledge of business operations.

(8)   Where practitioners are able to develop the kind of perspective described, they can make a substantial contribution to strategic planning and decision-making. They can also help senior management groups make sense of the organizational mission, objectives and plans.

Notes

(1) Faulkner, David and Johnson, Gerry, *The Challenge of Strategic Management.* London: Kogan Page, 1992.
(2) Mason, R., What is a PR director for, anyway?, *Harvard Business Review,* Sept.–Oct., 1974.
(3) Hicks, N. Internal myopia's warning Signs, *Public Relations Journal,* October, 1987.
(4) MacMillan, K. *The Management of European Public Affairs,* European Centre for Public Affairs, Occasional Paper 1, July 1991. Templeton College, Oxford: ECPA.
(5) Watts, Reginald, *PR Week,* 26 May 1994.

3

Options for the management of public relations

Choosing the right route

Public relations is part of the overall task of management. Organizations have relationships with important groups, such as their own employees or external groups such as government or the community whether or not they choose to manage them. But relationships are a resource and should be managed in the same way as other resources are. Matters of concern for management include the possible arrangements that can be made for managing public relations, and what the role of senior management should be in the day-to-day management of the function.

Studies of the choices made by major companies in the USA and the UK indicate that the majority, over 70%, choose to staff an internal public relations department either with a single practitioner or with more staff. In addition, in-house departments will, in the majority of cases, also draw on external help from consultancies and specialist agencies.

Occasionally, companies may decide to manage their public relations activities by handing them all to an outside consultancy. A recent example of this approach is Philips Electronics in the UK, which placed its corporate communications department and all corporate public relations activity with an external consultancy. However, generally there are strong doubts about this approach, which may leave public relations to be managed by a consultancy that, despite good intentions, cannot be fully briefed on company concerns.

Reporting relationships have an important bearing on the effectiveness of public relations practice. Studies from the European Centre for Public Affairs at Templeton College, Oxford, and the International Association of Business Communicators, have shown the importance of a direct reporting relationship between the senior public relations manager and the senior management. The most effective practitioners are those who can become close to management at the chairman and chief executive level.

Each company has to define its public relations strategy in the way best suited to its needs. However, there are several common issues to be faced:

- where public relations sits compared with other functions;
- the role public relations plays in supporting marketing;
- programme management and evaluation;
- choosing and using external consultants;
- dealing with the particularly complex European market.

The role of the senior public relations manager

Public relations as a respected function in its own right is in an embryonic position compared with better-established functions such as marketing, production or finance. That can make the job of the person in charge less clear cut. They can be heads, managers or directors. They can enjoy widespread responsibility and be on an equal footing with their fellow directors, or they can be used simply as messengers. Some can be in charge of the entire corporate communications network, or have responsibility for media relations alone.

In the USA, for example, heads of communications, corporate affairs directors, public relations directors – whatever they are called – have vastly improved skills and play a central role in corporate activities, with some reaching the board. They are being elevated to the same level as the chief financial or legal officers. Europe lags behind in this. But there is a growing band of enlightened companies where best practice predominates.

The qualities these chief communications executives have to possess include an interesting mix of functional, managerial, organizational and negotiating abilities. And as they become more senior and increasingly associate with other senior executives as equals, there is greater emphasis on improving the communications skills of all management.

In the final analysis, of course, the senior communications executive can only be truly effective with the backing of the chairman or chief executive. The head of public relations, or chief communications officer, should have a direct line to the top management, if not a direct reporting relationship.

This is a crucial relationship, and must be close since the role that the head of communications can play cuts across all the major functions. After all, not only do the company heads set the tone for corporate communications, they can spend almost three-quarters of their time on communication/presentation of one sort or another. In public companies chief executives have to be closely involved in dealings with investors, bankers, analysts and the financial press. Relationships with employees, customers, senior government officials and the local community also have to be nurtured.

Chairmen or chairwomen are, above all, the keeper and protector of the corporate reputation. That is why they need the advice and expertise of a professional communications manager.

The terminology is not the same everywhere and every company is different in terms of what it does at the centre and what it does in the subsidiaries. There is no pattern and there could not be, because every company's style is different.

Deciding the role of the senior communications officer thus depends on the size of the company, the nature of its products and its business objectives. In many companies the communications managers increasingly have strong dotted reporting lines to other public relations personnel all over the world. That stems from the need for consistency allied to technological advances in communications: if an event occurs in Germany which will have an impact on the corporate reputation around the world, effective and coordinated action needs to be taken to deal with the ripple effect as the news travels from country to country.

Figure 3.1 shows the structure of communications departments of leading companies in 1992. The staffing levels and the functions that they handled varied widely. This highlights the fact that each company has to define its public relations strategy in the way best geared to its needs. That means resolving:

- determining the relationship of public relations and the other functions;
- the role of public relations in the sensitive areas of investor relations, internal communications, crisis management and maintenance of the corporate image;
- finding ways to evaluate its effectiveness.

Having a public relations function is not new. It has been around in some form or another for a long time. However, in far too many companies it has been done extremely badly. Often that has been a reflection of the lack of concern about communication from the top of the company. Public relations as a function can be compared with where marketing was in corporate thinking 10–15 years ago, that is seen as a 'soft' area which, since it cannot easily be quantified, is largely undervalued. The calibre of in-house people at all levels reflected this and accounted for the fact that the best people tended to gravitate to consultancies.

Corporate Communications Departments 1992

The following list outlines the areas overseen by the central communications departments of a number of companies and their size. Admittedly a rough guide, it nevertheless reflects their diversity, while pointing to some underlying similarities. The staff numbers given after the company name in most cases include secretarial support. Unless indicated, the public relations people in the divisions/subsidiaries report on a dotted line basis to the centre.

(1) **Cable & Wireless**   19 staff
  Director of Public Affairs reports to the Chairman
  - Investor relations and corporate communications – includes government/ community affairs and sponsorship (New York also has investor relations office)
  - Employee communications and publications
  - Public relations – mainly media relations and organizing events
  - Corporate advertising

(2) **Vickers**   7 staff
  Director of Public Affairs reports to the Chairman
  - Media relations manager
  - Public affairs manager – brochures, annual report, budget manager
  - Administrative assistant
  - Publicity assistant
  - A/V manager

(3) **W. H. Smith**   27 staff
  Director Corporate Affairs reports to the Chairman
  - Public relations corporate: City, government relations, corporate advertising
  - Public relations consumer: brand support
  - Community affairs
  - Sponsorship
  - Charitable/educational involvement
  - Investor relations
  - Some internal communications

(4) **Fiat**   200 staff
  Head of External Communications reports to the Chief Executive/Chairman
  - Relations with institutions, including governments, EU, etc. Also industrial relations at a high level
  - Press office, domestic and international
  - Corporate ads and image
  - House publications
  - Rome office – presence in the capital
  - Public relations – mainly protocol
  - Cultural activities

(5) **Reed**   8 staff
  Director Corporate Communications reports to the Chairman
  - Investor relations support for finance director, chairman
  - Media relations
  - Government relations – legislation, lobbying
  - Corporate charitable work
  - Group printing and production
  Subsidiaries have strong public relations functions

(6) **American Airlines in Europe**   5 staff
  Regional Public Relations Manager Europe reporting directly to HQ in Dallas with dotted line responsibility to the Vice-President International Service

- Media relations
- Internal communications
- Public relations for Sabre reservation system

(7) Henkel 42 staff
Director Corporate Communications reports to the Chief Executive Officer
- Visitors' department
- Economics department
- Press relations
- Corporate image advertising
- Publications/videos

A separate department handles investor relations and reports to the director of finance management – it works closely with corporate communications

(8) Taylor Woodrow 12 Staff
Director of Corporate Communications reports to the Chairman
- Handles overall communications strategy, management counselling, communications input to investor relations and public affairs, external relations and research
- Government affairs
- Advertising and marketing services – corporate advertising, corporate identity and design, group publications, annual report, and corporate gifts
- Events and services – sponsorship, corporate entertainment, charity trust, exhibitions, photographic/audio/visual
- Media relations and publications (including some internal communications)

(9) Guinness 13 staff
Director of Public Affairs reports to the Chairman
- Public relations, including events, sponsorship, publications, photography, editorial support and budgets
- Public affairs, including government, Whitehall and Westminster liaison
- EU affairs (Brussels office)
- Press relations

(10) Mercury Communications 29 staff
(Subsidiary of Cable & Wireless)
General Manager Market Communications reports to the Marketing Director
- Press and public relations
- Advertising
- Audio/visual
- Market communications planning
- Sponsorship (including corporate hospitality)
- Events

The Public Relations Manager has dotted line responsibility to the Cable & Wireless Director of Corporate Affairs

(11) Abbey National Building Society plc 20 staff
Corporate Affairs Manager reports to Executive Director (Group Services) with dotted line responsibility to Chief Executive
- Public affairs
- Corporate affairs
- Investor relations
- Events and presentations
- Quality service unit (TQM)
- Customer relations
- Video unit

Figure 3.1 Corporate communications departments, 1992. (*Source*: EIU)

That is slowly changing. In the USA, for example, heads of communications, corporate affairs directors, public relations directors – whatever they are called – have vastly improved skills and play a central role in corporate activities, with some reaching board level. The sorts of issues that communications officers deal with in the USA are indicated by Figure 3.2, which shows trends in organizations and structures in leading US companies, as well as the function of senior communications executives and the activities reporting to them.

Europe lags behind in this. But there is a growing band of enlightened companies where best practice predominates. This role has been developing over the last few years and is breeding a new type of corporate executive, far removed from the yes-man or yes-woman of past years. As Colin Thompson, director-general of the Public Relations Consultants Association, has noted,

> 'The public relations people are most likely to be the first to know what is really going on. Because they have to sow the seeds with groups like the shareholders, staff and so on so they become quite important people. The individual that is employed as a press officer, who is probably very good to have a beer with someone on the local paper – that person is disappearing. Nowadays it is much more professional.'

The qualities these executives have to possess include an interesting mix of functional, managerial, organizational and negotiating abilities. The following comments from senior in-house public relations executives from a number of leading European companies sum up this intriguing role:

- 'We are a combination of ambassador and salesperson all rolled into one.'
- 'You have to prove that you can make a difference to the company's ability to do business and make a profit.'
- 'It is about attitude, about advocacy – everybody has a side of the story to tell and your ability to do that has an impact on the way your company appears.'
- 'We have to tell them when they have no clothes on.'
- 'We are not the conscience but the worriers of the company.'
- 'In our department we make things happen.'
- 'We can be out during the week talking to all the different product lines more frequently than the chairman so we can begin to see a pattern emerge.'
- 'You can hear things across your product lines or across the areas you work in so you can try to put two and two together and get four before anyone else.'
- 'We are in touch because we read all the press.'

- 'We are like the court jester in the king's court.'
- 'You have to have a terribly lively curiosity.'
- 'You have to have a very thick skin.'

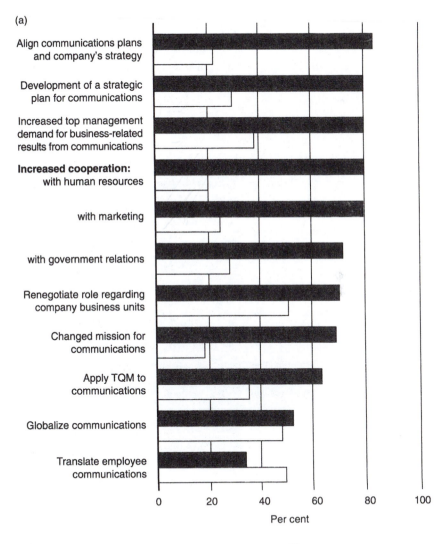

(a)

Align communications plans and company's strategy

Development of a strategic plan for communications

Increased top management demand for business-related results from communications

Increased cooperation:
with human resources

with marketing

with government relations

Renegotiate role regarding company business units

Changed mission for communications

Apply TQM to communications

Globalize communications

Translate employee communications

Per cent

■ Trend relevant to 1989–95 period   □ Projected for 1992–95

(b)

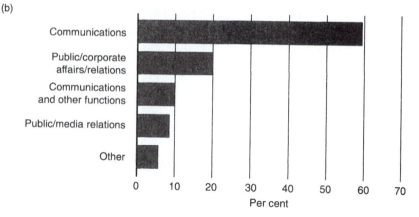

(c)

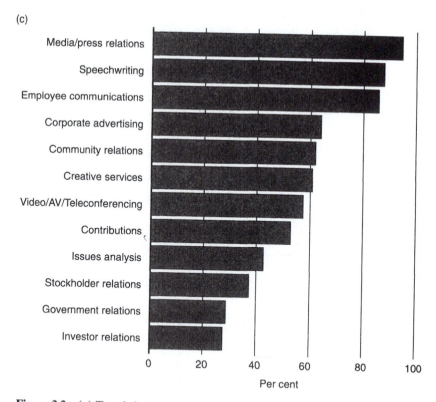

Figure 3.2 (a) Trends in organization and structure (base = 156); (b) Function of senior communications executive; (c) Activities reporting to senior communications executive (base = 157). (*Source*: The Conference Board)

Charles Cook, managing director of Grandfield Rork Collins, described the sort of in-house people he saw headhunters and clients actively seeking:

> 'They are probably in their mid-40s, and are professional communicators who have actually done something else as well. It may have been a spell in line management, it may have been a spell in the financial sector, and a combination of the two is even better. It is probably no longer an ex-journalist, which was, of course, the more traditional background.'

They are also likely to be increasingly well-paid – salaries of up to £100,000 are still rare but becoming less so.

Case 3.1   Guinness, 1992

Guinness is one of the world's most profitable alcoholic drinks companies. A few years ago it was on the brink of the corporate abyss. By 1992 it had successfully pulled itself back from the brink.

The Guinness chairman had three main board directors responsible to him: one in charge of the brewing interest worldwide, one running United Distillers, and the finance and administration director. Chris Davidson, public affairs director, sat right at the heart of the corporate structure. Not only did Davidson have a strong relationship with the chairman, to whom he reported, he also worked very closely with other senior people.

How did public affairs relate to public relations? As Davidson explained:

> 'It is probably semantics, although we would probably describe public *relations* as being a function of marketing, supporting our brands, while the public affairs side is fundamental to the future of the business in that it relates to the strategic direction of the business. Public affairs works closely with the chairman and the board in smoothing out the playing field where we

continues

continued

operate. I am a public relations executive, but we use the differentiation of public affairs because of the way we are structured.'

This structure was important because Guinness was very much a 'brands' company. The publicity done for the brands came under the marketing budgets, while each operating company also had its own public affairs director. There were, however, dotted lines to Davidson so that consistency of voice was assured.

Davidson's department at headquarters reflected the communications concern of a large, international company. He had a manager of public relations, who oversaw areas like events, sponsorship, publications, photography, articles and speeches, plus support work and budgets. Then there was a manager of public affairs, responsible for government liaison in both Whitehall and Westminster. Next came the head of EU affairs to deal with EU issues, an area very important in an era of growing regulation about what drinks companies can – and increasingly cannot – do in terms of promotion, and a manager of press relations. Davidson used a football analogy, with his three 'strikers' in the press, UK and EU government matters providing a service to the group as a whole, although, as he pointed out, 'Most of our concerns are much wider than the UK/Europe. Our area of greatest concern today is probably the Asia/Pacific area because of the opportunities which are available.'

Guinness displayed all the hallmarks of the modern company balancing centralization and decentralization at the same time, where there was a strong connection to the central culture balanced by adherence to the demands of the different marketplaces. The operating companies worked on the same principle: at United Distillers, for example, where there are carefully devised central guidelines for handling the different brands, with local adaptations made for local conditions.

The same applied to everyone who worked in public affairs/relations throughout the group, who felt part of the same function but responded to the demands they faced. There was no formal manual outlining obligatory behaviour: 'It would be difficult to provide a booklet that would describe everything we do because so many issues we face we cannot plan for 12 months in advance. The whims of government mean that the ground rules can change very quickly,' noted Davidson.

The effectiveness of public relations can be very hard to measure. In Davidson's case, it operated through a fairly formal document which covered the issues the board agreed should be dealt with over a year by Davidson's department, apart from unforeseen occurrences, of course. That had become a rolling system, whereby each year Davidson could be measured on how those issues had been handled and whether the

continues

continued

goals set had been reached. New ones could then be agreed for the following year, which became the basis of the department's budget – for example, what sort of work should be done in the sensitive area of alcohol abuse.

In 1987, Davidson pointed out, the research showed that Guinness was the UK's best known company – but not for the right reasons. That began to change in 1987. By 1990 the Guinness reputation was number one in favourability.

A report[1] produced in 1991 by communications consultancy Smythe Dorward Lambert on the rise of powerful in-house corporate communicators underlined the growing importance of these senior corporate communications executives. It argued that there has indeed been a noticeable shift in major companies away from employing the old-fashioned style of 'PR hack' who deals only tactically with the end result of decisions, towards what the report calls 'corporate navigators'. They are probably not on the board, but are nevertheless at the very heart of corporate planning and activity. They are increasingly called on not only to ensure consistency of voice, but also to have a hand in defining just what the message is.

The report noted that these corporate communicators tend to:

- work in rapidly changing organizations;
- have small, tight teams but good budgets;
- have to balance being advisers and facilitators with the need to be implementers;
- focus on internal communications as much as media relations;
- be a key part of the executive team.

It concluded that the major issues confronting this new breed are the need to:

- gain commitment to communications from the top management;
- clarify their tasks in organizations that are devolving responsibilities and fragmenting;
- find ways to measure their effectiveness.

Their jobs can encompass a wide variety of responsibilities:

- managers of their immediate department;
- managers of dotted line relationships with other public relations people throughout the company, including subsidiaries around the world;
- marketing director of the corporate brand;
- public relations practitioners in their own right;
- coordinators of all the intangible elements that make up a company's ethos under direction of the chairman;
- overseeing the hiring of and the relationship with outside consultancies;
- acting as sounding boards;
- making sure internal and external communications are consistent in conjunction with personnel/human resources managers.

Mike Beard, director of corporate communications at the construction to property group Taylor Woodrow, believed that one of the main differences between the communications role and other senior ones in an organization was that

> 'everyone is an expert in our field. Everyone has a basic belief that they have the expertise. Take two things, finance, first. How many people can really read a balance sheet or understand complex financial instruments? So the finance director and his team have something that others don't really understand. And there are computers. When the computer services director is presenting to the board, after he has got beyond his first megabyte, people feel that because they don't really understand, they had better be a bit cautious before challenging it. But, of course, everybody reads the newspapers so is an expert on them, everybody watches TV and is an expert on it and on advertising. Everyone has to write memos and letters so are experts on writing. With a lot of things we do, everyone feels they are experts. So you get far more of a challenge. Interestingly, you don't usually get it from the chairman or chief executive, but from a little bit further down the organization.'

Diplomacy and the ability to get on with people are obviously crucial qualities. As Werner Baier, Henkel's director of corporate communications, pointed out, 'It can be very tough on a product manager who has a good idea and there is some guy from head office saying it may not be such a good idea.' Or, as Beard noted wryly, 'One of the oldest lies in the business is "I am from head office and I'm here to help you".'

The public relations framework

It is difficult to generalize, but a 'typical' structure might encompass the following:

(1) At the top sits the head of public relations, or director of corporate communications, reporting directly to the chairman/chief executive officer.

(2) Under him/her can be a department of some substance which covers a wide range of topics, or one which is quite lean and handles only essentials. This particularly characterizes companies that have a strongly centralized headquarters in a different country and/or those using public relations to spearhead their way into a new market.

(3) Product/brand publicity/public relations is pushed down to the operating companies. The public relations people there probably report to the marketing director, although there is a strong dotted line to the centre.

(4) There might also be a head of public affairs/relations in a division, as at Guinness, depending on how autonomously the operating companies are.

The more senior position of the head of communications, and the increased association with other senior executives as equals, means there is more emphasis on improving the communications skills of all management. At the same time more resources are being put into public relations training for all the public relations staff. As Peter Walker, chairman and chief executive of consultancy Pielle pointed out,

> 'The drive for better training is from these senior people because they are under pressure to have effective and efficient departments. There also has to be a succession built into the organization. If you don't have a successor at that level it is an admission of failure.'

More management courses – at Harvard Business School, for example – incorporate public relations/communications as a topic, to sit alongside the more traditional areas of finance, marketing and human resources, while it is not uncommon today in large companies for career planners to rotate people through public relations departments. Another role the centre can play, apart from educating other executives in communications skills, is to make sure that senior managers in subsidiary companies understand just what sort of communications resources exist in-house, before resorting to using outside consultants.

A strong central communications function also acts as a protector and promoter of the corporate brand, and shows how it can give added value to a subsidiary's business. But it stretches beyond that: it is about educating all management into the relationship of the corporate brand with all the relevant parts of the company. As Jan Shawe, director of corporate affairs at what was then Reed International, argued, all senior management should have this element of corporate awareness in their make-up: 'I think they should be broadly numerate, they should have an idea of human resources and how to make the best of people, and they should have an eye for the company's public face.'

That means the head of communications has to be listened to. Terrence Collis, former director of public affairs at Vickers, believed the best way to earn the respect of other managers in a company was by proving how effective the role can be. He earned his spurs by being instrumental in helping Vickers fight off a predator, and by playing a major role in the campaign to win a major defence order from the UK government (see Case 3.2). The company underlined how important it considered his function by putting Collis on the executive committee.

Case 3.2   Vickers, 1992

In 1992 Vickers was a medium-sized engineering group involved in defence, automotive, medical and marine activities. The chairman and chief executive, Sir David Plastow, made effective communication a central plank in the way Vickers functions. To this end, Vickers was one of the few companies where the director of public affairs, Terrence Collis, had a full seat on the executive committee, which comprised the main board directors plus three other directors, including Collis. Collis was one of the few senior communications officials who not only had clout, but who was seen to have it. Why did Plastow include him?

> 'Several reasons. We need to have stable and consistent signals going to various groups. Investor relations is at the top of the list. Then we have to have regular well-informed presentation of the company in the context of customers all over the world. Thirdly, there is presentation to interior audiences as well.

continues

continued

And we can't do it without having him in that position. I have seen other places were the public affairs role means writing a press release and big news gets suddenly thrown at the media relations department. I don't know how you can work that way. Terry's office sits literally between the finance director and mine. So he is into everything fully. There are no secrets. Though he is not on the board, he has a regular slot to appear there. There are no surprises for him – and he can come back to me and influence what we get up to.'

Collis was called public affairs director but reckoned, like Chris Davidson at Guinness, that it was more a question of semantics than anything else – although his role was far more than 'chief public relations man' in the old-fashioned sense. Because he sat on the executive committee and had responsibility for public affairs/relations throughout the group, whether directly or by dotted line into the product divisions, he could ensure a consistency of message in what is a quite diverse company. Collis commented: 'There are standing orders about what they do and what they have to tell me about, like anything that may hit the nationals and may affect the share price. The worst thing for a public relations man is not to know. If a journalist calls, you never want to be embarrassed.'

An important way to keep in touch with the communications network was a two-day workshop with up to 20-odd people run once a year by someone from the outside. Both people in public relations and those in parallel areas like marketing came along and discussed anything from very basic concerns to more philosophical issues. He also got involved in executive briefings, while trying to inculcate what he called the 'David Plastow philosophy of public relations' into the operating businesses: 'It takes time. They can be unwilling to put resources into public relations because they don't see the long-term benefits. And I can't make them. I would rather do it by influence, by convincing, by discussing. I cannot just be the chairman's mouthpiece. There has to be mutual respect.'

Collis believed that the effectiveness of this approach was demonstrated not only by research that shows Vickers was rated highly by the City as a company with good communications, but also more concretely by success in two major campaigns in which he was deeply involved: a fierce proxy battle with New Zealand share raider Sir Ron Brierly at the Vickers 1990 annual general meeting, and the winning of a major order for Challenger tanks from the government. In both cases, said Collis, 'The important thing was to keep a grip on what is being said and who is saying it. The fewer people between the people making the decisions in the company and the audience the better.'

Cross-border communications

Nowhere does an international outlook count for more than in communications. Regardless of nationality, professionals who have created cross-border public affairs/public relations networks are at the forefront of helping their organizations present a coherent and consistent approach, particularly in an embryonic and complex market like Europe. 'When you're trying to get a company's affiliates to speak with one voice in the EU, it can take the ability to think like a Belgian one minute and an Italian the next,' said an American, born in South America and now working as a communications consultant in Europe. This quality is difficult to understand and not always appreciated by senior management from the USA or Japan.

This still relatively small breed of communication experts increasingly consider themselves 'European' and are most comfortable in multicultural contexts. They share the ability to rise above national conflict – real or imagined – without ever losing sight of the need to take national considerations into account. After all, when taking Europe as a whole, the 'British way of doing things' simply will not work in France, where the French, as a rule, resist taking direction from anybody. And understanding the way to get messages across in Italy may be next to impossible for a Spaniard, even though management may have made the mistake of thinking that 'after all, Italy and Spain are both Latin countries'.

The crucial factor is the balance of real power and responsibility. For instance, an international organization seeking to staff a revamped 'public affairs division' looked for a new director who was 'a strategic thinker; innovative and entrepreneurial; with an ability to lead and manage people'. But in real terms, the organization offered a job with no power – over money or people. No innovative and entrepreneurial manager would commit to it.

Cross-border communications departments demand those rare people who are multilingual and multicultural. They also need credentials if they are to be effective. Working experience in one of the company's main lines of business helps. Legal training is another good qualification. In any event, it is very important for the head of corporate communications to be able to work effectively with other disciplines in the company: marketing, finance, legal and personnel, for example. This is why, organizationally, corporate communications – or corporate affairs – should be accorded the same importance as other staff departments in the company.

Organizing the function across borders

If the company is European, the central corporate communications function should report directly to senior management. If the company is non-European, the function should still report to senior management, either in Europe or – if there is no executive responsible for all the company's European operations – at home base.

In status-conscious Europe, in particular, the title must carry weight outside the company. It also must convey to all and sundry, but especially those in government, that the person has the authority to speak in the company's name. And perhaps most important, the title and the job itself must have the weight to be respected within the company, with other managers.

There are various options. For example:

(1)   If the president of the company is the main articulator of the company's reputation then the head of communications should be the president's trusted counsellor when it comes to articulating the company's point of view.

(2)   Another option is to keep the president of the company in the background and use the head of communications to personify the company image.

(3)   A third variation is to keep both the president and the head of communications in reserve, and apportion responsibility for different types of communication among managers: communications; government affairs; internal communications, etc.

(4)   Other companies – usually highly decentralized or transnational – empower country managers to speak in the corporate name, using the central corporate communications function as a resource.

Deciding which of these four options to choose depends on the size of the company, the nature of its products and the objectives. It also depends on the kind of people involved. If the company president is not comfortable in public – although being a good communicator is becoming more of an demanded attribute of the senior job – then a strong head of communications comfortable and operational in a cross-border environment is essential. If, on the other hand, the company president has no problem taking centre stage, a strong head of communications who can tell the chief what to say, when and to whom can be invaluable.

Cross-border, and particularly pan-European, reputation-building is a relatively new discipline, so experience is a quality that counts for a lot. It is an area where instinct can be as important as intellect.

Staffing the function

Communications/public relations manager, government/public affairs manager and internal communications manager: these are three of positions making up the framework of a modern communications department. They radiate from a central pole – or corporate communications department – at headquarters into the different markets on a national, regional and increasingly global basis.

Communications manager

The communications manager can be the person who produces, or supervises the production of, the communications materials (position papers, speeches, articles/videos for media placement) that affiliates will use to make known the company point of view. Communications support to above- and below-the-line marketing programmes in different countries should be part of this person's responsibility. Combining marketing and corporate communications under one manager at headquarters is the only way to get the synergy the company needs to make the most out of both types of communications in different markets.

The communications manager should have an international outlook and an understanding of the different cultures and languages that make up his/her area of responsibility, as well as a good understanding of the business and a good rapport with the people marketing products/services for the company. The communications manager at regional headquarters – in Europe, for instance – necessarily should have close ties to – and the support of – counterparts in other parts of the world, as well as at corporate headquarters.

Corporate media relations and advertising can come under the responsibility of communications manager – with or without the help of an associate.

Internal communications manager

Depending on the size of the company and the extent of its presence, an internal communications manager can ensure consistency of corporate information to employees. Some companies farm out such tools as employee newspapers and bulletins. Others delegate employee communications to country/plant managers.

Government affairs manager

If the manager of communications is an inside job, the manager of government affairs is an outside job. It means being on the road, lobbying and helping company affiliates coordinate their own lobbying efforts. Most companies lobby nationally in the company name and through the country manager. The government affairs manager at regional headquarters is the linchpin that ensures there are no contradictions and that what emerges in the end is a seamless position on key issues that affect the company's business.

This is particularly important in Europe, where the European Commission is in the midst of formulating directives that can have serious implications for companies. An important part of the government affairs executive's job is thus keeping senior management at corporate, as well as regional, headquarters informed of developments in the EU and at national level that are relevant to the business.

Public relations on the board

Whether corporate communicators should be elevated to board level is beginning to be an area of some debate as the role becomes more recognized for its strategic input.

Tim Halford, then group public affairs director at Grand Metropolitan and now at Trafalgar House, is a fervent adherent of the argument that communications people should not sit on the board: 'I believe in small effective boards whose objective should be to run the company strategically and clearly.' His ideal board would comprise the chairman, chief executive and finance director along with the senior operational executives and strong non-executives. While he conceded that there could be a general purpose executive on the board who drew together all the strings of areas like management development and external affairs, he shied away from the American concept of putting corporate communications people on the board: 'They have boards of 20 people. That's not lean effective management.'

The Vickers' solution was to give the director of corporate affairs a full seat on the executive committee. Not only did this confer status, but it also allowed him open access to what was going on – which, Vickers believed, was essential in a job where information plays such a crucial role.

John Lavelle, director of the UK's Institute of Public Relations (IPR) and ex-Nestlé management, has made getting public relations into the boardroom one of the IPR's leading issues. He said:

'It seems that for too long, even in my general management days, the public relations function was writing speeches for the chairman or answering complaints about products. Twenty years ago I was told that marketing was something you learn as you go along. Public relations is still like that.'

One unwelcome result has been that bright young graduates who wanted to go into public relations have in the past primarily headed for consultancies rather than companies.

Dr Kevin Hawkins, W.H. Smith director of corporate affairs, believed that while public relations might creep on to the board under the heading of community affairs or corporate communications, straight public relations directors on the board will be few and far between. Partly, that is, because some companies have relatively small boards, and partly because 'the whole thing has grown so quickly in such a short space of time that there are a lot of people around who quite frankly are not of the right calibre to be main board directors'.

Why companies use consultants

The way that companies choose and use public relations consultancies is changing as never before, as squeezed budgets are accompanied by a deepening understanding of the central role communications plays in securing competitive advantage.

The fact that many of these in-house managers have also had spells in consultancies means that their knowledge of how consultancies operate is rooted in reality. In other words, they take a pretty hard-headed approach, demanding improved understanding of the client business and demonstration of specialist skill, better performance, and more accountability. Some have brought the public relations in-house, dispensing with outside help except on an *ad hoc* basis. Others increasingly demand that their consultancies accept work and compensation on a project-by-project basis, rather than being kept on a retainer.

According to Graham Lancaster of Biss Lancaster, clients are indeed far more tuned in to how to use PR consultants both because they are more sophisticated and because the recession has forced them to concentrate on getting value for money; and that, he said,

'has forced PR companies to respond accordingly. The recession has forced out some consultancies, either because they were marginal or because of property and other issues and I think we are seeing a leaner, fitter and better consultancy world as a result. I believe the profession is earning its spurs more.'

Case 3.3   W.H. Smith and Abbey National

In 1991 W.H. Smith, a leading retailer, and Abbey National, a building society turned plc, had something in common: both preferred to build up good-sized in-house teams rather than to employ a raft of outside consultancies.

W.H. Smith

W.H. Smith had just under 30 public relations staff in its department, which serviced what is a diverse spread of businesses, including retailing of books, magazines, stationery, recorded video and music in the UK, distributing of newspapers, magazines and office supplies and a growing retail business in the USA and on the continent. According to director of corporate affairs Dr Kevin Hawkins, the group used an external agency for government relations:

> 'Otherwise we are self-sufficient. The company felt there were synergies in having central resources as opposed to fragmenting them around the business units. And I have not been overly impressed with consultancies, who grew so fat in the 1980s that they took on people who might not have got jobs otherwise.'

The public relations function had become established as a more integral part of the business over the last five to six years. It had to prove its worth to – at times – sceptical executives. As Hawkins said:

> 'In any company where you are growing and developing it is inevitable that some people tune into that wavelength and others take longer. My perception is that over the last two years the subsidiary companies and senior executives have begun to realize what sort of hard contribution good public relations in the widest sense can make to the business. However, one always has to guard against being seen as a high cost overhead away from the coal face.'

The team, most of whom have had experience in external consultancies, dealt in a wide range of areas, from the strategic to the tactical. That could mean speaking on issues like the Net Book Agreement or Sunday trading, to devising brand promotions for the individual companies. They had 10 'clients' in all. A complicating factor was that although there is an overall W.H. Smith vision statement, each company retained its own image and philosophy. Nor was the work readily assured: as divisional public relations manager Valerie Hart noted, 'We

continues

continued

had to pitch for Our Price Video against two outside consultancies. And we won it. We are not cheaper because we are in-house, so we must be doing something right.'

Abbey National

Stewart Gowans, then manager of corporate communications at Abbey National, was wary of using external consultancies because he found them 'patchy in standards. There is no such thing as a good consultancy – there are instead good people in them.'

The strength of his department meant that consultancies were only brought on board when it was over-extended or needed specialist skills. When Abbey decided to target youth with its current account, for instance, it used a consultancy that had expertise with the youth press. And while Gowans agreed that the way clients commission consultancies can be at fault, the consultants could have just as much to answer for: 'They say they can do everything when they cannot. They over-promise, their training can be bad, and they have staff who are variable in skills. They mushroomed in the 80s and over-extended themselves.' He also believed there was something wrong with the hierarchial structure of consultancies: 'I think they should be more like lawyers or merchant banks where you are unaware of the structure, and where you get involved with a few talented people who are organized into a team. You get service.'

The former director of corporate affairs at Vickers, Terrence Collis, believed that:

'If you think you need an agency, think very, very seriously about it for a long time. Then don't do it. If you have another serious think, and decide you really might need one, you have to decide exactly what you want them to do and why:

- Am I just trying to offload work?
- Is there some expertise I don't have?
- Am I using them as a stalking horse to get something done internally because the chairman won't listen to me but might listen to that fancy chap from outside?
- Do I need outside thoughts – which can be a very valid reason – or third party endorsement?'

The decision to use an external consultancy should be preceded by a thorough examination of the health of the company's communications and grounded in a clear understanding of objectives and of the skills and resources necessary to achieve them. There are a number of reasons, both strategic and tactical, for hiring a consultancy:

Strategic

- strategy development
- second opinion
- strategy implementation
- standby for major developments.

Tactical

- filling experience/capability gaps
- access to contacts
- extra pair of hands
- stalking horse – the consultancy puts something forward for the in-house executive to present to those above him/her.

It is important to break down what might be vague objectives like 'boosting our profile in the media' into their component parts:

- WHY does the profile need to be raised?
- WHAT is the profile compared with the competition?
- WHO is in charge of media relations?
- HOW does he/she go about it currently?
- HOW can it be improved?
- WHAT outside help is needed?
- HOW much can we spend?
- HOW will we evaluate a programme?
- WHAT will it involve in terms of management time?

The areas where companies turn to consultancies cover a wide range and can include the following.

Financial public relations

This can include takeover bids, investor relations, preparing for a quote either in the UK or abroad, privatization.

Public affairs/corporate affairs

This can cover strategic communications planning, corporate communications and internal communications. It means dealing with the company's different audiences at the corporate level: government, press, public organizations, the City, shareholders, consumers, trade unions, general public.

Consumer public relations

All aspects of brand/product/service promotion to consumers, from press relations, to launch, to competitive monitoring.

Business-to-business

The same as for consumer but dealing with other companies instead of general consumers. This requires a different approach.

Lobbying

Watching out for and acting for particular interests at the local, national, EU level.

Crisis management

This ranges from contingency planning to implementation to damage limitation.

Events management

This is a specialism in handling conferences, exhibitions, presentations, etc.

Sponsorship

Using sponsorship as a way to boost either the company or the product name.

Services

This can cover any service needed in handling the client's account, from design, print production, direct marketing to audiovisual.

While different countries will use a different mix of skills, a few of the more lucrative growth areas for consultancies across Europe include health-care, technology, public affairs/lobbying, and the perennial favourite, helping clients understand the media.

Financial public relations was a flourishing area in the mid-1980s. While the recession dampened down the sort of takeover/merger activity which helped it thrive, it is establishing itself again. It is one of the areas where UK firms, with their experience in takeover/merger work, have a depth of expertise. It is one of the more complex and sensitive briefs since it covers dealings with stock exchanges, professional investors and the financial media, and it may include the small shareholder depending on the ownership profile of the company.

It is also increasingly likely to be an international audience. As Charles Cook, managing director of Grandfield Rork Collins, said,

> 'At one end of the scale it is making sure that the financial press understand what is going on with your client. At another level it is helping organize analyst presentations for twice yearly results. That is not just a nuts and bolts job because I think you need general understanding of accounts and figures to be able to talk to the finance director and chief executive at results time to help them bring out the best messages for that presentation.

'At a more exalted level it can mean communicating directly with the institutional investors, at which point I think consultancies have to be very careful regarding their relationship with the house stockbroker. It is not our job, in my view, to seek to replace the broker in any sense. We see ourselves in communications terms as being the third of the corporate advisors with the brokers and merchant bankers.'

The sheer complexity of relationships with government at all levels, allied to the burgeoning of the EU bureaucracy, has also proved a boon to consultancies, particularly lobbyists of all hues. Some companies handle the work in-house by having permanent members of staff in strategic places like Washington and Brussels. Others will work through their trade associations. Whether external help is necessary depends on size, location and business sector.

The publisher Reed International, for example, used in 1991 external consultancies in both Brussels and Washington DC. In Europe it used a UK-based lobbyist to monitor legislation and regulations that could have a major impact, like the Social Charter and restrictions on advertising. The US consultancy was a small firm that specialized in looking after the needs of foreign-owned companies, including potential legislation that could affect the group, and also acted as Reed's eyes and ears.

There is another area under this heading which the bigger, more international consultancies are targeting: acting as advisors for small countries anxious to make their voices heard on the international scene or attract foreign investment. The consultancies act both as lobbyists and, because of their international reach, almost become the equivalent of a diplomatic service. This can obviously backfire if consultancies work for countries with less than savoury practices.

Dealing with the media is usually considered the prime function of public relations. It cuts across all specialities, since a company's reputation is built up not only by dealing directly with its publics, but also by its profile in the media. That is why many companies hire consultancies to advise on media relations, or act as a sounding board or monitor. But allowing outside consultancies to take over that relationship rather than just advise or act as a sounding board is fraught with dangers:

- the company can lose control over what is really happening;
- the image it gives of the company as unable to deal with questions directly is often unfavourable;
- it can be an unnecessary expense.

Most companies nowadays at least have a press officer to field enquiries. Some do not, and that can be an indication of a lack of understanding of the importance of public relations in general.

Finding the right consultancy

Finding the right consultancy to carry out work can be just as time-consuming as developing a tight, carefully thought-out brief – although the former will be far harder without the latter. For such an intense 'people' business, it is not surprising that many clients say that they find consultancies through:

- personal recommendation
- professional reputation
- knowledge of particular individuals
- client list.

But using such a personal approach does not mean clients should not do their homework, as follows, before they hire a consultancy, particularly with the rise in specialization.

(1) *Investigate the consultancy's background:*
- how long has it been in existence?
- its ownership profile? Is it part of a much larger group, and is that group financially stable?
- how stable is it? Has there been much turnover at the top?
- is there tangible evidence of an understanding of your business?
- does it have the spread you need, that is, across Europe or further?
- is there clear evidence of an understanding of the political arena in which the company operates?

(2) *Consider its reputation*
- has it worked in your sector before and with what results?
- what do journalists think of its abilities?
- what were the experiences of other companies which have used it?
- what is the rate of client turnover? How many clients have left in the last year compared with new ones taken on?

(3) *Consider its financial framework*
- look carefully at its financial structure
- see whether there is an open and transparent method of billing
- check its fees compare with other consultancies of a similar size
- what about its margins?
- what about fee income per person employed – a rough measure of productivity?

(4) *Look at its structure*
- what is the age profile?
- what is the background of the key players?
- is the firm dominated by one or two high profile founders?
- does it have a codebook/manual to enforce standards?
- does it exploit modern technology in an effective manner?

- has it had to go through its own restructuring? If so, what did that involve?
- does it offer what seems like too wide a range of peripheral services?

There has to be a fusion of personalities between consultancy and company, particularly between the people who will deal together on a day-to-day basis. In addition, recognize the role intuition and instinct can play in making a choice.

Case 3.4 Sutcliffe Catering

When Lynette Eaborn, group marketing manager for Reading-based Sutcliffe Catering, one of the UK's top three contract caterers, went looking for a new public relations agency, she knew exactly what she wanted: a consultancy that could demonstrate business-to-business experience with food and generate media coverage. She used a combination of recommendations from friends and colleagues and mail shots to find suitable consultancies to ask to pitch. She was particularly interested in the possibility of hiring a regional agency because she had such a good experience with a local firm in another marketing service. She also wanted one that was neither too big in which Sutcliffe would get lost, nor too small to handle public relations work, which is worth a fifth of her overall marketing budget.

In the end the shortlist came down to two, one in London and one local. 'Both seemed to have great ideas, they showed experience and enthusiasm. It was a very hard choice.' She decided that the solution was to visit each of them and chat to everyone, from the receptionist to the account executives who would work for her. To help her, she made up a little checklist against which she could score the consultancies. It included:

- straight thinking
- creative ideas
- the people on the account
- how much hard work they had done
- enthusiasm
- how well they answered the brief
- loyalty to Sutcliffe and their own firm
- overall confidence in their ability to deliver.

Eaborn believed that 'It helps to know what you are looking for. Clients do get the PR they deserve.'

Many clients do find consultancies through personal recommendation, professional reputation, or client list. At Mercury Communications, for example, public relations manager Doug Walker watched campaigns and other public relations activities: 'If I see something clever and inspired, I would probably backtrack to see who is responsible.'

Guinness is one of the few top companies that does not use an external consultancy at the corporate level but relies on in-house expertise. But, said Murray Loake, press relations manager, if he did need one – to do with health issues, for example – he would use both the grapevine and also talk to one or two journalists in the area and ask who the good public relations operators were. He would also use directories like Hollis. Loake, who has worked in both consultancies and companies, is clear about who he would choose: 'The consultancy with the best contacts, the most experience, good background, and a reasonable fee.'

There are other more formalized sources of consultants. In the UK, for example, the PR Register offers a confidential and objective service, while the Public Relations Consultants Association has a system that can help clients build up a shortlist according to PRCA members' skills and expertise. But they can only refer, not choose – so clients who want to get the consultancy that will suit them best need to ask some pretty detailed questions.

Using consultants

As with most relationships, that between the client and the consultancy can rapidly lose its ardour if clients find that the promises made during the pitch do not quite match reality.

Clients are as much to blame if they get shoddy service from any outside agencies. But ask users of public relations consultancies, whether in companies or journalists, for example, why they have a less than favourable view of public relations consultants and the answers will be unsurprising:

(1) · *Over-promising* – perhaps the most common trait;
(2) · *Inefficiency* – whether about returning phone calls, targeting press releases, or organizing press conferences;
(3) · *Lack of knowledge* about the client company/business;
(4) . *Inconsistency of service* – including using junior executives to do jobs that senior ones should;
(5) · *Over-charging* – as one former consultant, now working in-house, says: 'They think of a figure and then double it';

(6) •*Concentrating too much on grabbing new business* at the expense of existing clients;

(7) • *Unsound management* of their own companies.

The sad fact is that this sort of behaviour by the worst obviously tarnishes the growing band of consultancies which work hard to achieve high professional standards, reinforced by the efforts being made by the professional bodies both in the USA and Europe into pushing best practice in both consultancies and companies. But, while many of the faults cited above could be attributed to all types of consultants, there are probably several reasons why public relations consultants come in for more flak than most:

- Journalists deal more with public relations people than any other form of consultant so their weaknesses are under a brighter spotlight.
- Public relations as a management tool has its origins in some rather dubious practices which it has yet to outlive.

Graham Lancaster, chairman and chief executive of Biss Lancaster, argued that one of the biggest problems clients and consultancies have is a mismatch of expectation on both sides, which can lead to problems at one of several stages of the relationship:

(1) *The pitch* – consultancies can over-pitch because they want the business so much: 'You try and be realistic but it is hard.'

(2) *The brief* – 'Most clients are very experienced about writing briefs for ad agencies, for banks, for accountants – but not for public relations. The client might give you the ad brief or business plan and say that's what we want to achieve. But how does the public relations fit in into that?'

(3) *The client* oversells to his/her manager. 'If there is an expectation beyond what is achievable and in relation to the budget, problems can arise later on.'

Jan Shawe, director of corporate affairs at Reed International, and someone who had worked on both sides of the public relations fence, believed that there has been a vast improvement in the client–consultancy relationship:

> 'A lot of in-house people now know better how to use external consultancies. And I think they are much better as well. I think there has been a supreme shift in the service they offer and if I contract an outside consultancy I have a very good idea what I want from them. I don't just ask them to carry out the scripture on my public relations needs and then give them a pot of money. I know what my objectives are and work within very fine parameters.'

Box 3.1 The Mercury suppliers' charter

All marketing communications suppliers have to adhere to Mercury's Suppliers' Charter, a commitment which is matched on its part by Mercury. It includes the following elements.

Mercury's suppliers must commit to:

(1) agreeing with Mercury the objectives, budget and timescale for a project before starting that project;
(2) quoting an all inclusive price (clearly specified total);
(3) delivering to specification within budget and in time;
(4) measuring with Mercury the success of projects against objectives;
(5) accepting that whereas the professional opinion of its suppliers will be valued and considered Mercury will decide what is in its best commercial interest;
(6) using Mercury's procedures for budgeting and invoicing;
(7) promptly advising Mercury of any potential conflict of interest which arises at any time;
(8) abiding by industry codes of practice;
(9) adhering to corporate guidelines in all market communications;
(10) providing output consistent with Mercury's brand positioning.

Mercury will commit to:

(1) supplying a full written brief for a project with sufficient notice to allow the project to be executed most efficiently and to the requested standard;
(2) supplying authorized purchase orders to proceed, specifying cost and time for a project, at the time when the budget is accepted;
(3) accepting that changing the brief during the course of the project may change the cost or time needed for completion of the project. In the event of such a change, written authorization will be given to cover these changes;
(4) paying itemized invoices up to the agreed budget promptly;
(5) working in partnership with suppliers to address issues that need resolution;
(6) giving regular feedback on performance;
(7) rewarding high performance with appropriate additional work as available;
(8) being a reference account for high performers.

What more knowledgeable clients are doing is establishing a structural framework and code of practice within which their suppliers can operate. In the marketing communications department of Mercury

Communications, for example, there is a 'suppliers' charter' covering all marketing communications (see Box 3.1). According to Mercury's Doug Walker, 'It has worked very well. And it is probably more effective internally than externally in making people think through objectives, messages, target audiences. It means that agencies can't take down briefs on the back of a fag packet which cuts out a lot of fuss and bother.'

Relationships that do work and are kept fresh over a long period of time can give the client a lot of added value.

Using consultants on a pan-European basis

Sooner or later, the time will come when the implementation of a pan-European communications strategy will require reinforcement in major markets in the European Union. Companies marketing and operating in Europe have been using outside communications consultants for years. Today, however, the successful choice of consultants will depend, as never before, on their ability to function on a pan-European basis.

There are a number of factors to take into account:

- the nature of the work – whether it is a simple, single focus exercise like image building or issues monitoring or one that will entail a complex coordination job;
- the profiles of the individuals in each location;
- the actual location of the offices;
- whether the network has carried out any similar exercises for someone else with proven results;
- how much the client is prepared to pay for coordination (consultants will have to travel and meet to coordinate effectively);
- which part of the client company will be in charge;
- how sophisticated the network's communications facilities are;
- the fact that Europe is by no stretch of the imagination a homogeneous market.

As A Plus chairman John Aeberhard warned, 'What companies – particularly US companies – have got to come to terms with is that there is a multiplier effect in Europe. They have to recognize that it will cost more to hit the same sort of market area as the USA because it is not just a question of doing different translations, but that they are different markets.'

A lot can depend on the project. US consumer goods company Gillette is very centralized in its communications, with public relations run out of its Boston headquarters. When it decided to launch its new Sensor shaver that had been 10 years in development, its research convinced it that demographics made it feasible to run an integrated campaign across both the USA and Europe. It coordinated its public relations through an international network, spearheaded by the consultancies in Boston and London, which gave it international consistency, but allowed local adaptations in different shaving markets. It turned out to be one of Gillette's most successful product launches.

The issue of who controls coordination is one that will become increasingly central to international public relations. Giving responsibility to an international account executive in one of the big networks is one solution, but that demands complete confidence in the network's capability. Alternatively, clients can plug into a network but coordinate themselves and/or add outside consultancies where the local satellite seems weak.

What some companies do is put together their own network based on choosing local firms in each market. That is the option selected by Lizann Peppard, regional public relations manager in Europe for American Airlines. Before Peppard arrived at the beginning of 1990, American Airlines had been using a big international network as a one-stop European operation with London as the focal point, where one person could activate Europe with supposedly the same standards across the board. Peppard ended that relationship and built up her own network. She chose mainly smaller consultancies both because of the more personal contact and involvement, and because of their specific expertise. In Germany, for example, she used a small but specialist travel consultancy with only three to four people, while Spain was a one-man band. Others could be added to the network when they were needed.

She based her choices on both personal chemistry, and the ability to provide the fast service which American demands. Running her own network not only gave her control but also cut costs. Peppard commented: 'Quite often the coordination fee is a hefty part of the total and it is not a piece of money that is achieving anything. It is hard enough to quantify what public relations does anyway.'

The American Airlines approach will obviously not work for all companies. The solutions have to depend on the complexity of the programme or project. Even if a company has decided to exploit a network already in place, it is crucial to investigate all the members individually – there can be wide variations in service and skills. And careful thought has to go into how much to leave to local management initiative, who probably can contribute:

(1)   established links with influential groups including media, unions, governments at different levels;
(2)   a subtle understanding of market conditions and restrictions;
(3)   a grasp of culture and understanding of language;
(4)   an understanding of what sort of programmes work and what do not.

External communications consultants in Europe are a very mixed group. Each EU member state seems to have its particular strength as far as the profession is concerned and that should be taken into account.

If the corporate communications function at regional headquarters has been positioned correctly and is equipped to function as a regional resource, then the choice of consultants in each EU market can be made in tandem with the company's senior manager in each country. By this time, communications objectives should be defined, with a pan-European strategy in place. Consultants, if and when they are chosen, can contribute at the national level.

Sometimes, vaunted pan-European capacity is more cosmetic than real. The client still basically gets a collection of national units, connected through a 'European headquarters' that does the selling and sends out the bills. 'They come in with a "flying squad" trained to sell and blow the minds of line management,' recounted a bemused corporate communications manager. 'But once they have the account, you never see the "flying squad" again, and you find yourself dealing with junior people who have never worked for a company in their lives, don't understand the way we have to communicate internally, and cannot think beyond national borders.'

Some clients prefer one or two international agencies to simplify and strengthen European coordination. Others put creative quality first and hire the best available agency for the local market. Either way, the strategic pan-European communications component is difficult to implement.

When the communications push comes from North America, companies may be tempted to extend their US contracts for public relations and advertising so that they cover Europe. This is not always a good idea. Management charged with opening up or expanding markets in the EU is held accountable for results. These results more and more will depend on management's ability to use cross-border communications in a cost-effective manner.

It follows that management for Europe should be empowered to structure communications support in Europe in line with its own objectives and operating conditions, within the constraints of budgets and available human resources.

When US-based management decides to offer – or impose – its US agency on European management, the arrangement usually does not last very long – even if headquarters is paying. One London-based corporate communications director for a financial institution headquartered in New York admitted,

> 'My boss, the vice president, corporate communications, in New York is a very good friend of the chief executive of the public relations agency that we use in the States. We are using them in Europe too – for the moment. But after enough time has elapsed to build a solid case, we will make our own choice and we'll get the US management to support what we need.'

When a company comes to Europe with no home-based connection to a communications consultant, a big name often comforts management at headquarters and on the spot. When the company is truly global, with Europe an important but not the only priority, the use of global communications combinations are easy to fall back on. Unfortunately, expatriate managers, parachuted in to make a success of Europe, usually do not know how to use such global networks of communications consultants and only end up complaining about how much they cost.

In the pan-European arena, UK-based public relations companies are trying hard to expand their pan-European links and provide US capability as well. In the end, however, their image is still very British on the continent. This can have its advantages, notably with some directorates of the European Commission. Otherwise, UK-headquartered agencies can find it difficult to do business on behalf of clients in countries like France, Italy and Spain.

Common language is another advantage cited by US-headquartered companies that use London-based communications consultants. But common language does not necessarily mean common mentality, and 'Anglo-Saxon' can still be a pejorative term on the continent.

Except for a very few UK companies that are truly international, using a UK-based consultancy to provide communications support on the continent can turn out to be a mistake.

The multiple agency approach

There are networks of agencies with informal links that operate in different EU countries. But these ties usually mean no more than: 'If you send me business, I'll send you some – when I can.' For lack of a central point for quality and cost control, pan-European strategy and direction have to come from the client.

In the 1970s and 1980s, managing a team of 10 or 12 public relations agencies across Europe was fairly common for communicators operating out of a company's European headquarters. But as time went on, this type of arrangement became increasingly difficult to manage.

If a company has the resources to bring all its agencies together periodically, and if the company's management of pan-European communications is effective, the multiple agency approach to cross-border communications can work. Companies do it and are happy with the arrangement – provided they have the talent and the clout in-house to keep independent agencies on track for the corporation in the EU, as well as for national country management.

There are at least four other preconditions when the company decides to manage a network of independent agencies:

(1)   There should be an agency retained in each EU country where the company has a marketing or an operating presence – even if only for monitoring purposes.
(2)   The company should have a long-standing relationship with each agency.
(3)   Local company management should be encouraged to use – and contribute to the cost of – the agency in each country.
(4)   Each national agency should receive the same brief on issues that matter to the company, on guidelines for communicating with the media, and on positions relevant to public policy that could affect the company's bottom line, both nationally and internationally.

An alternative is to opt for an international household name, like Burson-Marsteller, for example. A key advantage of a network like this is access to the agency's offices outside Europe: in Washington DC (for public affairs and lobbying), in New York and in Japan. Global resources like these can be useful, particularly to companies head-quartered in the EU with only embryonic ties of their own to markets outside Europe. Another advantage is that global firms like Burson-Marsteller and Hill & Knowlton supposedly have close links to advertising agencies.

In theory, this relationship should make it easier for public relations and advertising to work together on behalf of a client's overall communications strategy. In practice, this type of synergy is only rarely achieved, and when it does work it is usually because the client has made the effort to ensure that both disciplines work together.

Using one agency's facilities across borders ostensibly contributes to consistency of communications. On the other hand, current (and former) clients most often cite three disadvantages of international public relations agencies operating in Europe:

• quality of service varies widely from country to country
• costs are excessive
• image is 'too American'.

Burson-Marsteller/Europe is one international agency that refutes the 'too American' charge by pointing out that nearly all of its offices are staffed and managed by nationals. In several countries, Burson-Marsteller has been chosen to manage government accounts, which, the theory goes, could not go to non-national agencies for political reasons. On the other hand, maybe the governments in question – like companies in the private sector – simply chose the best consultant on the national scene for the job at hand. International consultancies like Burson-Marsteller offer worldwide resources and virtually 'one-stop' access to a large selection of services: opinion research, corporate positioning, crisis communications, employee communications, events planning, alliance building, financial and investor relations, and community programmes.

Without some form of network, it is very difficult for a company to achieve pan-European communications – and consequent reputation-building – capacity. Some companies turn to individuals, however, for particular services: strategic communications counsel; publications audits; surveys of opinion leaders where interview candidates have to be approached personally and confidentially; organization of pan-European image-building events; and support through sponsorship.

Sensible corporate communications people assemble a stable of writers, familiar with different issues and capable of producing communications to deliver the company's strategic image-building messages in a consistent manner to people of different nationalities within the EU. This type of international writing is essential to effective pan-European communications, because it can be offered as a resource to country managers (for consistency), to senior management at corporate headquarters (for information about EU issues as they evolve) and to regional management for corporate communications purposes.

'The weak link in most pan-European networks of consultants is the ability to communicate clearly and directly on complicated issues,' said the corporate communications manager of a large US company operating in Europe. 'National or international, most public relations agencies usually cannot grasp the importance of certain issues to the company's bottom line. There is the problem of confidentiality. And you usually end up paying too much for a document that can't be used on a European level.'

Fitting into a globalization strategy

With the possible exception of the UK, most communications consultants in Europe today are working to develop and reinforce their ability to provide clients with pan-European service.

At the same time, Eastern Europe beckons – along with Asia, North America and even Latin America. If the globalization of business is a reality, then globalization of communications strategy and programmes cannot be far behind. Pan-European reputation-building is a platform for some companies' international expansion. For others, already operating on a global basis, a pan-European image is an integral part of a greater whole.

Eastern Europe is a special case that interests more and more companies. Professional communications help can be found in Vienna or in the East European countries themselves. 'But,' warned a pharmaceutical company's communications manager, 'you can't expect quality of service to be comparable with what you can demand in the EU.'

Today, companies say, the measure of quality of service that counts anywhere is comprehension of international objectives and strategy, creativity, and the ability to implement an agreed communications plan as part of an international team.

In the end, the choice of communications consultants will come down to chemistry: between them and local management, between them and corporate communications people at regional headquarters. Once a team is in place, it is important to know how to manage it. Even when an international firm is used, regional corporate communications people must be allowed to drive the teams of national consultants across the region, in close liaison with the company's country managers.

In an age of increasing integration, companies will have to have the in-house structures that enable them to coordinate all external communications activities, not only across borders but across disciplines as well. That means a sophisticated matrix of responsibility overseeing and aligning the output of all marketing services firms, including public relations, advertising, direct marketing and sponsorship, in the name of complete consistency.

Box 3.2 Checklist for choosing outside consultants in Europe

Here are the steps to follow when the time comes to help local management select a national consultant:

(1) Make sure that local management does not have unrealistic expectations. Go over objectives and strategy once more, pinpointing areas that require additional resources.

continues

continued

(2) Determine whether these needs are really national or whether they can be met by the company's own communications resources – in other countries or at regional level.

(3) Decide whether a national consultant is needed on a long-term or project basis. Many companies prefer to avoid making long-term agreements with consultants because they like to use 'horses for courses': different kinds of consultants for different assignments. The disadvantage of this approach is that it makes it more difficult and costly – in terms of time and money – to ensure cross-border consistency. Obviously, once a consultant has proved to be competent and useful, short-term commitments can be converted into longer-term contracts. If this is a possibility, the consultant should be told at the start.

(4) No matter what local management says, do not underestimate the advantages of the continuity that a long-term relationship with a consultant can bring to the process of building a cross-border reputation for the company (and/or its products). It takes time for a consultant to get to know a client's business. And it takes time for a client to come to trust a consultant.

(5) Investigate and meet at least five national consultants before selecting three to present to country management. Try to find three that are very different from each other. This technique tends to concentrate the minds of country managers who do not quite know what they want.

(6) Visit the premises of the three consultants on your shortlist. You should be able to judge the quality of the people who work there, whether they are committed and happy and well-equipped (professionally and technically) to work on your company's behalf.

(7) Ask to see the consultants' client list. Beware a list that mixes current with past clients. Ask how the consultant would deal with a conflict of interest – especially if you see one coming. Like other kinds of infidelity, if the consultant is willing to dump a current client in order to win your business, you can be sure that he/she will dump you if and when something better comes along.

(8) Ask for references by name, and contact the consultants' current clients. Examples of proposals and work done are less reliable indicators of competence, and, unless experience is presented in the form of anonymous case studies, confidentiality may be a problem. Every country in Europe, for example, has a national public relations association, with professional rules and standard charges. A membership check is a good idea, with the proviso that, when it comes to providing strategic counsel and implementation of programmes that go beyond traditional public relations, some of the best consultants in the country may not be part of the national public relations associations.

continues

continued

(9) Ask about billing and reporting procedures. Activity reports should be sent to the client monthly, at least. If they are sent out more frequently, this tends to add to costs – and to the pile of unread material on corporate communicators' desks, especially when reports come in from 12 different countries, say. Initial briefings usually are not charged (unless the consultant has to travel out of the country to the company's regional headquarters). After that, the company should be prepared to pay for a proposal and its presentation. Some agencies (notably international ones) build this charge into subsequent charges if they get the business. But it is usually preferable and clearer for all concerned if proposals (and/or trial assignments) are billed separately from contracted fees. Expenses should be billed at cost.

(10) Look for agencies that have total national capacity and are not just well connected in the country's capital. This is very important in countries such as Germany, where much is accomplished at state level. It is less important in Italy, where most professionals are to be found in Milan (though they should have a Rome office), and the Netherlands. In Belgium, linguistic differences matter. In the UK, beware the 'senior consultant' unwilling to look beyond London. Depending upon what you want to accomplish, UK consultants should have the capacity to work with media and politicians in other parts of the country. The same is true for France and Spain, where power is slowly but surely being diffused out from Paris and Madrid.

Summary

(1) Public relations is part of the overall task of management. Organizations have relationships with important groups, such as their own employees, or external groups such as government or the community whether or not they choose to manage them. Relationships are a resource and should be managed in the same way as other resources.

(2) Each company has to define its public relations strategy in the way best suited to its needs. However, there are several common issues to be faced:

- where public relations sits compared with other functions;
- the role public relations plays in supporting marketing;

- programme management and evaluation;
- choosing and using external consultants;
- dealing with the particularly complex European market.

(3)   Public relations as a respected function in its own right is in an embryonic position compared with better-established functions such as marketing, production or finance. That can make the job of the person in charge less clear cut. They can be heads, managers or directors. They can enjoy widespread responsibility and be on an equal footing with their fellow directors, or they can be used simply as messengers. Some can be in charge of the entire corporate communications network, or have responsibility for media relations alone.

(4)   The senior communications executive can only be truly effective with the backing of the chairman or chief executive. The head of public relations, or chief communications officer, should have a direct line to the top management, if not a direct reporting relationship. This is a crucial relationship, and must be close since the role that the head of communications can play cuts across all the major functions.

(5)   A 'typical' structure might encompass the following:

- At the top sits the head of public relations or director of corporate communications, reporting directly to the chairman/ chief executive officer.
- Under him/her can be a department of some substance which covers a wide range of topics, or one which is quite lean and handles only essentials. This particularly characterizes companies that have a strongly centralized headquarters in a different country and/or those using public relations to spearhead their way into a new market.
- Product/brand publicity/public relations is pushed down to the operating companies. The public relations people there probably report to the marketing director, although there is a strong dotted line to the centre.
- There might also be a head of public affairs/relations in a division depending on how autonomously the operating companies are.

(6)   A strong central communications function also acts as a protector and promoter of the corporate brand, and shows how it can give added value to a subsidiary's business.

(7)   Nowhere does an international outlook count for more than in communications. Regardless of nationality, professionals who have created cross-border public affairs/public relations networks are at the forefront of helping their organizations present a coherent and consistent approach, particularly in an embryonic and complex market like Europe.

(8) The way that companies choose and use public relations consultancies is changing as never before, as squeezed budgets are
accompanied by a deepening understanding of the central role
communications plays in securing competitive advantage.

(9) The decision to use an external consultancy should be preceded by
a thorough examination of the health of the company's communications and grounded in a clear understanding of objectives and of
the skills and resources necessary to achieve them.

(10) Finding the right consultancy to carry out work can be just as time-
consuming as developing a tight, carefully thought out brief –
although the former will be far harder without the latter. For such
an intense 'people' business, it is not surprising that many clients
say that they find consultancies through personal recommendation
and professional reputation. But using such a personal approach
does not mean clients should not do their homework before they
hire a consultancy, particularly with the rise in specialization.

(11) One of the biggest problems clients and consultancies have is a
mismatch of expectation on both sides, which can lead to problems
at one of several stages of the relationship. What more knowledgeable clients are doing is establishing a structural framework
and code of practice within which their suppliers can operate.

(12) Companies marketing and operating in Europe have been using
outside communications consultants for years. Today, however,
the successful choice of consultants will depend, as never before,
on their ability to function on a pan-European basis.

(13) The issue of who controls coordination is one that will become
increasingly central to international public relations. Giving
responsibility to an international account executive in one of the
big networks is one solution, but that demands complete
confidence in the network's capability. Alternatively, clients can
plug into a network but coordinate themselves and/or add outside
consultancies where the local satellite seems weak.

Note

(1) *The Rise to Power of the Corporate Communicator*, Smythe Dorward
Lambert. London: 1991.

4

Public relations programme and human resources management

How public relations should work

Public relations activities are initiated in response to events, or develop almost logically out of business and organizational objectives. In the jargon, they are reactive or proactive. In reaction, they are concerned with problems or opportunities that have arisen. They may be carried out in response to crisis, or to deal with unexpected criticism or activities on the part of competitors.

As far as possible, however, public relations should anticipate problems, issues, events and opportunities before they arise. This approach is emphasized in issues management, a specialism of public affairs, itself a specialized branch of public relations.

Public relations should be managed to support the achievement of strategic objectives of the company. And objectives for the public relations programme itself should be formulated to ensure they tie in with these overall corporate aims. Following this approach also leads to more comprehensive programme management, including taking account of the consequences of the programme for allocation of time, budgeting, human resource management and evaluation, subjects that will be dealt with in this and the next chapter.

Perhaps the biggest challenge facing public relations practitioners today is managing programmes across borders consistently and effectively. This is particularly complex when it comes to Europe, not only because of the multicultural aspect, but also because different markets are at different stages of development.

Programme management in Europe

There are seven steps to take before beginning to design a pan-European communications strategy. These steps apply to any exercise – whether for a company, a product, a trade association, an international organization or an individual. There are no short cuts. The process will take time. In the end, it will cost money. Executives should systematically follow these procedures whenever they prepare to set their company's image-building goals.

(1) Take a cold, hard look at what you wish to accomplish. Set objectives down on paper. Try to express them as a projection of and support for the objectives spelled out in your company's business plan. Objectives can range all the way from building sales for a particular product, to resolving a conflict in a particular region or community, to creating an image that will favour overall business development for the company.

(2) Define your company's current position. Before conducting formal (and costly) image-tracking studies (that usually involve employees, customers and suppliers), poll your company colleagues in different disciplines: finance, personnel, marketing, legal. If they have trouble defining the current perception of your company – or have no idea what you are talking about – there is work to be done. Survey employees in different countries.

(3) If you can, go out with sales people. What arguments are used to convince customers? How could these arguments be reinforced by corporate communications? How could corporate communications be used to convey additional arguments for buying your company's products/services? How could these arguments be communicated to governments and regulatory authorities?

(4) Look at the way the competition communicates and the way it is perceived. Results of your initial investigation will help you to see what your company can do to set itself apart.

(5) Look at the way your own company communicates. Is there a policy? Is there consistency across markets? Who is in charge? Where does the buck stop? If you put all your company's printed communications (annual reports, brochures, press releases, employee newspapers, personnel advertisements, and so on) on a table, can you tell that they come from the same company? Do your corporate communications add value to your product advertising

and promotions? Are you communicating in markets where you are not yet established?

(6) Analyse media coverage of your company, its products and your industry. This analysis should help to identify the qualities that can help build an effective public relations programme – *vis à vis* the competition – in the EU's single market.

(7) Determine how much freedom there is to create an appropriate pan-European corporate strategy. If your parent company is head-quartered outside the EU, what does it have to offer in the way of a platform for reputation-building in Europe? Is the image of the parent company an asset – or a liability? Can communications materials used by the parent company be adapted for use in Europe? Can communications policy be extended?

Usually, there is no reason why certain elements of a non-European parent's identity cannot be used in Europe. But if a company operating in the EU is able to create an identity for itself distinct from its parent's (in the USA or Japan, for example), so much the better. This is parti-cularly true when the parent runs into difficulties – with layoffs, for example, or crises in the home market.

Communications professionals agree that it is bad policy for com-pany executives operating in Europe to lack the freedom to speak for the company when necessary. It is practically impossible to communicate a pan-European position when Europe-based people have to check back with New York, or Tokyo, or Toronto. But this does not mean that a US or Japanese or Canadian identity cannot be advantageously used as an umbrella over a pan-European identity that creates consistency of image and communication in EU national markets.

It is a question of evaluating the parent company's image, and using what is appropriate for Europe. Even if a subsidiary has to start from scratch, there should be some tie-in with the parent company's identity. When the parent company is headquartered outside the EU, the objec-tive should be a global programme, with Europe as a component part.

Case 4.1 Gillette

Gillette is one of the more centralized consumer goods companies. Both marketing strategy and promotion guidelines come from the USA for both the USA and Europe, which Gillette is treating as one area to a large extent – the 'North Atlantic region'.

continues

continued

During the period 1983–87 Gillette – significantly in advance of many other organizations operating in the European arena – carried out a major programme of pan-European branding, packaging and advertising, as well as a restructuring of its entire Western European marketing and selling operations.

The head of Europe decided that men's shaving was a category where the marketing could be done on a very similar if not identical basis throughout Western Europe. He recognized that in the shaving process, what men are looking for and what they want have more similarities between and among countries than differences.

The first real test of his ideas came in 1986 with the pan-European launch of the Contour Plus razor, where the same brand name and advertising was used across Europe. The advertisements consisted of a very simple set of dramatic visuals to position the new product apart from its razor predecessors, with voice-overs in 16–20 different languages. It was a very successful launch, and led to a firmer strategy of taking promotional budgets from each country and centralizing them in the London head office.

As duplicated functions were eliminated, gradually consumer marketing and manufacturing responsibilities were centralized in the London headquarters. Country managers were encouraged to begin focusing their efforts exclusively on selling and on becoming experts on the trade.

The resulting effect on profits meant that Gillette headquarters in Boston decided that the successful strategy formulated by the European operation should be taken further. It reckoned that there was not really that much difference between the way people approached shaving in Europe or North America.

The result was the formation of the North Atlantic group, run from Boston headquarters and comprising the USA, Canada and Western Europe. This now gave the centralized marketing team the total North Atlantic media budget to use.

The culmination of this centralized approach came with the launch of the Sensor, which, with its spring-mounted twin blade technology, had been in development since the early 1980s. Formulating the promotional campaign was a mix of the simple and complex, a question of devising a promotional strategy that would work in both the USA and Europe. There had to be some local adaptation in terms of public relations and how to get the message to the media, but the underlying theme stayed the same. The template was created in Boston for the entire programme.

The public relations objectives were:

- to communicate that Gillette had a breakthrough product
- to create anticipation
- to generate trial when the product hit the market.

The thrust of the media strategy was to get maximum news appeal on an international basis. A comprehensive guidelines manual was done

continues

continued

to serve as a blueprint, while design elements were developed for use across all countries, with translations. Printing was done in the USA. Press materials included news and feature releases, photography, technical illustrations, fact sheets, and a video news release package.

Meetings were held with representatives from both the company and the public relations agency people from around the region. This was followed by weekly and then daily contact between the lead agency in Boston and the others to make sure that the message stayed consistent while taking account of local needs. For example, while several countries held formal news conferences, others approached the media individually or held small-scale briefings.

What made this more complicated was the number of different stories to tell. The financial media was interested in the corporate story, the marketing press in the marketing story – big budgets and an international launch – technology writers in the technology because Gillette had taken out 22 patents, and the consumer press in the consumer story.

The company held a press conference simultaneously in six markets. The publicity was so extensive that two months later *Fortune* named it as one of its 10 products of the year.

The new razor was mailed to important people in each market, including Donald Trump, George Bush – then president – and Hugh Hefner. In the UK it was sent to every member of parliament and the public relations agency followed this up with a Best Groomed MP Award. The UK consultancy also coordinated a pan-European survey on male grooming, looking at both male and female attitudes. While the results differed from market to market, the survey was well received everywhere.

The resulting launch in early 1990 surpassed Gillette's expectations and resulted in an avalanche of publicity. It sold more in nine months than it expected to sell in a year. In fact, demand for the Sensor was so overwhelming it created supply problems.

Gillette has recently followed up the Sensor launch with a new range of men's toiletries. The principles are the same: marketing guidelines have been set centrally from Boston, with the actual media strategy and buying, along with trade promotions, left to the local market.

The company believes certain factors contribute to making such a highly centralized approach work effectively:

(1) suppliers have to be willing to create parallel organizations to meet the client needs and demands for consistency and quality;
(2) the company has to be absolutely committed to ensuring that it gives back to the country managers – who have given up a lot of their autonomy – something better than they would have on their own. It has worked so well, in fact, that the company has begun to allow what it calls more controlled flexibility for the country managers.

Working with European audiences

The complexity of the European market makes it worthwhile to examine the five principal audiences that need to be targeted by pan-European corporate communicators:

(1) government
(2) media
(3) employees
(4) customers
(5) EU bureaucrats and political leaders.

In the USA, current jargon calls these targets 'stakeholders'. In Europe, communications professionals tend to use 'opinion leaders' or 'decision-makers'. Of the three terms, 'decision-makers' is probably the most apt in the European context because, sooner or later, decisions by representatives of each – or all – of these groups will affect company strategy, tactics, growth and profits.

The challenge is to know when and how to communicate with the five targets in order to build a positive and consistent communications strategy across Europe. Depending on the country – and the region and locality – the interests of each target can be different. Yet overall, there is indeed a pan-European dimension to each group of decision-makers, which progressive companies operating in Europe are beginning to address. The trend applies to business-to-business as well as to consumer-orientated marketers of products and services.

Government

Government or public affairs in Europe is a delicate assignment that can require working with (currently) 12 different national governments – 18 if the European Free Trade Association (EFTA), is added, and 22 with the Czech and Slovak Republics, Hungary and Poland. There is also, of course, the former Soviet Union. The sum total of communications with these countries' governments creates an impression – an image – that can make or break a company in Europe.

In addition to national governments, there is a need to communicate with regional authorities (in Italy and Spain, for example) and at the state level (in Germany). In Belgium, the process is complicated by political parties and regional administrations organized along linguistic (Flemish and French) lines. In France, more and more can be accomplished at regional level, even though, sooner or later, decisions will be made – or ratified – in Paris.

Companies with manufacturing facilities in different European countries are careful to keep lines of communication open with local governments and political leaders. These people can, in turn, communicate positively on behalf of the company all the way up the line to regional or provincial level, and with elected local representatives to the national level or the European Parliament.

Media

In the context of public affairs, national media can be a useful tool. But here again, relationships count. In some countries, it is virtually impossible to communicate via the media without a personal contact on the periodical in question. When it comes to orchestrating a pan-European media campaign, without using advertising, the challenge is even greater.

The way a company deals with the media in Europe is part of the company's corporate positioning. The long-haul counts. Relationships need to be built and nourished with regular information, and, sometimes, prior access to news that the company plans to release more fully soon after.

Privileged access to top executives is a perk that European journalists covet and zealously protect. To the frustration of their US-headquartered competitors – and communications professionals from Anglo-Saxon countries – French, Italian, Spanish and Swiss company presidents will often give their favourite journalists the inside scoop ahead of anybody else. It works both ways: access to top company sources is journalistic stock in trade; first-hand access to journalists helps the company to control what is printed. 'This is the way the game is played,' said a European media relations specialist. 'You just have to know how to play it'. All corporate communications targets want to know who they are dealing with. This is particularly true for companies of non-European parentage and may be the principal justification for taking the time and the money to build a pan-European image.

Employees

There are four factors to keep in mind:

(1) National – and now EU – legislation increasingly makes labour a fixed expense in Europe.
(2) Improved employee productivity can provide the necessary competitive edge in the global marketplace.
(3) Qualified labour is hard to find and a challenge to keep.
(4) Companies are judged by the people they employ and the way those employees are treated.

A clearly defined corporate image cuts across all four factors and pays off in terms of reinforced employee loyalty when:

- acquisitions need to be made
- production must be concentrated
- payrolls need to be reduced
- costs have to be contained and output increased
- new employees need to be recruited
- wages must be negotiated
- issues need to be addressed
- government approvals have to be won.

Ten years ago, the word transnational filled board chairmen with fear, as international organizations, unions and consumer groups demanded more disclosure, more social responsibility, and more proof that companies operating across borders were not engaged in nefarious activities designed to defraud the common weal. Today, the virtues of the transnational company are being communicated to employees by enlightened managements all across Europe, with applause and recognition from public authorities.

Customers

In Europe today, more than ever, customers want to work in partnership with their suppliers. The key to success is the ability to work together to solve specific problems.

'When Du Pont provides customers with solutions, not just products, it graduates from being a supplier to being a business partner,' the corporation's 1990 annual report pointed out in its review of Du Pont in Europe. Communications in the corporate name can be designed to build and cement alliances with customers. This concept is not limited to business-to-business marketing. American Express uses the problem-solving approach when communicating with busy, successful prospective cardholders with little time.

In terms of communications with consumers, it is important to respond to the fact that European markets have changed. The 1990s will be the balance-sheet decade, and only those who give the consumer what they promise will survive. Instead of worrying about making a living, customers now focus on the quality of life. Consumers respond to values, to convenience, to style. And their tastes are infinitely variable.

The umbrella that covers these infinitely variable tastes can be a carefully constructed corporate image – or a trademark – that becomes a vehicle to convey particular messages to customers. It can be a brand, like Coca-Cola, or a venerable name, like Dior.

The EU and its institutions

A lot of money has been wasted in the past in an effort to make companies headquartered outside the EU into 'European' companies. It cannot be done. A more limited – and achievable – objective is to build a pan-European image for a company and its products, irrespective of the company's parentage. This is vital because working successfully with the EU means communicating a European identity. Nobody knows this better than those information technology companies competing for a chunk of the main technological programmes at European level. It is where concerted pan-European image-building can pay off.

For example, after debating the problem of what to call themselves, companies that belong to the EU Committee of the American Chamber of Commerce in Europe came up with 'European companies of US parentage'. The term reportedly originated at Philip Morris Europe where it had been in use as part of corporate communications policy since 1978.

Apart from parentage, there are other elements of a pan-European identity that concern the EU:

- job creation
- contribution to exports
- investment
- research and development
- technology transfer
- tax contribution
- historic presence
- geographic presence
- respect for the environment
- relationship of the company's European operations to operations in other countries (notably, Japan and the USA).

It is a mistake to think that EU bureaucrats can quantify these characteristics, or even attribute them, when they have to make decisions that affect particular companies. 'They know us pretty well', is a common, but not necessarily correct, assumption when the European Commission is involved. A European 'fact-sheet', summarizing key elements of a company's presence in Europe, can never be used too often with the EU.

For at least three reasons, executives should make sure their company has a positive pan-European reputation and image, and that it is communicated to EU institutions:

(1)   The decision-making power of the EU will reach into virtually every aspect of corporate strategy for Europe in the 1990s. Under

EU competition rules, for example, the Commission can review all deals where the firms' aggregate worldwide sales exceed ECU5 billion ($6.1 billion) and where each company generates sales of more than ECU250 million inside the EU. Community merger inquiries start with a one-month review, when companies request clearance. If the Commission questions a merger's impact on competition, it can launch a full-scale inquiry.

(2) The EU is modifying its structure, with (at times fraught) negotiations currently taking place on economic and monetary union as well as on political union, and companies might as well be part of the process – as much as possible.

(3) For companies, a new credibility is attached to the EU.

Case 4.2   BellSouth, 1991

In 1991, BellSouth was in the process of positioning itself to compete in the European market for telecommunications. As one of seven regional operating companies divested from AT&T in 1984, BellSouth had built an image for itself in the USA based on dynamic management, technological expertise and financial performance. Of all the 'baby Bells', BellSouth was perceived to have pulled ahead of the pack – in the USA.

How well did this image transfer to Europe? BellSouth had been operating in Europe since the acquisition of Air Call in the mid-1980s. But Charles Menatti, a BellSouth international vice president for Europe, began building on the company's European marketing experience from a Brussels base.

A dual national (Italy–USA) with two passports, the bilingual Menatti knew that, for his company's business in Europe, the right image would depend on establishing long-lasting relationships. Having 'an international mentality' helped, Menatti believed. So did hiring European nationals to represent BellSouth in key markets to start with and more later. Unlike some of its AT&T siblings and competitors, the first baby Bell to attack the European market made a point of not just exporting expatriates to Europe.

Menatti moved from Paris to Brussels for BellSouth International in February 1991. He brought 15 years of international business experience to his job and to BellSouth's European development.

There was a lot to do. BellSouth was a $14.3 billion company, a leader in wireless communications technology and in directory publishing (with over 41 million directories published around the world). BellSouth's strengths included expertise in the deployment of

continues

continued

market-focused technology and the delivery of high-quality 'customer care' programmes. Technologically, the company had taken the lead in deploying fibre-optic cables to transmit data, video and voice.

Bell companies were then prohibited from developing programming for network distribution in the USA, but not in Europe. So far, technically the market was wide open and, in a highly competitive environment, the spoils would go to the company that customers believed would deliver the best value, reliability and service.

Keeping the European market open – at the highest level – was one of Menatti's challenges, one where image is very important in the cultural context of Europe and Europe as One Market. As Menatti said:

'BellSouth has a lot going for it from a technological and business point of view. We are service providers and one of the most innovative and progressive in the business. But, at the end of the day, our image and reputation are in the hands of the people that represent the company on "the front line".'

BellSouth executives knew that it would take time before the company could say that it was strategically placed in the European market. 'We work at being desired partners,' Menatti said, and BellSouth had developed partnerships around the globe. As telecommunications infrastructure is modernized in Western – and Eastern – Europe, alliances now and in the future would be critically important to the success of the company.

For the time being, much of the company's image-building was being done through one-on-one contacts in key markets (at national government level and at the European Commission), using communications material from the USA. Communications strategy was managed out of BellSouth headquarters in Atlanta, Georgia, but the company's European management implemented the strategy in different countries. Within the overall guidelines, there was room for adaptation to individual market conditions.

In a new market, with a relatively small target group, mass media advertising and classic pan-European public relations were not cost-effective for a company like BellSouth in 1991. Once the market was penetrated and producing, the situation could change. To build his network of contacts, Menatti used local consultants, law firms, accounting firms and partners.

Planning was begun early for the Telecom '91 conference, because it delivered high-level participation from the private as well as the public sector. Trade publications for PTT/government officials would be most useful but were lacking in Europe, Menatti found.

The groundwork for BellSouth, then, consisted of building relationships – and conveying expertise and reliability. Image-building means working person by person and country by country, with due attention to EU institutions.

The importance of a proper plan

When line managers sense a need for public relations to sustain their efforts, action-orientated tactics usually come to mind first. To be successful, however, corporate communications should respond to pre-agreed objectives and a strategy to achieve them over a prescribed period of time. Too many companies put the cart before the horse.

For example, one financial services company based in Switzerland decided to expand its business in Europe. What was needed was a brochure, management decided – or two or three: one for each type of service provided by the company, plus one for the company itself, in at least two languages. Design consultants were contacted and told to produce the required brochures. No objectives had been defined. No communications targets had been identified. No messages had been spelled out or coordinated. There was no agreed strategy to achieve precise objectives. 'Just make sure the brochures look good,' the designers were told.

Without asking whether or not a package of glossy brochures was what the company really needed and, obviously, without proposing alternatives, the designers proceeded to submit a budget that management found difficult to accept – because there was no context of realistic objectives and measurable results. The inevitable 'scaling back' process began. Two brochures, instead of four; 20 pages instead of 40, and so on. The inevitable result was disgruntled designers and company executives convinced that all consultants are not trustworthy. The brochures still sit on the managing director's bookshelf, an eloquent example of corporate communications gone wrong at substantial expense.

Keeping country managers in tune with headquarters

Sometimes, the needs of a particular country market move faster than corporate communications policy (and imagination) at headquarters permits. The following example neatly illustrates the resulting corporate dilemma.

This is what happened at a well-known French supplier of computer software for the banking industry. Corporate headquarters in Paris decided to build European growth market-by-market, with no overall corporate connection. But the company's Italian subsidiary felt that an international image, stressing certain company characteristics, would help build credibility and sales in a market crowded with strong, local competition.

A proposal was developed to use corporate image to help sell the company's products and services, distinguish it from its competitors, and contribute to its growth. Strategy called for communications to build an image by conveying the benefits to customers of the company's international resources and long-time presence in the Italian market, product quality, accessibility and willingness to 'tailor-make' products and systems to meet customers' software needs. The proposal included a mechanism to measure results of the image-building campaign after two years, and provided for the Italian market to use its own resources to finance the image-building exercise.

The Paris headquarters said no. 'Corporate image-building should be done out of headquarters,' the company's executive in charge of 'corporate communications' declared. Although technically he was correct, it is usually better to start somewhere rather than not to act at all. Because the Italian subsidiary's proposal suffered from the 'not-invented-here' syndrome, it could not go ahead and the company's valuable image-building capital was not used.

Striking the right balance between central and local control is the key issue when it comes to designing any cross-border marketing strategy whether for a company or for its products. Determining factors inevitably will be the nature of the company's products, the structure of each national market (and size of market share), the shape of the competition, and the rate of evolution of issues that can affect the business franchise.

A cross-border communications strategy can have a central core – or umbrella – of objectives with a series of national spokes that extend into different countries. One challenge is to design a strategy that meets the needs of all disciplines within a company. Another is to design a strategy that can work in all markets, when a company's presence may not be the same in all markets and when issues and attitudes tend to evolve at different speeds in different markets.

Box 4.1   Public Relations Society of America

At the 1993 Public Relations Society of America (PRSA), Barbara H. Hines, executive vice president, consumer marketing division of Porter/Novelli, outlined the prerequisites for a successful multinational campaign.

continues

continued

(1) Identify public relations goals based upon global business objectives. Core communication messages should reflect these goals and be consistent across borders. Consistency is crucial, even though programme implementation and tactical elements may differ in different markets. The key messages for all target audiences are best developed by the lead agency in consultation with the client, with local markets providing comment, adaptation and translation.

(2) Select local partner agencies or representatives to oversee local implementation. This is critical to make sure that the multinational programme reflects cultural, linguistic and budgetary differences. While ideally the lead agency should recommend local ones, typically the client presents the main agency with a slate of local agencies from local country management. In small countries, the management itself may carry out the public relations programme.

(3) Assign responsibility for multinational programme coordination to a single agency. This helps cost efficiencies, early problem detection, message consistency and feedback on a country-by-country basis into a central point. The coordinating agency can also act as a sounding board.

Coordination is essential throughout the campaign. The lead agency should review all programme drafts, press materials and media strategies from the other agencies, who should also forward copies of monthly status reports to make sure there is a comprehensive record of editorial coverage.

(4) Develop a programme 'blueprint' for distribution to all local agencies/representatives to ensure a framework within which local programme implementation can vary. It should include:

- overall business brief
- programme timetable
- objectives
- strategies
- target audiences
- core messages
- executional options
- key contacts, addresses, phone and fax numbers (home if possible to cope with time changes)
- core materials delivery schedule.

If possible briefings should be held face-to-face or using interactive video-conferencing. They should include both local agencies and management.

continues

continued

(5) Develop prototype design elements for use by all associated agencies/representatives. This includes press covers, letterheads, mailing labels and, where appropriate, invitations to ensure consistent imagery and reinforce brand identity across borders. This work can either be done by the lead agency or by the local agencies using original artwork. However, if necessary, to cope with local conditions or preferences, local agencies can develop alternative design executions within the programme blueprint.

(6) Develop prototype press materials for use by all local agencies. Core written materials developed by the lead agency should be offered to all the associates. It can include:

- news and feature releases
- fact sheets
- backgrounders
- brochures
- core speeches/presentations
- media question/answer documents
- photography captions.

(7) Core visual materials should also be offered, including photography, illustrations or technical drawings and any audio material. Product photography, however, should have no visible English language packaging which would limit the applicability to other countries. With audio material, English language should be on a separate track and accompanied by scripts to allow other countries to re-record and add translated audio.

Winning support from line managers

Experience shows that there are certain obstacles to overcome in winning support from line managers. First, communications are supposed to be within the competence of everyone in an organization. A personnel director may not presume to know how to build a production line but communications, after all, are supposed to be part of his/her job. This is true for practically every management function in the company.

Without going through the basic steps of analysing the current situation/image of the company, establishing objectives and creating a plan to accomplish those objectives, those on the front line tend to take a tactical rather than a strategic approach to the problem.

The task of executives trying to communicate consistently across borders is to make sure that action-orientated managers have a hand

(and a vested interest) in designing any cross-border communications strategy – and helping to implement it effectively.

Local managements too often resent what they perceive to be meddling in their markets. The way to handle this is to co-opt country management, to show, with support from regional management, that local authority to communicate really is being increased – within a regional strategy – for the benefit of the company as a whole. It may take time – and closely averted trauma – before local management confidence in a corporate communications function can be won.

One company with a product under fire in the EU used performance appraisals to make country managers accountable for implementing pan-European communications/public affairs strategy. Budget participation helped too: 'If they're helping to pay for it, they tend to be more cooperative,' said an EU public affairs director about his company's country managers.

As consultants, Burson-Marsteller Europe has found that, 'Increasingly, the management of European public affairs is moving from fragmented national strategies to European strategies.' This turns out not to be a strategy that is centrally designed and imposed throughout Europe. 'Rather, the emerging methodology is based on networking – or the orchestration of national responses,' said Larry Snoddon, president of Burson-Marsteller Europe.

Another example of the way national responses can be 'orchestrated' centrally was the pan-European strategy of the Chase Manhattan Bank. Operating out of headquarters in London, the bank's corporate communications department coordinated advertising and public relations to build a pan-European image.

Using image surveys

One way to begin to build a pan-European strategy is to refer to the audit or image survey of the company and its products used to set objectives. Can the survey serve as a base line against which results of strategy and action can be measured? If not, a more formal audit may be necessary. Audits/surveys should be conducted on a national basis, with a pan-European perspective. This means selecting opinion leaders, media, financial analysts, and so on with cross-border influence, as well as customers with a multiple-country presence within the EU.

Objectives will determine the identity of respondents. They should be chosen and approached with a view to going back to them (or their organizations) in at least two years' time. Depending on objectives, surveys/audits can be conducted in the company's name or anonymously, with the company listed as one of several others. (This alternative is used when a comparison is needed against competitors, for example.) Results will vary from country to country and should be analysed for positive, or negative, points in common. A list of key words will emerge, and this list can be used to delineate the current image of a company/organization or a product.

An example of such a list for a company might be as follows:

- powerful
- polluting
- foreign

An example of a list for an organization might be:

- clean
- hardworking
- dull

When compared with a company's mission statement and the objectives it would like to achieve, the list of key words can look like this:

Current image	*Target image*
• powerful	• dynamic
• polluting	• responsible
• foreign	• international

The organization's strategic list of key words could look like this:

Current image	*Target image*
• clean	• clean
• hardworking	• effective
• dull	• essential

Research could reveal that a product is considered to be:

Current image
- superfluous
- expensive
- national

Image-building strategy could be designed to achieve a different perception of the product:

Target image
- innovative
- reliable quality
- international

When strategy calls for the target company image to reinforce target product image, the result can look like this:

Company positioning
- dynamic
- responsible
- international

Product positioning
- innovative
- reliable quality
- international

Variations are infinite, but the basic strategy is the same: definition of the target image for the company and its products, and consistent communication of the target image across borders.

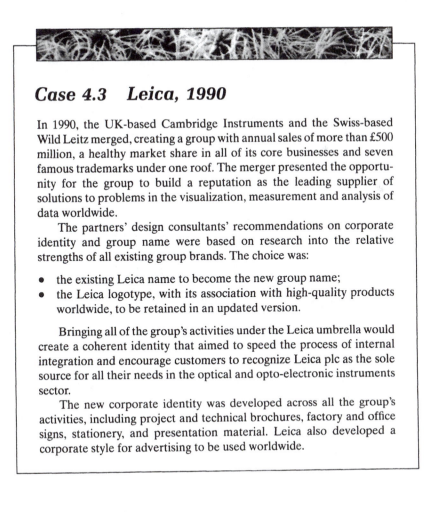

Case 4.3   Leica, 1990

In 1990, the UK-based Cambridge Instruments and the Swiss-based Wild Leitz merged, creating a group with annual sales of more than £500 million, a healthy market share in all of its core businesses and seven famous trademarks under one roof. The merger presented the opportunity for the group to build a reputation as the leading supplier of solutions to problems in the visualization, measurement and analysis of data worldwide.

The partners' design consultants' recommendations on corporate identity and group name were based on research into the relative strengths of all existing group brands. The choice was:

- the existing Leica name to become the new group name;
- the Leica logotype, with its association with high-quality products worldwide, to be retained in an updated version.

Bringing all of the group's activities under the Leica umbrella would create a coherent identity that aimed to speed the process of internal integration and encourage customers to recognize Leica plc as the sole source for all their needs in the optical and opto-electronic instruments sector.

The new corporate identity was developed across all the group's activities, including project and technical brochures, factory and office signs, stationery, and presentation material. Leica also developed a corporate style for advertising to be used worldwide.

Making strategy work

Before a strategy can begin to pay off it must be implemented. And a strategy for communicating effectively across borders cannot be implemented in a vacuum. It is necessary to create a concept, select the tools to communicate the concept, draw up a budget and commit to a timetable. Then the corporate communications function needs to be defined and managed.

Much will depend on the way the company is organized. As one Brussels-based public relations manager remarked, 'It does no good to talk about "empowering" people to fulfil their responsibilities as part of a pan-European network if the company itself still is organized hierarchically.'

Much also depends on the extent of a company's presence in certain markets. If the EU is a new market, for instance, then executives hired to penetrate it will have to begin to implement communications strategy themselves. To a great extent, the company's eventual reputation will depend on the people it hires to work in a market where first impressions count and companies are personified.

Or a company can be widely exposed in terms of investment and different product lines. The time will come when it will be necessary to ensure that there is an overall identity to use. A corporate communications function will have to be built from scratch.

Another turning point may come during and after a merger or acquisition. If both partners have existing corporate communications functions, effective organization becomes critical. There may be differences of philosophy and there must be a rapid and clear evaluation of the best way to deal with the combined partners' communications needs.

Then there is the company that gets to the point where it makes sense to combine marketing and corporate communications so that they reinforce each other.

Coordinating the flow of information

Delegating to national level is effective, but only if an overall communications strategy applies, so that the same information is given at the same time to the same people in different countries. If the overall alternative is to work, a constant flow of information is necessary – from headquarters to countries, from countries to headquarters and among the countries themselves. Electronic networking is essential to this type of information flow, but networking cannot replace face-to-face meetings and pan-European conference calls can become global conference calls when circumstances warrant.

The task is to create a multi-country team of professionals, who network with one another as well as with important external groups. Their work will build trusted relationships and allow the company to participate constructively in the community as well as in the political process at the country and EU level.

Investing in computer links, cross-border communications training, and regular regional information meetings with communications colleagues and marketing management will cost money. But if the investment produces a consistent strategy and coherent action in major markets to accomplish business objectives, return on investment can be enormous. When this return can be quantified, so much the better.

For example, an international consumer goods company with marketing and production facilities throughout the EU suddenly saw its leading product slapped with a surtax in France. For country and regional management, the French government's move was a national obstacle to overcome. More – and better – marketing effort surely could compensate for any impact on sales.

At regional headquarters, corporate affairs looked at the EU as a whole. What they saw presented a challenge and an opportunity. The French surtax set a dangerous precedent that could be copied by other countries. Further, their knowledge of the Rome Treaty told the company's corporate affairs people that the French surtax contravened specific articles.

The task then became to convince French and regional management that the company had more than a national problem; to do the arithmetic to convince French parliamentarians and ministers of the impact on current revenues from the product if sales fell because of the surtax; to confirm the legal basis for a Treaty of Rome violation; to identify decision-makers in France and in Brussels with influence on the implementation – or cancellation – of the surtax; to prepare briefing papers to help present an objective and documented case against the surtax to the targets identified at national and EU level; and to communicate with those targets, on a one-to-one basis and through the media.

At a time when lobbying was virtually unheard of in France, senior national management lobbied French parliamentarians, with regional corporate affairs department support and resources. Specially written articles were placed with the media, documenting the folly of tax increases that would reduce sales of articles already generating hefty tax revenue for the national budget.

Simultaneously, the company talked to comparable decision-makers in another member state where jobs and export revenue depend on producing for the French market. Copies of resulting media coverage were circulated in France and at the EC.

Finally, the French government got the message: from the top at the EC (during a French presidency), from the directorates concerned and via the member of the French parliament responsible for liaison with the EC.

The result was that the French surtax on the company's product was discontinued. The contention (prevalent outside the EU) that the Union has no power over member states was disproved. And the bottom-line efficacy of a pan-European strategy, implemented by regional corporate affairs in close liaison with national management, was confirmed.

Convincing country managers

At one US-based multinational, it took seven years before the company's European corporate affairs department became credible enough with country managers to be used as a policy and communications resource. Affiliates were contributing to the headquarters budget but were not seeing any results for their money. There are three lessons here for national and regional management:

(1) Corporate communications/public affairs should not be used like firefighters. The department should be brought in at the business strategy level, not after the fact.

(2) Results take time. There is no quick fix.

(3) When the implementation of a cross-border communications strategy pays off, results should be attributed to the credit of the people concerned.

In the end, the only thing that matters is mutual trust and confidence built up over time among the company's country managers, corporate communications at regional headquarters, and consultants.

Short reporting lines are essential. There is nothing worse for a national communications professional (or a consultant) than to be sitting in the middle of a public maelstrom waiting for approval before action can be taken or a response given.

Within clearly spelled out guidelines, country managers or their in-house communications counsellors should be empowered to speak for the company within individual markets on matters that affect the company (and its image) in that country. If issues are anticipated, there will be time to use corporate communications at regional headquarters as a resource, so that pronouncements are coherent from country to country.

With rare exceptions, outside consultants should not be used as spokespeople. They should advise on appropriate national strategy and implement action within that strategy. The ultimate source of information always should be the company. Consultants who receive queries should alert national management and regional corporate communications at the same time. Responses should come from national management. The result should be a consistent chorus of authoritative company voices, all saying the same thing.

Human resource management

Part of the programme management involves the allocation of people to activities. This is an especially demanding task for the managers of public relations consultancy teams, and the managers of larger in-house departments. There is a need to balance the skills of available staff, their working level and time against the requirements of the programme.

The group of qualified people able to work in public relations practice is relatively small, for a number of reasons. At this stage of the development of the practice, there is still no clearly recognized or required programme of preparation for work in public relations. The most able practitioners are those who have an aptitude for it and who, in the course of their careers, have acquired the experience that has enabled them to progress in their career.

The size of the pool of available practitioners has a number of consequences. One is that there is strong competition for the small number of able practitioners, particularly at senior levels. Another is that salary levels for the same staff can be quite high.

The pool is augmented in a number of ways. In what a number of US academics have called 'encroachment', staff from other areas, such as marketing, legal services or strategy, may be drawn into public relations practice. Encroachment may be a threat to the future development of the practice, because staff from other areas come in with recognized professional skills and may have a credibility that public relations practitioners still lack.

The pool is also increased by new entrants to the practice. A problem for public relations practice in the past has been that it has not been regarded as a career of first choice. This has meant that individuals have come into the practice as though by default: they have begun their careers in other areas, such as journalism, advertising or administration, and made a move into public relations at a later stage.

Public relations has also been seen, in some organizations, as a function through which staff from other disciplines can pass as part of a process of career development, or as a function into which staff who have outlived their usefulness in other parts of the organization can be retired.

In the past, because of generally held attitudes towards public relations, the practice has failed to attract the best and brightest of potential entrants, who are still creamed off into more established professional practices, such as law and medicine.

These problems are lessening. Now young people are attracted to the prospects of a career in public relations. University and college level programmes in the USA, Australia, Canada and the UK have made it possible for young people to opt for studies in public relations as a preparation for a career in the practice.

Career patterns

The pattern of a career in public relations is also becoming clear. A substantial number of entrants still come to public relations as a second or further career from other activities. For example, the so-described veteran campaigner, Des Wilson, prominent in the promotion of a number of social causes in the UK and the election campaign of the Liberal Democrat Party in the 1992 UK general election, recently moved into public affairs practice with Burson-Marsteller in London, and then to an in-house public affairs position with BAA plc, which owns and manages a number of the UK airports. This kind of career development is still common, and brings strong skills into public relations practice.

More young people are also choosing a career in public relations. Studies of the development of subjects for study at university level in the UK have found strong growth in interest in subjects related to communication. In the USA, there are scores of undergraduate programmes offering students the opportunity to major in public relations.

Undergraduate programmes, where offered in the USA, UK or elsewhere, tend to be multidisciplinary, with strong liberal arts or humanities components, as well as business, communications and social science content. Practitioners have mixed views regarding the value of these relatively new degrees. Studies in the USA and Canada of employers' expectations of entrants to public relations have found that employers still prefer entrants to have a preparation in an established discipline, related to business or organizational interests, rather than a degree in public relations. This situation will change as the new degree programmes and their graduates gain credibility.

Entrants to public relations through the new degree programmes, or through other routes, are expected by employers to present themselves well, have good communication skills (particularly for written communication) and to have judgement. Academics and others involved in the education and training of entrants to the practice expect them to have:

(1) analytical skills, based on knowledge of research techniques and experience of a variety of organizations and social situations;
(2) excellent and well-developed communication skills, for face-to-face communication, as well as for forms of communication requiring skilful use of words, images and design;
(3) an appreciation of culture and cultural differences: organizational, national and international;
(4) business, management and political skills.

It is quite clear that these skills cannot be developed solely within the confines of the classroom, and the most successful – and credible – education programmes are those which combine academic content with opportunities for students to gain practical experience through work placements or extended practical project work.

Women and public relations

A feature of the student group now working its way through degree programmes in public relations is that it is dominated by women. It is also an aspect of membership of the professional associations such as the International Association of Business Communicators and the UK's Institute of Public Relations that the majority of new entrants are women. The 'feminization' of public relations practice has been studied in the USA by the International Association of Business Communicators, and there are concerns relating to increases in the number of women entering the practice:

(1) Other occupations which have come to be dominated by women, such as teaching, tend to lose status.
(2) Women, though skilled in public relations work and, according to research findings, generally better qualified than their male counterparts, are paid less than men for similar work, and find that their career progress to more senior level positions in the practice may be blocked. They tend to hit a 'glass ceiling', which many will claim does not exist, but actually keeps them from reaching senior positions.

Prominent exceptions to these observations do not detract from the statistics which show that women in public relations are consistently paid less than men for similar work, or from the subtle prejudice which may be expressed against women progressing to senior advisory roles in many organizations. Studies of the progress of women in public relations careers in Canada have found that many women in public relations move on to their own businesses in order to make progress that they cannot make in the organizations in which they work.

Improving qualifications and training

Studies of the membership of professional associations, such the UK's Institute of Public Relations, have shown that the educational qualifications of members are improving. Better qualified people are now coming into public relations practice, and standards within the practice will improve over time. The need to improve standards has been recognized by the practice's leading figures. Peter Gummer, chairman of Shandwick, told a meeting of the International Public Relations Association in November 1990 that unless the practice, worldwide, took urgent steps to improve standards – by recruiting adequately qualified staff and providing proper training – its future would be doubtful.

Outside the practice, commentators such as Professor Leo Murray, director of Cranfield School of Management, one of the UK's leading business schools, have commented on poor standards found in public relations practice. In a comment (quoted with permission) on a study of the teaching of public relations in the UK's business and management schools in March 1991 he said that

> 'most directors/managers react very negatively to the term "PR". It conjures up the image of external agencies carrying out superficial tasks and usually to a very low level of competency and inordinately high costs. With notable exceptions the lack of professionalism of PR agencies and the poor quality of their operational staff is a byword.'

Against this opinion, standards of practice are now under close scrutiny, as attempts are made to bring consultancy and management practice in public relations up to publicly recognized standards such as international and national quality standards. Attention is being paid to qualifications and skills, partly through the development of training programmes, for which some of the more forward-thinking consultancies are gaining recognition.

Studies by the International Association of Business Communicators, the Public Relations Society of America and other national professional groups such as the Canadian Public Relations Society have identified the training needs at various stages in a public relations career.

A career in the practice involves preparation for entry – now increasingly involving degree-level study in related subjects such as business, communications, the social sciences or public relations itself – and entry itself. The early stages of a career in the practice require a grounding in all aspects of public relations.

Later, a career in public relations may lead into advanced specialization in areas such as public affairs or investor relations, or a move into the management of groups of public relations staff. As yet, it is rare for public relations practice to provide a springboard on to the more senior levels of general management, in the way that a finance director may use his or her position as a basis for progression on the chief executive officer's role.

At each stage, specific education and training requirements are apparent. After entry, training requirements are for development and refinement of basic skills, in the practice itself, in communication, in the basics of business and organization management, financial management, social research, consulting and project management. Following entry and this basic training programme, further development of skills in analysis, judgement and working with more senior levels of management are necessary to bring the entrant up to a full working competence. At this stage it is also necessary to develop project and programme management skills.

Studies of public relations careers – particularly studies carried out within the federal government in Canada, and among Canadian and UK practitioners – have found that at approximately five years into a career in public relations, practitioners are faced with a choice in their career development. This is between:

(1) developing specialist skills, or
(2) preparing themselves for a more general management role, in which skills in managing programmes, staff, budgets and in providing higher level, strategic advice to the organizations and clients they work for will become important.

Discussions of education and training of public relations staff have focused in countries like the UK on ways in which professional groups and employers can develop training programmes which meet requirements at each stage. These discussions have led to initiatives at the postgraduate level in university programmes, to the introduction of specialist masters' programmes in public relations and to emphasis on the MBA as a possible preparation for advanced work at the management level.

Education and training initiatives in place at the present time are tentative and experimental, but gaining in strength and credibility. The specialist master's programme at Stirling University introduced in the late 1980s now graduates practitioners who are well accepted by employers.

Additional features of careers in public relations

Other features of careers in public relations are that there are still few barriers to entry, and that it is possible for able entrants to progress very quickly to senior positions. This means that it is possible for an entrant with no formal qualifications to enter the practice and, through aptitude expressed in creativity, skills in problem solving and business management, to make very rapid progress. Among current practitioners, there are many who feel that this opportunity should not be closed off by an insistence on rigid entry qualifications. Others feel that it is important for practitioners to be at least as qualified in formal terms as the people that they hope to advise. This means entrants who have a first degree to which they may add significant business and management experience, and a further degree, probably an MBA or other management degree.

As public relations evolves, this argument will diminish. The practice is becoming a popular career choice. More, better qualified applicants are seeking entry into the practice, and employers will be able to choose among these to find the candidates best qualified to meet their requirements.

A final feature of a career in public relations is that because progress to a high level in the practice can be made quickly, young practitioners may find that, at an early age, they have few career options left within public relations. Alison Canning's experience provides an example of the rapid progress that can be made. An MBA graduate of City University Business School in London, she was recruited by one of the leading senior practitioners in the UK, Reginald Watts, to join Burson-Marsteller in London in 1983. After a short career which has included experience with the consultancy in New York, and with a sister company in the UK, she has now, at 34, been appointed chief executive in Burson-Marsteller's London office. Other examples can be found in-house, in large companies, where young practitioners have made similar progress.

The problem for these young achievers is what to do with the remainder of their career. They can remain to grow their jobs within the organizations where they have achieved their early success. They can make a number of lateral, senior moves. They can establish their own businesses. They can also look for opportunities outside public relations, although these are less obvious, and the opportunity to move into more senior management positions is, as we mentioned earlier, unlikely to be open to managers from a public relations background.

Several potential dangers attach to this phase in an able practitioner's career which relate to staleness, maintaining interest in the practice, satisfactory relations with senior management or clients where relations have to be sustained over a longer period of time. To avoid these career problems, practitioners need to create challenges for themselves, which might involve setting up independent business ventures, or making moves into teaching and training, or becoming more involved in the development of the practice itself. A favoured option in future may be to undertake further education and training to carry out research into the practice, or to prepare for a transition into other areas of management.

What can employers and clients expect from practitioners?

Cranfield's Professor Murray suggested that the poor quality of staff in public relations is well recognized. Employers and clients for the services of practitioners can check the quality of staff they are likely to work with by running through a checklist of the characteristics of the staff they employ, as in-house staff or consultants.

From an employer or client perspective, practitioners should be:

- educated, formally and through experience;
- analytical and questioning of problems presented to them;
- skilled in consulting: that is, practitioners at all levels should be able to clarify client or employer problems – even minor technical problems – and provide guidance towards dealing with them;
- effective in implementation: they must be able to do, or to get done, the fundamental tasks involved in public relations;
- capable project managers.

In working with consultancies, clients often complain that the staff who present to win accounts are often not the staff who work on their account. This problem should diminish over time as the quality of all staff assigned to accounts, and their general level of preparation for public relations work, improve. Training available for consultancy staff depends on the attitude of consultancy management groups to training, the resources they have available, and their willingness to devote resources to training.

Clients may want to check the training programmes in place within consultancies they wish to work with: this can be done at the time that credentials are checked. Training should be based on an analysis of the needs of staff for training, and should cover all aspects of public relations practice, from basic communication and research skills through to management level training.

In-house, employers making decisions regarding appointment of staff to public relations positions will need to consider a number of criteria, including:

(1) The scope of the position being filled. Public relations is too often regarded as a matter of media relations, and of the exercise of a limited number of specific communication skills. However, more can be expected than this: a practitioner can be an adviser, a source of research information and intelligence regarding important groups, and can be a link between the organization and these groups. It is important to define what is expected of the practitioner before the appointment is made, to avoid dissatisfaction later.

(2) The qualifications and skills of the person likely to be employed. While this is a standard approach in recruitment, it is less easy to be precise at this stage in the development of public relations practice because people with skills in the practice will have come from a variety of backgrounds, and will have developed differing repertoires of skills, partly as a result of the training and experience they have had.

Efforts to recruit to public relations positions will often be rewarded with many applications from people who believe that almost any qualifications and experience will make them fit for work in practice.

Human resource questions in public relations practice will be resolved as employers, clients, the professional associations and potential entrants become clearer about the tasks involved in public relations, and the qualifications, skills and experience needed to manage them. Attention to these details will be needed on the part of the professional associations, such as the Institute of Public Relations and the Public Relations Consultants Association in the UK. Some work has already been completed: in the UK, the Public Relations Education Trust, supported by the main professional associations, has developed a public relations training matrix to identify training needs at each stage in a career in public relations. Further work remains to be done, and this will be bound up with the development of the professional associations themselves. We will return to some of these points in the next chapter, which looks at the future of public relations practice.

Summary

(1) Public relations activities are initiated in response to events, or develop almost logically out of business and organizational objectives. As far as possible public relations should anticipate problems, issues, events and opportunities before they arise.

(2) Perhaps the biggest challenge facing public relations practitioners today is managing programmes across borders consistently and effectively. This is particularly complex when it comes to Europe, not only because of the multicultural aspect, but also because different markets are at different stages of development.

(3) The complexity of the European market makes it worthwhile to examine the five principal audiences that need to be targeted by pan-European corporate communicators:

- government
- media
- employees
- customers
- EU bureaucrats and political leaders.

In the USA, current jargon calls these targets 'stakeholders'. In Europe, communications professionals tend to use 'opinion leaders' or 'decision-makers'. Of the three terms, 'decision-makers' is probably the most apt in the European context because, sooner or later, decisions by representatives of each – or all – of these groups will affect company strategy, tactics, growth and profits.

(4) To be successful corporate communications should respond to pre-agreed objectives and a strategy to achieve them over a prescribed period of time. Too many companies put the cart before the horse.

(5) Striking the right balance between central and local control is the key issue when it comes to designing any cross-border marketing strategy whether for a company or for its products. Determining factors inevitably will be the nature of the company's products, the structure of each national market (and size of market share), the shape of the competition, and the rate of evolution of issues that can affect the business franchise.

(6) The task of executives trying to communicate consistently across borders is to make sure that action-orientated managers have a hand (and a vested interest) in designing any cross-border communications strategy – and helping to implement it effectively.

(7) One way to begin to build a pan-European strategy is to refer to the audit or image survey of the company and its products used to set objectives.

(8) Before a strategy can begin to pay off it must be implemented. And a strategy for communicating effectively across borders cannot be implemented in a vacuum. It is necessary to create a concept, select the tools to communicate the concept, draw up a budget and commit to a timetable. Then the corporate communications function needs to be defined and managed.

(9) Delegating to national level is effective, but only if an overall communications strategy applies, so that the same information is given at the same time to the same people in different countries. If the overall alternative is to work, a constant flow of information is necessary – from headquarters to countries, from countries to headquarters and among the countries themselves.

(10) Within clearly spelled out guidelines, country managers or their in-house communications counsellors should be empowered to speak for the company within individual markets on matters that affect the company (and its image) in that country.

(11) Part of the programme management involves the allocation of people to activities. This is an especially demanding task for the managers of public relations consultancy teams, and the managers of larger in-house departments. There is a need to balance the skills of available staff, their working level and time against the requirements of the programme.

(12) The group of qualified people able to work in public relations practice is relatively small, for a number of reasons. At this stage of the development of the practice, there is still no clearly recognized or required programme of preparation for work in public relations. The most able practitioners are those who have an aptitude for it and who, in the course of their careers, have acquired the experience that has enabled them to progress in their career.

(13) In the past, because of generally held attitudes towards public relations, the practice has failed to attract the best and brightest of potential entrants, who are still creamed off into more established professional practices, such as law and medicine. These problems are lessening.

(14) Better qualified people are now coming in to public relations practice, and standards within the practice will improve over time. The need to improve standards of practice has been recognised by the practice's leading figures.

(15) From an employer or client perspective, practitioners should be:
- educated, formally and through experience;
- analytic and questioning of problems presented to them;
- skilled in consulting: that is, practitioners at all levels should be able to clarify client or employer problems – even minor technical problems – and provide guidance towards dealing with them;
- effective in implementation: they must be able to do, or to get done, the fundamental tasks involved in public relations;
- capable project managers

5

Budgeting, control and evaluation

Budgeting

Treating the management of public relations as a matter of managing programmes of activities has implications for budgeting. To achieve identified objectives in known time periods allows for accurate budgeting for the costs of activities, resources and services involved, and the costs of staff time. Using programme budgeting techniques enables public relations managers to develop costs for all programmes, exert controls on expenditure, and evaluate programmes against costs. They also allow managers to establish more precisely how much an organization should spend on public relations activities – and to answer the question which frequently arises about how much should be spent.

Another question which arises is who should have control of expenditures on public relations activities. If the budget is held centrally within the organization and managed by a senior public relations manager it is visible and may be open to criticism or to misunderstanding, or to reduction as a central cost. This arrangement does leave control of the budget in the senior public relations manager's hands, and give some power to determine the way in which public relations will be managed. At the same time, though, other managers, because they are not directly involved in decisions on public relations expenditures, may not understand the reasons for these expenditures.

An alternative arrangement leaves budgets for public relations activities with line managers, who can either buy the services of a central public relations staff group, or buy outside services, or make expenditures themselves on public relations activities, with the advice of specialist staff, internal or external. Expenditure from their own budgets will involve managers more closely in the management of public relations activities. This alternative may be favoured for the reason that it does emphasize that all managers have some responsibility for public relations management, in the same way that all managers have some responsibility for human resource management.

Budgets also have a significant role as a means of communication. Commitment to make expenditures to achieve objectives will communicate the importance of those objectives throughout the organization.

Case 5.1   Chase

In 1990, the Chase Manhattan Bank ran an advertising campaign in Europe to get across the message that Chase had the cross-border banking and industry expertise to meet its global clients' needs in the new Europe. The bottom line was proof of performance in corporate finance.

One of a series created by Saatchi & Saatchi, the advertisement clearly positioned Chase as a 'pan-European' player in the global financial marketplace and reflected a deliberate shift in business strategy for the bank, which began preparing for 1992 five years ahead of the date set for the advent of the single European market.

The bank's business and communications strategy was focusing on four key business areas: corporate finance; risk management; private banking; and information and transaction services. 'Part of the effort is aimed at emphasizing the bank's industry expertise and the fact that we are a global bank that has been active on the European scene for a long time,' said Stewart Prosser, second vice president in charge of advertising.

In terms of corporate finance, target industries for Chase specialist teams – and the bank's corporate communications effort – were branded foods, chemicals, energy, insurance, media, and paper and packaging. Consequently, the bank's advertising and media relations activities focused on the trade press that served these industries, as well as on national business and economic media and on pan-European publications like the *Financial Times*, *International Herald Tribune*,

continues

continued

Wall Street Journal (Europe) and *Euromoney*. Local language media were used in France, Germany and Spain. In Italy, advertising would often run in English.

At Chase in Europe, advertising, public relations, sponsorship, events and internal communications were used individually and together to build and reinforce the image that the bank wanted to convey. 'We believe there is enormous benefit in this type of reinforcement,' Smith said. 'As a department of the bank, corporate communications is designed to provide a service for our business managers across Europe while we centralize resources and avoid duplication,' he added.

There could be national differences, but the bank's European corporate communications function was intended to provide an overall communications and positioning umbrella that ensured consistency and coherence of messages. The pay-off was measured via tracking studies that helped those responsible 'keep our communications strategies on target'.

Advertising and public relations consultants got the same brief and were managed out of London, in close liaison with New York. Hill & Knowlton was the bank's public relations agency of record.

Smith reported to Chase Manhattan's corporate communications executive at the bank's US headquarters. There, the function encompassed government and investor relations (which in London it did not), internal communications, public relations and resources marketing. Communications budgets for each geographic region were built up on the basis of overall business plans.

Sometimes, agreed budgets were supplemented to meet particular needs. When reports of the troubles of the US banking industry were hitting Europe's business pages, for example, Chase decided that it was important to communicate positively and reconfirm its commitment to its strategies in Europe.

As in this case, media advertising was often leveraged in direct mail packages that communicated with employees and customers. This way, pan-European advertising became the vehicle for corporate messages that were the same throughout the EU. Even though languages and operating conditions might vary from country to country, the reality of one market for financial services was recognized in a very appealing – and performance-related – way.

Control

Programme management and budgets tied to the programme of activities allow for tighter management control of public relations activities. Plans for public relations activities can be developed out of organizational plans and agreed with line managers, with budgetary arrangements planned at the same time.

Management control of public relations practice can be exerted in an examination of expenditures against pre-determined budgets, and of progress towards specific objectives against timetables. The setting of precise objectives activities allows for checks on progress towards objectives, and is a prerequisite for later evaluation of public relations activities.

Evaluation

It is all very well saying that a properly thought out and carefully carried out communications programme can have an impact on the bottom line. But how can it be measured? There is both a long-term and a short-term aspect to evaluating the effectiveness of public relations. Long term means measuring over time what can be small but significant shifts, while short-term evaluations can be carried out for specific campaigns. It is still a relatively new area, however. In advertising millions have been spent creating sophisticated measurement systems. Public relations has not enjoyed the same attention, although, as the next section shows, consultancies are struggling to come up with formalized ways to evaluate what they do for their clients.

According to one senior public relations consultant, evaluation is one of the big trends of the 1990s.

'By the mid-90s companies and consultancies will expect to be able to measure what they do – and I don't just mean through the media. It will be done through research, exactly as you measure advertising results. Some areas will be difficult. But because so much more of public relations is project-based, it is becoming increasingly possible to measure. And companies, as they invest more into their communications and become more aware of that investment, are more prepared to put money into measurement.'

Common factors in measuring both long- and short-term results include a clear understanding of the goals and then research into whether they were reached. According to Guido Bellodi of GCI Chiappe Bellodi in Milan research is the only scientific instrument:

'If you have an awareness programme, for example, you should measure what type of awareness you have before the therapy and what type after. You have to have a set of achievable objectives, and achievable is an important word because in my opinion both clients and agencies can overestimate the type of result wanted or offered. It is human nature to offer more than can be delivered. If the objectives are achievable you can end up happy or unhappy but you know.'

Box 5.1 The Conference Board report

Eight out of 10 participants in The Conference Board's 1993 survey of senior communications executives agreed with the statement that it is realistic for top management to expect communicators to demonstrate a link between their activities and business results. However, as one respondent pointed out, 'I have been in this field for 25 years, and I don't know any more about measurement than I did when I started out. It comes down to customer satisfaction, management vision and opinion surveys.'

Results from the survey suggest that areas like investor–government relations, along with sales/marketing support activities, lend themselves more readily to documentation than corporate advertising, employee communications and community relations.

In investor relations, indicators include changes in the share price, share appreciation versus goals, share performance measured against that of peers and analyst opinions. Surveys of advertising awareness, results from targeted marketing campaigns, sales completed or new accounts are signs of success for marketing and sales support programmes. Executives responsible for government relations can point to legislation or regulations passed, killed or amended.

The main methods used by companies surveyed by The Conference Board in the USA to evaluate results are shown in Figure 5.1.

Modern measurement techniques work even in the more elusive area of gauging corporate image. As Joan Wasylik, European corporate communications manager for US-based trading conglomerate Cargill, said,

'You can measure image with surveys, for instance, with the target audiences that are important to you. Say it is important that your customers in a certain business perceive you as reliable, giving quality, and so on, whatever the values are that

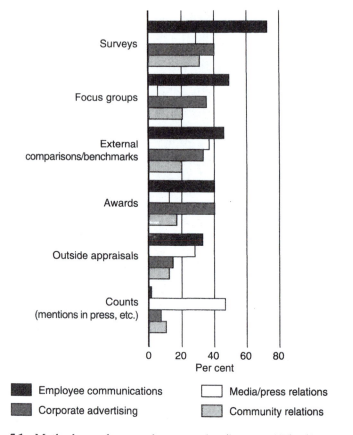

Figure 5.1 Methods used to evaluate results (base = 155). (*Source*: The Conference Board)

you want to make sure that they understand. So you measure that before you do your programme. You find out their perception of you now – for instance, you ask them to name the top three providers of that product or business. Then you do your programme – although this is very simplified – and at the end you measure whether you have made it to the top three.

'The perception that image has means that it is hard to put a monetary value on it until something goes wrong. The minute that happens, then you see the fruit of all you have done in preparation. So you are preparing against something you hope will never happen and in the meantime trying to show why this is important.'

Management should be made aware of two axioms of any professional communications plan: results take time and there can be no guarantees. It is, however, possible to conduct a baseline survey of a representative mix of respondents (for example, actual customers, potential customers, media and other decision-makers) to determine such factors as:

- how a company is perceived according to the market;
- what products or services are associated with the company in different markets;
- what (actual/potential) customers want when they choose a supplier;
- how respondents rate the quality of a company's products/services;
- how the company is perceived as an employer, potential business partner, and so on;
- how much and what kind of interest target media have evinced in the company to date.

Based on results of a baseline study, communications strategy can be elaborated and implemented over a period of time, usually two years. Then the study is run again to measure results.

A test can be run after one year, with all or part of the original sample. Strategy and action can be changed or reinforced, emphasis shifted or scope widened, depending on results. Public relations/communications budgets for the two-year period should be constructed to permit fine-tuning of the corporate communications plan, if necessary.

Opinion research and image tracking studies are expensive – especially when more than one market is involved. But when the corporate communications function is new, or when results-orientated management insists on measurement, such studies can help build credibility and support.

Coupons are a device that can be used to measure results of corporate communications, on advertising, for example, in connection with annual reports, or both. Beneath a message signed by chief executive Nelson Robertson, General Accident's full-page advertisement in the *Financial Times* in spring 1991 carried a coupon enabling readers to order copies of the insurance group's 1990 annual report. Based in Scotland, General Accident's business is worldwide. Coupon returns provide an indication of the international reach of the FT, non-UK readers' interest in the company and its results, plus the effectiveness of the advertisement itself.

At SmithKline Beecham, government and public affairs objectives were established annually and reviewed quarterly. Yet the difficulty of measuring results was acknowledged. 'We are committed to deploy all efforts to treat but not necessarily cure', said Michel V. Philippe, SmithKline Beecham's vice president and director, government and public affairs, Europe.

What users should acknowledge is that it can be awfully easy to assume that media coverage is the way to judge success, and that public relations can be used as an easy scapegoat when messages get jumbled, or when the media ignore company announcements.

Setting benchmarks

Increased pressure to find more formal ways of measuring effectiveness will probably arise from the quality movement, with its emphasis on research, setting benchmarks and then measuring achievements and results. Executives in charge of areas like marketing and communications which are often seen as budget black holes will be increasingly confronted with the very real question of a superior saying: how do you measure the effectiveness of what you do?

The Smythe Dorward Lambert survey of corporate communicators mentioned earlier[1] underlined the growing attention being paid to evaluation of effectiveness. The report predicted that these executives will want to go beyond broad-based measurement founded on opinion polling, for instance, and examine the quality of individual relationships with people in an organization since 'that dictates overall attitudes to the company and the propensity to buy from it, listen sympathetically to it or be motivated to work effectively for it'. That entails understanding of:

- attitudes on specific issues
- the effect of current communication practices
- what sources of information are valued and seen as credible
- gaps and inefficiencies in current practices.

The report noted that accuracy of measurement goes 'far beyond mere hunches' and can be instrumental in persuading senior managers how important it is for all of them to build up solid relationships and of their essential role in the communications process. It concluded that 'commitment to good communications can best be won in the way that every other management discipline wins; by putting a properly-researched case and demonstrating the competitive advantage to be obtained from having lively relationships.'

Box 5.2   Evaluating public relations

According to a 1989 paper[2] on evaluation in public relations practice from Cranfield School of Management, having appropriate means of evaluation would enable practitioners to:

continues

continued

- establish the value of their services;
- put an accurate financial value on their services;
- develop managerial controls on the effort invested in public relations activities for known returns;
- develop a more professional approach to the provision of public relations services.

The paper outlined five steps in the evaluation of public relations activities:

(1) *Initiation.* The activities are set in motion because of an opportunity, problem or difficulty, or by an organization's overall objectives.

(2) *Negotiation.* This involves discussion between client and consultant (or employer and in-house advisor) to clarify overall objectives, opportunities or problems to be faced and possible action. This sets the framework for evaluation.

(3) *Programme development.* These can be chosen to achieve agreed objectives or will emerge directly from the set objectives. Formative research may be need to tighten objectives, make them precise and measurable and help choose from available alternatives.

(4) *Programme implementation.* Tracking and other studies may be carried out during implementation, including media analysis to check that the right messages are appearing.

(5) *Programme evaluation.* It is crucial that a common approach is followed that recognizes that evaluation will be programme-specific and based on briefing discussions. It encompasses:
    - programme objectives;
    - results of interim measurements of progress towards reaching objectives;
    - results of measurement of impact on the attitudes and behaviour of key publics.

The paper stresses the key role played by research: 'Public relations is a research-based practice. All phases of the practice depend on research, broadly defined as the process of systematically gathering information for decision-making purposes, both formally and informally.'

It is used at the outset of a programme to refine objectives and contribute to decision-making about the programme, to provide measures of progress during the programme, and to establish whether results have been achieved at the end.

Finally, the paper considers some of the types of measures which can be used in public relations, both objective and subjective.

Objective:

(1) impacts on behaviour, such as buying or voting behaviour, or consumption patterns;

continues

---

continued

(2) measures of response, a specific behaviour produced by invitation or encouragement or by the presentation of information;
(3) measures of awareness, opinions and attitude, such as research carried out to gauge awareness of a new product;
(4) measures of media content, both amount and, more subjectively, interpretation;
(5) measures of readership, to see if readers have read and remembered content;
(6) measures of distribution, similar to the idea of the reach of a publication or television programme.

Subjective:

(1) client satisfaction
(2) judgement
(3) intuition
(4) 'gut feeling'.

Demanding more measurable results will apply to public relations practiced in both companies and consultancies. The problem is that consultancies are often held more to account for effectiveness than in-house teams and so come under more pressure to justify what they do.

According to Alan Parker of Brunswick Public Relations, companies that have good communications/public relations know that they do:

'A lot of people say that you cannot possibly measure it. Others say they can sell you research to measure it. But in the end there is a set of people who know if they have good public relations and those people will pay for it. They sit in boardrooms and they have a vision of what they want to get across to the marketplace. They know over a period of time if they are getting it across and if they are receiving the level of advice and consistent service which they need to help frame and communicate those decisions.'

One major obstacle has been costs: clients simply have not been prepared to put the money upfront to help consultancies develop evaluation programmes. As Peter Gummer of Shandwick has noted, discussions about evaluation can be somewhat misleading:

'Over the last 17 to 18 years I haven't found myself under constant pressure to evaluate what I do. Quite the opposite. We go out and do what the client wants us to do. If we find it impossible to produce the results, then we have a conversation about it exactly as we would any other activity. One of the things people will ask when they are spending £100,000 with a consultancy is, how do I know it shouldn't be £90,000 or £100,000? But in 99.9% of cases, it could cost £100,000 to evaluate if that £100,000 was well spent.'

It can be easier, of course, to evaluate some programmes more than others: brand publicity work, for example, can be judged ultimately on sales. Less tangible areas like corporate image can be evaluated through research over a period of time. One of the problems public relations faces in putting itself through the evaluation hoop is that it covers such a wide range of areas and addresses a variety of audiences. In one sense, product public relations is reasonably straightforward as it becomes more project-based. But others are less so, like corporate communications, internal communications, sponsorship, events management, lobbying community affairs and so on.

The problem with measurement of effectiveness is that it has to be a combination of hard fact and soft judgement. Modern technology is, however, beginning to help with the former. In the USA, for example, there are increasingly sophisticated methods for evaluating media results, while in the UK in particular bodies like the Public Relations Consultants Association and the individual consultancies are working on systems that change evaluation from being a rough, post-mortem technique into one which can be used as a continuous management tool.

Rigorous evaluation procedures will eventually be the norm. As Graham Lancaster of Biss Lancaster said, 'The benefit is that if we are forcing ourselves to do it, we are also forcing clients to do it. They are then not treating us as alchemists who can come in and work wonders. It is about managing expectations in advance.'

One solution for companies who want to use research but dislike the fact that it can take a huge chunk out of the public relations budget is to take a more enlightened and integrated approach, and allow the public relations firm to use the research from an advertising campaign to make the whole programme more effective. For example, when ice cream maker Häagen-Dazs launched its US premium ice cream with a series of striking and erotic ads, it generated an avalanche of publicity far beyond that normally accorded a mere food product. But the company was prepared: not only did it brief its sales force to be ready for questions about why sex was being used to sell ice cream, but it also sent every journalist who wanted to write about it a tub to prove that it really was as good as promised.

The ice cream is now used almost as a metaphor for indulgence and still generates those press clippings. According to the then marketing director Simon Esberger, a typical year in the life of his public relations programme in 1993 had been to have successful advertising which created a lot of comment that drove the public relations.

'The other way we can measure it is doing tracking studies, particularly during and after the ads, looking at awareness of Häagen-Dazs and trial. That went up just as much this year as last, even though the advertising was not talked about as much.

'So we are still happy with the PR. As part of the awareness we asked them where they first heard about it and almost as many people are still reading about us as seeing the ads. So that is another way to say the PR is working. If we get to the stage, however, where however good the advertising no one is coming to it through editorial we will start to think it is time to do a proper PR plan.'

According to public relations consultancy Paragon's marketing director Gordon Knight, measurement of objectives depends on those set for each programme. In Paragon's experience, the objectives fall into one or more of the following categories:

(1) The successful achievement of all the actions in the PR plan – did we do everything we said we would?
(2) The impact of changing attitudes among the target groups for the campaign – did we move things as a result?
(3) The effect in generating business interest – did the phone start ringing from potential prospects?
(4) The mitigation of a potential crisis – did we avoid a panning by a hostile and unsympathetic media?
(5) The re-rating of a share price – have we persuaded the investment community of the company's future prospects?
(6) The achievement of specific success factors – did we get the big order? Obtain planning consent? Fend off the bid?
(7) The control of budgets – did we do it all for what we said it would cost?

There is no doubt that many clients using public relations as part of marketing communications still rate it for its ability to generate the right sort of column inches. In the USA, according to David Drobis, world-wide chairman and chief executive officer of Ketchum, clients want public relations consultants to help them focus on their business but they also want to see media mentions:

'Publicity is still very important in the US. You hear buzzwords like strategy and evaluation a lot but – and I am exaggerating here – everyone in PR is saying let's be like McKinsey management consultants. While the clients are saying we would like a little bit of McKinsey we want to be in the *Times* too.

Box 5.3 The BT campaign

Paragon Communications (UK) has, since its formation in January 1981, adopted the principle that public relations is only effective if its results can be measured and its value to the client's business/organization demonstrated. The following illustrates how this can work.

Paragon Communications (UK) was charged with increasing public awareness of speech handicaps for BT. The challenge was to improve understanding among the general public of the communications problems experienced by the 2 million plus people in the UK who suffer from a speech and language difficulty and to communicate the support given to them by BT through National Speech Week.

The strategy was to focus on members of the community who deal most regularly with the general public – retail and service sectors – and to produce extensive branded support materials.

The action programme consisted of:

(1)   formation of a national Speak Week Coordination Committee with representatives from BT, Paragon and the speech therapy profession;

(2)   ongoing coordination and liaison with all 29 BT regional public relations officers, district speech therapy managers, associated charities and other relevant speech therapy bodies;

(3)   production and distribution of national Speak Week support materials – educational leaflets, badges, posters;

(4)   production and distribution of celebrity training video packages aimed at retail and service sector employees;

(5)   media campaign tailored to the general public, industry, and leading opinion formers including government.

The coverage generated total 'opportunities to see' among target audiences of 103 million (based on circulation and audience data) which clearly delivered the key messages.

'I would like to get PR a little further than inches but for most marketing people it is still about inches. They want to see ink, and ink that will help them sell their products. What we are trying to figure out is how that ink is moving towards product sales. In the US we are using marketing evaluation techniques, which we can tie in with our publicity programmes with some success.'

Walt Lindemann, senior vice president and director of research at Ketchum Public Relations in New York, has argued[3] that it is definitely possible to measure public relations – and to do so without spending inordinate amounts of time or money. The problem lies with practitioners who fail to think systematically about what is involved.

What Ketchum has done is develop a straightforward set of guidelines or standards called a 'Public Relations Effectiveness Yardstick'. It consists of several steps as follows:

Step One: Determine the goals or objectives of the public relations programme. What is it seeking to accomplish? This usually falls into four categories:

(1) You or your organization are trying to get certain messages, themes or ideas out.
(2) You would like these messages or ideas distributed to certain key or target audience groups.
(3) You envision distributing these messages to your target audiences via certain pre-selected or specific communications channels – perhaps through the media, by word-of-mouth, or by using a direct mail approach.
(4) And, ultimately, for what you say, for how you say it, and to whom, there are certain short-term or long-term 'ends' or objectives you are interested in accomplishing. Based on how and what you say and do, you would like those you reach to respond in a certain way.

Step Two: Determine the level of public relations measurement. Lindemann divides this into three levels of ascending sophistication.

(1) Level One measures what the public relations practitioner or organization actually did. It measures public relations 'outputs'. A basic measure, it gauges the amount of exposure the organization has received in the media, the total number of placements, the total number of impressions, and/or the likelihood of having reached specific target groups.
(2) Level Two is about measuring whether or not the target audience groups actually received the messages directed at them, whether they paid attention to, understood and retained the messages in whatever shape or form.
(3) Level Three, at the top end of the yardstick, assesses 'outcomes' like opinion, attitude and behaviour change. It involves, among others, using approaches such as:
   • pre- and post-tests;
   • experimental and quasi-experimental research designs;

- data collection methods like observation, participation and role-playing;
- advanced data analysis techniques;
- comprehensive, multi-faceted communications audits.

As Lindemann writes, there is no one simplistic method for measuring public relations effectiveness. But it is extremely important before evaluation that specific goals and objectives are set against which the results can eventually be measured.

Summary

(1) Using programme budgeting techniques enables public relations managers to develop costs for all programmes, exert controls on expenditure, and evaluate programmes against costs. They also allow managers to establish more precisely how much an organization should spend on public relations activities – and to answer the question which frequently arises about how much should be spent.

(2) If the budget is held centrally within the organization and managed by a senior public relations manager it is visible and may be open to criticism or to misunderstanding, or to reduction as a central cost. This arrangement does leave control of the budget in the senior public relations manager's hands, and give some power to determine the way in which public relations will be managed.

(3) An alternative arrangement leaves budgets for public relations activities with line managers, who can either buy the services of a central public relations staff group, or buy outside services, or make expenditures themselves on public relations activities, with the advice of specialist staff, internal or external. Expenditure from their own budgets will involve managers more closely in the management of public relations activities.

(4) Management control of public relations practice can be exerted in an examination of expenditures against pre-determined budgets, and of progress towards specific objectives against timetables. The setting of precise objectives activities allows for checks on progress towards objectives, and is a prerequisite for later evaluation of public relations activities.

(5) There is both a long-term and a short-term aspect to evaluating the effectiveness of public relations. Long term means measuring over

time what can be small but significant shifts, while short-term evaluations can be carried out for specific campaigns. It is still a relatively new area, however.

(6) Increased pressure to find more formal ways of measuring effectiveness will probably arise from the quality movement, with its emphasis on research, setting benchmarks and then measuring achievements and results.

(7) Having appropriate means of evaluation would enable practitioners to:

- establish the value of their services;
- put an accurate financial value on their services;
- develop managerial controls on the effort invested in public relations activities for known returns;
- develop a more professional approach to the provision of public relations services.

(8) It can be easier to evaluate some programmes rather than others: brand publicity work, for example, can be judged ultimately on sales. Less tangible areas like corporate image can be evaluated through research over a period of time.

(9) There is no doubt that many clients using public relations as part of marketing communications still rate it for its ability to generate the right sort of column inches.

Notes

(1) *The Rise to Power of the Corporate Communicator.* London: Smythe Dorward Lambert, 1992.
(2) White, Jon, *Evaluation in Public Relations Practice.* Cranfield School of Management, 1989.
(3) Lindemann, Walt, An 'effectiveness yardstick' to measure PR Success, *Public Relations Quarterly*, Spring 1993.

PART TWO

Special areas of practice

6

Media relations

The breadth and depth of the media

The importance of public relations has been heightened not just by the demands of the global business environment but also by the changing nature of the media and the fact that modern international companies are vast, complex, sprawling organizations made up of lots of varied elements. At any time any one of these elements can come into contact with the media. Unless there is a clear understanding of the corporate ethos and how that should translate into behaviour in all circumstances even one off-the-cuff remark can lead to global and damaging headlines.

Modern communications allied to an internationally competitive media means that it becomes increasingly pointless to practice fortress building and leak prevention. It demands a rethinking of how to deal with a hungry and amazingly diverse collection of journalists who themselves have different audiences to satisfy and different proprietors with which to deal. It is no good hoping the media will go away, or only be there to spread the good news. That does not mean media manipulation is impossible – practised spin merchants will always find gullible journalists they can sell to. But the sheer competitiveness of journalism now, and the scale on which it is practised, means that constant probing for weak spots will usually come up with something. As the Grand Metropolitan case study (Case 6.1) shows, it is essential to foster a professional relationship with the media because of the impact that relationship can have on corporate activity.

Case 6.1 Grand Metropolitan, 1992

Grand Metropolitan is major international company involved in three core areas of food, drink and retail. Although British-based, up to 60% of its profits come from the USA, mainly through the acquisition of Pillsbury in 1989. That had changed considerably from the company Tim Halford, former head of public affairs, joined in 1984: 'I was the first public relations man Grand Met had. It meant that the company did not have a very good reputation because it was not accessible. You had public relations people handling the brands but nothing corporate. And the public relations wasn't coordinated.' Halford, whose skills had been honed by spending some years working for Sir Arnold Hammer, the infamous oil magnate, was at first hampered by lack of resources.

Under the chairmanship of Sir Allen Sheppard, however, the company doubled in size, becoming much more US focused, and the communications side expanded and received much greater emphasis. It encompassed investor and government relations, as well as media relations which came under Halford.

Halford oversaw all external communications, a demanding job in a company as newsworthy as Grand Metropolitan:

'A lot of it is trivia. There is always speculation in market reports because we are such an active company. Why we are a bit different is that because we are in consumer products there is a lot to write about us. We are watched carefully which is why you need a senior person in this job. I have to know the chairman, the board and how they think. I will probably spend an hour alone with the chairman going through things during the day.'

Halford had to account for anything in the press: 'It is a real firing line. A lot of people find it rather difficult.' But he believed the media was a lot more sensible than companies thought: 'They can see through things that are false. The early days of public relations when you could get away with being misleading have gone. I think both sides are more streetwise. I also think that building up trust between the company/consultancy and media is vitally important.' Vitally important, because a half-true story written by an alienated or misinformed journalist could wreck a multi-million pound deal.

One reason for the pounding companies take from the media, apart from the breadth and diversity of it, is the spread of what is called the 'Anglo-Saxon' model of journalism: a determined quest for facts, facts and more facts as opposed to a more commentary-driven approach. Some also blame it on Watergate; that, however, was a result, not a cause, of a more investigative style of journalism that has been in the UK and USA for decades. And, interestingly, in countries like Poland and what was the Soviet Union, the media, having been cut from their bonds of censorship, are embracing this with zeal.

Relationships with journalists

Making generalizations about media relationships in different countries is as tricky as making any stereotypical comments. But most business journalists would probably agree that US companies are much more open and communicative, having understood the power of public relations for some time. However, that disarming openness can also be a smokescreen for dubious practices. In the UK, on the other hand, companies have not been noted for their dealings with the press, often using the press office to issue 'no comment' statements to almost anything. That has changed over the last few years as the enormous surge in hostile takeovers forced companies to realize the powerful role the media plays in winning the battle or warding off predators. This process will accelerate across Europe as more companies are confronted with the growing demand for more information from their range of audiences.

The UK is a good example of the gradual shift to a more open style. A quarter of a century ago companies did very little other than release their results if they were publicly quoted. They used press offices to ward journalists off. Then, at the end of the 1960s, companies facing hostile takeovers from asset strippers began to see that it was important to become known, since it was useless appealing to the City shareholders who had little idea of the company's *raison d'être*. It was no longer enough to keep the corporate eye glued only to the bottom line.

Box 6.1   IMRES survey

Companies should be more open, honest and willing to deal with uncomfortable news, according to a 1993 survey of journalists in 10 European countries. The survey, Media Viewpoint Europe 1993, was coordinated by Yankelovich Partners UK and covered 322 business journalists in broadcast and print. There were a number of interesting findings.

The criteria which almost all business journalists considered the most important in determining the quality of companies' media relations were:

- fast reaction to enquiries
- an open and honest media relations policy
- willingness to deal with unfavourable news
- comprehensible information.

Accessibility to a company's global management was rated by journalists as more important than an accessible press department, while a proactive policy of contact from the company was singled out in the UK and Germany.

Among the reasons most often given for rating companies' media relations work poorly were:

	% of those interviewed
• Little contact	20
• No contact	16
• Poor press dept	10
• Poor quality information, hard to use	8
• Irregular, inconsistent	6
• Not helpful/informative	5
• Not open, dishonest, secretive	3

Finally, the survey found that journalists prefer to ask for information rather than read it. The two sources rated most useful were personal or telephone interviews with managers and off-the-record background briefings from companies. And while interviews with managers are found more useful than ones with the press office, the press department is often seen as the first port-of-call for arranging access to management.

Written corporate sources considered most useful include annual company reports and press releases. Non-corporate written sources include research reports from banks and analysts, and press articles and reports. Business magazine journalists make more use of corporate background materials and relatively less use of news sources such as wire services, press releases or conferences, than newspaper journalists.

Over the last 15 years or so several factors have contributed to the growing awareness of the importance of media relations:

(1) the enormous strength of the pension funds as investors has demanded a radical new approach to investor relations including a rethinking of how to deal with the financial media;
(2) the rise of 'consumer power' and the growing number of programmes, newspapers and magazines that cater for the demand for more comparative information;
(3) allied to that, the increased coverage of business matters in a more populist format;
(4) the proliferation of special interest magazines;
(5) a realization that employees read papers and watch TV too.

Bad communications can often be a strong indication that something is going wrong with a company. The once-proud engineering group Hawker Siddeley had little chance against the powerful conglomerate BTR, which had honed its communications skills after years in the takeover field. Hawker fought back with a fatal combination of hesitant and confusing statements from senior executives, a press office given little backing and thus devalued, and a bad reputation for keeping shareholders poorly informed. Media comments went along the lines of the following one from *The Times*: 'Yesterday's defence document from the beleaguered and accident-prone Hawker was long on presentation and promise but conspicuously short of hard fact'.[1]

The need for consistency

There are too many gaps into which a corporate reputation can fall. What is imperative for companies is to close the gaps through consistency: after all, journalists speak to analysts who speak to politicians, who speak to journalists, and so on. For example, when the powerful UK-based conglomerate Hanson took a stake in what was considered the jewel in the UK industrial crown, ICI, Lord Hanson was taken aback by the ferocity of the reaction, which pitted his reputation as an 'asset-stripper', rightly or wrongly, against that of the research-based chemicals company. ICI was easily able to muster over 30 backbenchers in Parliament to speak up for it as well as packs of distinguished scientists. Hanson had failed to plug all the gaps, a fact highlighted by the leaking of a private letter he sent to one of his public relations advisers (see Case 6.2).

Case 6.2 Hanson/Bell

A private letter sent to his chief public relations adviser by British industrialist Lord Hanson towards the end of 1991 and leaked to a Sunday newspaper put under an intense spotlight the usually hidden relationship between client and consultant.

The saga began when noted takeover artist Hanson bought a small stake in the UK's premier blue chip company, ICI. Under criticism for being too slow to restructure thoroughly enough to handle fiercely competitive conditions and thus be seen as potential target, ICI nevertheless was able to marshall some strong allies in the face of a potential bid from Hanson. It became a communications war, where each side dug up the dirt on the other. Ironically, despite Hanson's undoubted financial track record, ICI was able to position itself as the heartland of British industry, the company where long-term commitment to R&D was essential to the UK's corporate health. Hanson was depicted as an asset-stripper whose financial transactions were creative, to say the least.

The denouement came when someone leaked a private letter Hanson wrote to his chief adviser, Sir Tim Bell – one of the most high profile people in the business thanks to his close association with the former prime minister Margaret Thatcher – lambasting him for letting ICI's advisers, Brunswick, run circles around them. He had believed he was paying for media contacts, not weekly strategy meetings. This extraordinary letter highlighted just what can go wrong when there is a lack of clear understanding of what public relations is, and how to use it. The letter outlined Hanson's belief that public relations is about selling the story more than conveying reality. It also displayed a misunderstanding of the role of advisers. At that level, and at that cost, using them as media messenger boys rather than as strategic sounding boards shows that somewhere there had been a confusion in the brief.

This rebounded badly on Hanson, to the point where there were serious questions about the company's future. And the cascade of articles that followed, although highlighting the 'hidden persuaders' who play such an active role in bids and deals, were almost unanimously – and ironically – in favour of the public relations consultants.

'Lord Hanson must think public relations consultants are miracle workers. Judging by his intemperate letter of complaint to his PR advisers, he believes they can turn unfavourable facts into favourable coverage. He seems to have forgotten that Sir Tim Bell, Brian Basham, and Roddy Dewe, all of whom he employed in the wake of Hanson's acquisition of 2.8% of ICI, are mere mortals. They can no more turn bad news into good than water into wine,' stormed *The Independent*.[2]

continues

continued

> The shock to the Hanson system was obviously severe. One result
> was that in December of that year, *The Sunday Times* magazine carried
> an unusually lengthy article on the company, with all the senior people
> wheeled in to talk to the journalist, while the front cover had close-ups
> of both Lord Hanson and his partner Lord White. Both the size of the
> piece and the positioning spoke volumes for the fact that the company
> had begun to realize that having what is a very successful financial track
> record is simply not enough if the image is out of line.

The importance of understanding the relationship between journalists and the public relations people who are either in the company or
representing it outside cannot be stressed enough. It is a common reflex
action by journalists to say that all public relations people are terrible.
They call them both manipulators and blocks. They are inefficient, they
never call back and if they do they are useless. They are also such easy
targets for abuse. But scratch a bit deeper and most journalists will admit
that, well, of course x, y and z are notable exceptions, and that they
indeed use public relations people quite heavily, if only for background.
As David Fausch, vice president of corporate relations at Gillette in the
USA, and an ex-*Business Week* journalist, concluded in 1991:

> 'One lousy public relations person can poison the well for the
> good ones. Like any group of professional people – accountants,
> investment bankers – the standards vary. But we seem to be con-
> sistently down there with car salesmen. Since reporters deal with
> public relations people more, they see one bad one and that's it.'
>
> 'It is a vicious circle: a lot of public relations people have
> been undervalued and untrained. Therefore they give bad
> service, so journalists rate them poorly, and hence form a bad
> opinion of the company, which probably deserves it for under-
> rating the importance of communications. Ask any business
> journalist which companies over the years have been consis-
> tently bad at public relations, and nine times out of ten those
> companies have either disappeared, been taken over, or changed
> out of all recognition.'

What lies behind the consistently bad assessments given by journalists about public relations people in numerous surveys?

(1) Journalists see public relations people as failed journalists – an
     increasingly false assumption.

(2)   There are still some very dubious public relations practices.

(3)   There is still too much public relations done which is not carefully targeted to its journalistic audience, that is public relations people who send the same press release to both a national newspaper and a local radio station without adapting it for different audiences and get the names of the contacts wrong in both instances.

(4)   All public relations people, just like all journalists, get tainted by the worst excesses in both professions. The corollary to that is that some journalists can get very defensive to avoid admitting that they can be lazy, unwarrantedly arrogant, not let facts ruin a good story, or have a hidden agenda (that is proprietorial interference forces a story to have a certain bias).

(5)   Journalists can feel guilty that they do indeed rely a lot on public relations people. In the UK, the infamous 'Friday night drop' to the Sunday papers, whereby City public relations advisers give exclusives to favoured journalists and play one paper off against the other – currently being examined by the Stock Exchange for possible leaking of price-sensitive information – is something the recipients do not talk of openly or proudly.

(6)   Journalists live with an image of public relations which is based more on past perception than modern usage.

(7)   It can be hard to have an objective assessment of public relations people when at their best they are almost invisible. There has long been an unwritten rule that public relations spokespeople are never quoted, for example, though that is changing as in-house communicators have much higher executive status.

This last point is worth elaborating. If, for example, an advertising agency does an advertisement for a company which gathers a lot of publicity, the agency can justifiably boast about it and win awards. If, on the other hand, a public relations practitioner writes a superb speech for a chief executive, the chief executive is not going to announce that he is not the real author. That is why, when public relations people do take on a higher profile than their clients – as the financial public relations consultants have done in the heady 1980s and early 1990s – the knives come out.

Sir Tim Bell probably has one of the highest profiles of all public relations practitioners, and has become almost a brand in his own right. He does not enjoy it, he says:

'I think it is terrible. Both Bernard Ingham (Prime Minister Margaret Thatcher's press secretary) and I are public figures because we worked for Mrs Thatcher. What is bad about it is first, the risk we might start taking ourselves seriously, which would be awful. Secondly, it is bad for us because there are loads of journalists who will abuse any public relations person they can find because they know they are dependent on them. People always bite the hand that feeds them. I spent 25 years being insulted for working in advertising and yet those ads are what pays for all the TV programmes. Now I have spent five years being abused in public relations when we fill their columns and they hate it.'

The role of consultants

As mentioned above the common assumption that public relations people are failed journalists is losing steam. Nowadays the skills needed for a more strategic approach to clients mean that writing skills and an understanding of the media alone are only a small part of what is demanded. A sign of this is the entry into public relations of other professionals such as lawyers and accountants. Journalists still do 'cross the line', of course. David Brewerton, a respected business and city editor on both *The Independent* and *The Times* joined Brunswick Public Relations in 1991 after opting for a move into financial public relations. As he recalled, when he breached the divide,

'There were certain flutters about it. Everyone was surprised because I had a reputation for hating public relations people. I didn't – but I did think many of them were pretty useless. I thought – God, these flakes go into business, they purport to advise people, but do so badly. I could do better.

'I soon realised how relatively little the press knew about what was going on. I was surprised at the access I was given to some of the deep problems companies had, and the long-range planning that goes on to deal with them and culminates in an announcement.'

One of the big problems, he thinks, is the term 'public relations' itself, which covers anything from the most mechanical press release house to a chief adviser to the chairman of a huge corporation: 'But we will only change perceptions by actions, not by name.'

The more strategic role played by these senior consultants, both in-house and outside, means convincing heads of companies to admit problems as openly as possible. As Sue Bohle, of the LA-based Sue Bohle consultancy, said in 1991:

'We are not supposed to be a block. We really have to advise clients what they should do against their wishes. I think there is more understanding of the need for visibility than in the past, but they still need counselling because they are nervous. I ascribe to the philosophy that if an interview with a journalist has been thought through we can know if it will be negative. I also ascribe to the theory that if in 80 articles three or four have a negative jab one shouldn't be worried because the visibility across the board will be better. The job of a journalist is to be objective so unless you are 100% covered on all bases someone will point out that you have a weak spot and it is out of your control to be able to hide that.'

Case 6.3 Wellcome

Sometimes even extensive contingency planning and media training can prove ineffective in the face of a media onslaught.

This happened with Wellcome, the drugs group, with its controversial HIV treatment AZT, its second-best seller.[3] The UK Medical Research Council (MRC) had called a press conference following a Franco-British trial which suggested that AZT did not, as had been widely thought, slow down the onset of AIDS. Wellcome, which assumed that giving out any information would wait until both sides had reached an agreement, was caught unprepared. Moreover, its chief executive was in the USA and two non-executive directors were on holiday, leaving the research and development director to cope along with a newly arrived finance director and two press officers.

What made things worse was that the press officers lacked information to counter the MRC claim, and to compound the problems, gave out inaccurate information about potential damage to sales. The share price slumped by 51 pence, while prescribers and users of the drug were understandably dismayed.

The company hit back with press conferences and meetings with AIDS activists. They were rated unsuccessful because of their confusing presentation and were followed by accusations from the MRC that the company had manipulated the data. The chief executive was open about the communications mistakes the company had made and was quoted as saying: 'We've learned a lot in the last few years, but we still have some way to go.'

It needs a strong personality to stand up to an annoyed chairman staring at a crop of negative headlines. As Werner Baier, director of corporate communications at German detergent to chemical conglomerate Henkel explained:

'With the German press you have to prove that you are credible, trustworthy, that you don't lie and can give good background, and can give and take on a serious basis. We cannot be manipulators. You have to live with negative headlines and not over-react. If my boss were to say "couldn't you avoid a negative headline" I would say no – and I wouldn't. But he is not going to ask me. And senior management are learning to trust my judgement.'

The journalist/public relations relationship can be very complex and subtle and, to some extent, self-serving on both sides. As Raymond Wilson, who has worked in public relations both in the government and in the private sector at TSB and the Norwich Union, argued,

'You can't use the credibility built up over months and months of working with journalists in trying to push something that clearly has no credibility or weight. So from time to time, you err into the shade, as long as the relationship with the journalists is good enough to know that while they might not believe what I am saying, they will toe the line because it is a long-term relationship. Certainly in government you get the sort of occasion when someone is appointed or in the private sector when a director is fired, but the line is they are moving on to do something else. Because I know I can't go off the record, it is a matter of holding the line. If I give way at all, I know the journalist is going to do his/her job and have a spokesman admitting that so and so has got the push. And that puts my reputation on the line internally.'

Media relations across Europe

There is still a lack of truly pan-European media. Television crosses borders, of course, and is used effectively by marketers of consumer goods and services, particularly to the young. But except for music videos and sports, pan-European TV suffers from a lack of good programming.

As for newspapers, all are more national than pan-European. *The European*, published in English in London and widely distributed all over Europe, is British rather than European although it is working towards a more regional flavour. The *Wall Street Journal* (Europe), read for its news of US industry and stock markets, is used more frequently by pan-European advertisers because of the quality of its readership. The same goes for the *International Herald Tribune*, now trying to become the world's first global newspaper and The *Financial Times*. *The Guardian* in London carries regular pages of reports from other European newspapers.

Some national newspapers are pan-European, without losing their national identity. This is true of *Le Monde* but not of *Le Figaro*. Spain's *El Pais* came on the scene nearly 15 years ago as the country's first truly national newspaper. Now it can be found all over Europe and is widely read for the quality of its editorial content and opinion.

Fiercely independent, Switzerland's *Neue Zürcher Zeitung* is widely quoted and can be considered pan-European because of its influence on editorial opinion in other European newspapers. *Frankfurter Allgemeine Zeitung* is read for its business clout all over Europe, and *Handelsblatt* is culled regularly for leads by business editors in European and North American capitals.

For business news, there is really only one truly pan-European daily and that is the *Financial Times*. Pan-European periodicals include *The Economist*, because of its prestige, and *Euromoney* and *Institutional Investor* for the financial sector. Newspapers in major European capitals carry sections with European sectoral news and developments that help to compensate for the variable quality and relatively limited circulation of the European trade press. A notable exception is the trade press that services the food and packaging industry. Supplements to major dailies also are becoming a useful medium for pan-European communications.

The power of European media should not, however, be under-estimated. As experienced reputation-builders in Europe have learned, decision-makers often do not know what they think until they read it in the paper. In 'Latin' countries like France, Italy and Spain, image influences consumer decisions perhaps more than any other factor except price. In 'Anglo-Saxon' countries and countries in the so-called D-mark zone, a positive reputation can see a company relatively unscathed through bad times.

And in Europe particularly, where decisions have everything to do with political justification, reputation can make the difference between success and failure. In this atmosphere, the company that can position itself as a valuable European player – with national commitments in more than one EU country, 'transparent' in its dealings with all segments of European society, willing to communicate and accessible to its target groups – clearly will end up with a positive reputation. The trick today is to make that reputation pan-European.

Box 6.2 Advertorials

Pick up a glossy magazine or newspaper supplement and there will almost certainly be at least one double page spreads that looks like a regular editorial page but is headed up either 'promotion' or 'advertisement'. These hybrids – unattractively but aptly called advertorials – are being used with increasing frequency by a growing number of companies. Traditionally the preserve of either high-technology clients with a complicated message to get across to potential customers, or companies promoting food or fashion which aim at women's titles, over the last few years the use of this technique has spread to encompass new sectors like financial services, alcohol and automobiles.

One major reason why marketing departments are becoming more receptive to ideas for advertorials is that publishers are pursuing them more aggressively at a time of shrinking ad budgets, while they are being treated far more professionally in a bid to persuade clients that this is a creative opportunity to spread their message to their target audiences. Pouring more imagination into them allied with raising production standards has also been a means whereby the commercial executives of magazines and newspapers can try to convince sceptical editors who strongly disapprove of blurring the advertising/editorial line of their worth.

What advertorials are about is control – controlling the message in an editorial format. Positive editorial coverage of a company and/or its products in credible publications is the best publicity any company can hope for, but often proves elusive. A successful advertorial, its proponents argue, can pinpoint the way the company delivers its message to the heart of its target audience.

That story also has to be complementary to the overall brand strategy, not just be there to entertain or explain a complex message, although entertainment and education are both important elements, as is crafting advertorials to fit in with editorial style. For example, United Distillers (UD) ran a series of advertorials about Gordon's Gin in national titles, along with one in Scotland. Each one was individually tailored to fit in with the publication. The message the advertorials were there to enforce was straightforward: Gordon's is a quality product, an institution. The educational and entertaining elements came from the story about Gordon's Italian connection: Gordon's gets juniper berries from the Umbrian hills, so the message was that Gordon's only uses natural ingredients and is a quality product.

High technology was one of the main sources of early advertorials – unsurprisingly, the products are complex and need to be explained with some technical detail to get the story across. That is not so easy with traditional advertising.

continues

> *continued*
>
> Advertorials can also to some degree circumvent journalistic indifference to what a company is doing because editorial coverage has already been so extensive. In the case of a company like Compaq, whose swift growth in the computer market attracted many inches of editorial space, that very success can lead to journalists wondering how they can write something different about Compaq. There can be diminishing returns from an editorial point of view. So advertorials let the company present things editorially but with bought space. While they should be strongly labelled, information is being given to readers in a format that looks familiar.

The impact of new technologies

The key to effective media relations is thus to regard the relationship between organization and the media as a negotiation of interests which should emerge from an association built over time, rather than hurriedly created in times of difficulty. Building that relationship requires management attention to details such as the interests of the journalists and the publications and media outlets they represent, the information the company itself has to offer, and the policies and procedures developed to release information to the media.

Media relations will undergo some profound changes as and when the impact of 'information highways' works through to the way companies interact with journalists – not least because of the way the media themselves will be affected when the various technological strands of communications merge.

It is quite possible that in a few years' time what is now regarded as newspapers will be delivered electronically to the home television set, as a fax is now delivered through a telephone line. It may also become possible for consumers to choose the contents of their 'information package', or accept the package that is prepared by a central news collection agency. Even if organizations can convince journalists of the merits of the information they offer, that could be stopped at the next decision point when consumers decide on what they want to see. Companies will therefore have to find other, more effective ways of communicating with information consumers.

Consumers will have other means of gathering information about companies in which they are interested. Already, journalists can have instantaneous access to information about companies anywhere in the world through a range of on-line databases.

But it is not just journalists who will be watching a company's progress: on Internet, the world's largest computer network, 20 million people conduct conversations on any number of topics and issues. So former relationships through the mass media formed by companies with their various audiences will change to links based on a larger number of possible communication channels and more responsive forms of communication.

Summary

(1) The importance of public relations has been heightened not just by the demands of the global business environment but also by the changing nature of the media and the fact that modern international companies are vast, complex, sprawling organizations made up of lots of varied elements.

(2) At any time any one of those elements can come into contact with the media. Unless there is a clear understanding of the corporate ethos and how that should translate into behaviour in all circumstances even one off-the-cuff remark can lead to global and damaging headlines.

(3) Modern communications allied to an internationally competitive media means that it becomes increasingly pointless to practise fortress building and leak prevention. It demands a rethinking of how to deal with a hungry and amazingly diverse collection of journalists who themselves have different audiences to satisfy and different proprietors with which to deal. It is no good hoping the media will go away, or only be there to spread the good news.

(4) One reason for the pounding companies take from the media, apart from the breadth and diversity of it, is the spread of what is called the 'Anglo-Saxon' model of journalism: a determined quest for facts, facts and more facts as opposed to a more commentary-driven approach.

(5) Bad communications can often be a strong indication that something is going wrong with a company.

(6) There are too many gaps into which a corporate reputation can fall. What is imperative for companies is to close the gaps through consistency: after all, journalists speak to analysts who speak to politicians, who speak to journalists, and so on.

(7) The more strategic role played by public relations consultants, both in-house and outside, means convincing heads of companies to admit problems as openly as possible.

(8)   There is still a lack of truly pan-European media. Television crosses borders, of course, and is used effectively by marketers of consumer goods and services, particularly to the young. But except for music videos and sports, pan-European TV suffers from a lack of good programming. As for newspapers, all are more national than pan-European.

(9)   The power of European media should not, however, be underestimated. As experienced reputation-builders in Europe have learned, decision-makers often do not know what they think until they read it in the paper.

(10)   Media relations will undergo some profound changes as and when the impact of 'information highways' works through to the way companies interact with journalists – not least because of the way the media themselves will be affected when the various technological strands of communications merge.

Notes

(1) *The Times*, 6 November 1991.
(2) *The Independent*, 16 October 1991.
(3) Abrahams, Paul, A question of misjudgement, *Financial Times*, 14 April 1993.

7

Marketing communications

The marketing/public relations relationship

The relationship between marketing and public relations/communications is often confused. One reason has been the lack of understanding about what marketing itself is, with the use of the term often synonymous with sales or advertising. And because marketing is reckoned merely to be about selling or creating images, then public relations becomes an even tackier part of the mix. It gets rated as a relatively inexpensive way of obtaining publicity for a product, but as an add-on, not major, technique.

That is changing as marketing itself moves up the strategic scale and is considered to be more of a framework in which the company should operate. This, in turn, shifts the perception of public relations, transforming it into more of a management service, according to Peter Walker, chairman and chief executive of public relations consultancy Pielle: 'The marketer, who is no longer a converted salesman, looks at the future. Public relations has to be alert to issues, perceptions, the changing environment and the impact on corporate reputation.'

This is not to disparage brand publicity but to understand better what role it should play. When the brand publicity is well thought out and integrated its payback can be multifold. The launch of Grand Metropolitan-owned Häagen-Dazs ice cream attracted a lot of extra attention because of ads which showed a nude man and woman intertwined. According to Graham Lancaster, chairman and managing director of Biss Lancaster, which handled the publicity, it worked so well for three main reasons:

(1) the managing director took an integrated approach to marketing communications so that it included product excellence, distribution and the right positioning;

(2) there was a good working relationship with the advertisement agency and Biss Lancaster;

(3) Biss Lancaster exploited the research done for the advertisement campaign to help it with its approach: 'The research clients can invest in tends to be related to advertising. It is not often they can justify doing it purely on the PR side so we can take a lot out of the research and make it go further.'

He could see clients beginning to understand that public relations can be used to squeeze a lot more added value out of advertising campaigns: 'They look at the J.R. Hartley/*Yellow Pages* campaign, or the Nescafe coffee saga and say – how can we get that massive added value? Well, it isn't by accident.'

The demand for integration

There has to be tight coordination among different groups for a more integrated approach to be effective and be consistent with the communications policy as a whole. That might mean the marketing director having control over all brand public relations with regular liaison with the in-house communications overlord. It has also led to the evolution of the 'marketing communications' department, a relatively new way of organizing what has been called the marketing department. The structure arises both from a desire for more integrated communications overall, and from the realization that the term 'marketing' in its true sense is more than just a tactical communications technique.

What is important is that the relationship between marketing and public relations is defined, understood and accepted. At building society Abbey National, for example, corporate affairs is independent of marketing in the retail operations, even though marketing is the dominant part of the company and involves most of the media relations work and staff communications. In fact, corporate affairs not only has the final say on what is reported to the media, but can play a very proactive role in product development. That means dealing with product managers in a way calculated not to raise hackles and convincing them that only emphasizing the strong points of products and ignoring any weaknesses to the media is not always in Abbey's interests.

The aim is to keep everything consistent with your core values. Abbey has 150 years of branding and image and it can easily be destroyed. So marketing and public relations people have to stay in close contact.

Case 7.1   *Digital Equipment Corporation International, 1991*

By 1991, Digital Equipment Corporation International had moved from a centralized to a decentralized communications function in Europe. The function had evolved from almost pure marketing communications to corporate relations, which included communicating with national governments, the EU, the media (trade plus the business press), financial analysts, academia and the general public as well as actual and potential customers.

In terms of organization, it was significant that David Cooper, director, communications and corporate relations, reported to the president of Digital Equipment Corporation International (Europe). Cooper worked closely with the heads of the company's affiliates in EU member states, as well as with the European headquarters marketing function headed by a vice president, marketing and sales (Europe). For Digital in Europe, marketing communications and corporate relations were inseparable. One reason was that decisions to purchase Digital's products and services often were made at the highest level in companies and organizations. Opportunities to communicate with decision-makers had be created, nurtured and sustained until the company's image began to pay off.

Digital is one of the world's largest suppliers of networked computer systems, software and services. The company does more than half its business outside the USA. Digital's image-building objective in Europe then was to create an image to reinforce a position of leadership in the market for open, multivendor systems and services.

Customer requirements for data processing equipment had changed since the 1970s. Customers were looking now for choices – for a supplier that would work with them virtually to tailor-make networked computer systems and help cut costs. 'In the 1990s,' Cooper said, 'the most commonly asked question is and will be, "How can I protect my investment in information technology and bring it up to date at the same time?"'

continues

continued

Digital wanted to be known as a company that listened to its customers, its employees, its 'third-party partners' (like software houses) and its associates in joint ventures. The company also wanted to be on the list of potential suppliers when large purchasing decisions were made. These objectives underlined communications/corporate relations strategy at Digital Equipment Corporation International in Europe.

The company did very little advertising, though a worldwide campaign stressing Digital's 'open advantage' was set to start before the end of 1991. Industry-wide trade shows were another tool that Digital used minimally, although there were some where it had to be. On the whole, Digital prefered to organize its own showcase called DECville in Europe, where customers and decision-makers from all the company's markets in Europe could be brought together in an exclusive and image-building environment.

To avoid reinventing the wheel in each European country (Digital operated in 19, including former Czechoslovakia and Hungary), communications/corporate relations used a classic transnational model. 'You analyse where your resources are strongest and you transnationalize them for the region as a whole,' Cooper said. 'We tell our people, "If you want to drive something, drive it on behalf of Europe."' Sales promotion tools were a good example.

> 'We've said there is a set of communications materials that is common to all countries. There are different languages, of course, but, basically, a VAX family brochure is a VAX family brochure, no matter where it's used. For pan-European events, the biggest ones we do are organized out of Valbonne, France, so let's transnationalize this type of event out of Valbonne. Instead of each market's doing all its own advertising, pan-European advertising is "transnationalized" out of Paris.'

This pan-European approach to communications had distinct advantages, Cooper found, apart from saving money. 'It empowers people. It gets them thinking internationally and, hopefully, it gets rid of the concept of an ivory tower [headquarters] sitting in Geneva.' Provided it is all networked – which Digital is – there would be few problems. Still, Cooper made sure that his communications team came together at least once a quarter, and that the team was involved in communications planning and budgeting for the region, as well as in implementation. 'We work to a common plan,' Cooper said.

He tended to use communications people from Digital's larger markets (France, Germany, Italy, the Netherlands, Sweden, Switzerland and the UK) as 'coaches' for the company's other European markets. All this was not as simple as it sounded, Cooper admitted. It had taken nearly two years to put a working cross-border communications system in place at Digital Equipment Corporation International (Europe).

continues

continued

'First, we had to sell the concept to people. Communications people, by definition, are creative. Creative people, by definition, like to create. And creative people, by definition, don't like to take somebody else's work. So it's extremely difficult to get creative people actually to behave in this way.'

To succeed, Cooper recommended that managers:

(1) involved subsidiaries' communications people in the process;
(2) made sure that reasons for assigning different tools to different markets were clearly understood;
(3) used subsidiaries' communications people to help develop the transnational plan and budget;
(4) kept all concerned continually informed; and
(5) accepted that not all communications could be transnationalized.

'Some things have to be done locally,' said Cooper, like public relations.

'PR means people-to-people. It cannot be transnationalized. So we suggest to subsidiaries that in their hiring plans and their training plans they might want to invest more in PR than in a sales promotion specialist, for example, because communications to support sales can be done cross-border, on a pan-European level.'

If results of Digital's approach to communications in Europe were measured, one indication of success would have to be that, three years previously, the company's total communications organization in Europe had employed about 230 people. It was now down to 165. The communications function at Geneva headquarters occupied 50 people five years ago. By 1991, there were eight.

Case 7.2 Mercury, 1992

Mercury Telecommunications was formed by a consortium in 1981 as part of the government determination to open up telecommunications to more competition. It had four product lines covering corporate, business and consumer, data and personal products, with their own marketing budgets, while alongside that there was also a regional structure to deal with the large customers. It was a complex matrix which had grown up in a largely uncoordinated fashion, where the sheer energy which

continues

continued

had to be funnelled into getting established as well as a focus on the technology had precluded a more integrated approach to communications.

By early 1990 the main role of Mercury's advertising and public relations department seemed to be one of firefighting. While there was a press officer with a clear role, others were called something vague like a publicity officer. But its subsequent evolution mirrored the general trend towards coordinating communications about both the company and its products.

By 1991 the department consisted of up to seven groups with 29 people. They included public relations, advertising, audiovisual, direct marketing, planning, sponsorship and events.

The department had three key roles:

(1) guardian of the Mercury brand: making sure the brand values were understood and percolated throughout the company, both externally and internally;

(2) carrying out corporate brand programmes, including brand building – corporate advertising, for example – and sales support, including corporate video/product videos, brochures, and exhibitions;

(3) coordination: ensuring that customers did not receive different messages from different parts of the group, for example.

That meant getting everybody to think in terms of the company's audience and developing programmes that worked across the whole audience. A precondition of that was fusing the customer databases that existed in the separate divisions into one centrally coordinated one.

Integration was also important for public relations. As the then head of the department noted,

> 'In my view public relations takes in the raw ingredients from anywhere in the company – whether the department or the product lines – and presents them to the public saying "wasn't this good". That is a very simplistic way of putting it, of course. But I say to the public relations people that it is not something separate from the rest of the department, it runs through the whole lot and they should be constantly trawling to see what is going on.'

Her goal was thus to break down the mental barriers between disciplines.

In some sectors public relations plays a well-understood and leading role in a company's marketing profile. High technology companies are a good example of this. As Mike Copland, managing director for the consultancy A Plus pointed out:

'It is such a dynamic sector. A generation of computer systems these days lasts a couple of years. And you have a constantly changing set of players. If you take the 10 leading high technology companies in 1969, 1979 and 1989, except for IBM the list would probably be very different.

'And there aren't really any standards, although we are beginning to move towards them. So you need to educate people and advertising isn't a very good medium for that. You are trying to explain and get people around to your way of thinking. That is why public relations is particularly dominant. Companies like Compaq, where computers have become a commodity, spend a lot on advertising. But in other areas like client server architecture or aspects of data communications, people need to be educated.'

The changing face of consumer public relations

Clients are increasingly seeking ways to make established brands stand out in the midst of cluttered and competitive markets where grabbing consumer attention for even new products is never assured. The premium is on the unconventional, creative approach – but one that actually works.

Biss Lancaster's Graham Lancaster has called it adding saliency: 'I define it as a relevance to lifestyle, creating a reason to request a brand, whether it is a specific, genuine unique selling proposition or purely a brand that cannot be ignored.' And this franchise extends beyond consumers to the powerful retailers: 'A lot of our clients are looking to us to create both end user awareness and through the same route make those activities clear to the multiples that this is the case, that there is a franchise for this product out there which they ignore at their peril.'

An additional force driving consumer public relations is the increasingly hard commercial edge of media owners, said Lancaster: 'We are finding that media owners are becoming extremely commercial and very sophisticated in what they look for, whether it is readers' offers, advertorials, joint sponsorship or lending their name to an awards scheme.'

That is also reflected in dealings with journalists. The days of the press conference trumpeting some new product, or variation of an established one, are just about over. Instead, public relations practitioners have to find stories that are genuinely targeted because 'if everyone has it no one wants it', pointed out Lancaster, just as supermarket buyers want promotions created specially for them.

It is all about tactics and finding creative hooks. While there are more and more consumer magazines, because of a product's price and its style it might be suitable for only 10. And because those magazines are very discerning, the match between techniques like advertorials or competitions and the publication's personality has to be spot on.

Public relations consultancies are also beginning to form closer relationships with the broadcasting world as regulations about sponsorship and promotions loosen. Burson-Marsteller in the UK, for example, has formed a partnership with the ITN network for corporate television, which on one level is about creating video news releases, electronic press releases, and syndicated broadcast material, but even more attractively for Burson, gives access to ITN's studio and distribution resources.

The techniques chosen can depend on whether the brand is established, has something new to say, or is a new product altogether. The more competitors in a field, the more the onus is on a high degree of creativity. And although new products might not have this problem, they need to be explained, which can be an uphill task unless it is from an established brand with a heritage.

What this is all about is targeting in an age of tight budgeting and fragmentation of both media vehicle and audience, according to Joseph Romero, of Paris-based communications consultancy Broad Romero:

'Nobody wants fluff any more. Everything has to be very focused, very targeted and very tight. Particularly because of the recession, companies want effective consumer communications, not just a lot of dust in the eye. They are looking for strategies that actually get the product out there. I think a lot of communications today has to be based on very strong information and be linked to any number of concerns people have today.'

Those concerns can stretch from the environment to helping others. Exploiting them as an adjunct to consumer communications is already a wide-scale practice in the USA. Defined as 'issues-led marketing', there is growing interest in Europe because brand differentiation, like brand loyalty, is increasingly difficult to achieve. This is particularly the case when there is not much to judge between different products in terms of their attributes. So nothing tangible can make the difference. Techniques like promotions and direct response can only buy short-term gains.

Companies have thus to grapple with finding innovative ways to command consumer loyalty, and to do so across borders in what are increasingly segmented markets.

Using corporate values

Evidence for this segmentation comes from a compelling study[1] published in January 1994 by Research International Observer (RIO) on the teenagers of the world. RIO is a biannual qualitative research programme carried out through Research International companies around the world.

It concluded that although teenagers are often thought to be more homgeneous globally than other groups, this is not absolutely the case. Not only are there differences, the report notes, but today's young people are considerably more sophisticated and complex than their predecessors, having to adapt and defend themselves in a fast-changing world.

There are shared needs, requirements and motivations – those that are the result of the transitional period from childhood to adulthood. However, the report's authors argue,

> 'At a wider, macro-level, the circumstances and context of being a teenager are not the same all over the world. The local environment in which teenagers live and grow impacts significantly on their attitudes and beliefs, shaping their values and aspirations for the future. The result is a rather more diverse and less homogeneous group of consumers than many have anticipated, with differing sets of value systems.'

There are a number of implications for the way companies communicate with this group:

(1) Corporate values are the key. Establishing what the report calls a 'meaningful brand-consumer interrelationship' demands that companies establish, communicate and substantiate a coherent set of corporate values. Mutual trust and respect between the brand and the teenager will bring a longer-lasting relationship than short-lived success based on 'fad' brands.

(2) Brands have to allow for self-expression not only as products, but also in the way their attributes are communicated.

(3) Increasingly, an 'adult-to-adult' dialogue will work better than attempts to talk down to teenagers.

(4) Teenagers will react positively to more unusual attempts to attract their custom and attention. Those serious in their desire to reach them need to look beyond traditional advertising-based methods of communications such as direct marketing, electronic media, point-of-sale, sponsorship and so on.

Case 7.3   Exxon

Determining the real impact of effective communications on the bottom line is hard enough with consumer goods. In the business-to-business arena, it can be even tougher to judge added value.

The answer for Exxon Chemical is integrated communications, as the manager of marketing communications, Marcel Daniels, told a conference in November 1993, 'Communications for a Changing Europe'.

Exxon Chemical is one of the four operating divisions of Exxon Corporation. It produces basic chemicals, performance products and polymers. With sales of about US$10 billion, a third of that from Europe, it mainly supplies chemical building blocks to various processing industries around the world.

Exxon Chemical begins each communications programme with a marketing objective and an itemized plan, which is translated into a communications objective, and then strategy. Budgets are defined, and once approvals are given, the plan is finalized.

The result of this, explained Daniels, is the annual 'Communications Plan book' which goes into as much detail as needed. As he noted, 'Going through this process has several advantages, not least the inclusion of the respective marketing/sales/technology departments in the preparation of the strategy, so there is hardly any second-guessing.'

Daniels then described how the process actually worked. Every three years the biggest plastics fair in the world is held in Dusseldorf. The latest one took place in 1992. So when the communications department was preparing its 1991 plans, it focused on the fair as a recurring highlight in a three-year strategic programme whose objective was: 'Present the company as a readily approachable, responsible quality supplier of polymer raw materials who listens and responds to customers.'

The message that they wanted to get across was that 'Exxon Chemical is a quality supplier and works very closely with its valued customers so that both parties benefit to the maximum extent from this resulting partnership'.

The approach was a fully integrated campaign, consisting of international trade media advertising, direct marketing, public relations and internal communications. The theme was the mutually beneficial partnership of Exxon with its customers. It was visualized by a jazz duet theme which had been successfully pre-tested. Crucial to the eventual success of the campaign was the constantly updated marketing database, which consisted of several thousand customer and prospect names, as well as 150 media contacts.

continues

continued

> The media plan aimed at trade press in major European countries leading up to the fair. Full information packs about the fair and Exxon Chemical were sent out about six months before. Direct marketing was two-pronged: first, a 'teaser' mailing, with a brochure explaining the theme of partnership, while the second had an invitation to the fair with a reply card and information about Dusseldorf. Exxon Chemical staff received information folders showing the advertisements, while training sessions were organized for those who would be on the stand.
>
> Comprehensive records about contacts made at the fair were kept. As Daniels pointed out, whether or not the contacts would result in more business was not straightforward to measure: this is typically a business with a lengthy and complex decision-making process. But, having said that, the results indicated that there was more than an average degree of confidence that those contacts would lead to more business.
>
> Finally, as he noted, the communications department carried out a communications survey with customers to get some first-hand feedback. Because the campaign had generated so much goodwill and had become so recognizable, it was decided to carry on with it.

The corporate brand

The power of brands and branding hit companies squarely in the balance sheet during the heady days of takeovers in the 1980s. Examples of predators paying four times asset value to get hold of brand portfolios were not uncommon. Takeover fever also generated what for many companies was quite a new concept: the corporate brand as an entity in itself. Potential targets would suddenly start telling shareholders with a vengeance that under the anonymous corporate name or set of initials sheltered profitable portfolios of delightful goods and services. At the same time, companies were coming under pressure to stop hiding behind the corporate façade.

What many companies failed to realize was that corporate identity is not just the image. One way they reacted to takeover threats, therefore, apart from beginning to associate the corporate brand with the different products and services offered, was to have a new logo designed.

The problem with logos is that they are almost too easy; not easy in the sense that a designer need only make a few scrawls that look appropriate. But easy in that logos and corporate identity can become a substitute for the really hard job of making fundamental and deep-seated changes to the corporate culture. That cultural change has to be both perceived and believed by anyone associated with the company – from investors, government and journalists to staff, customers, suppliers and communities. A new corporate identity can then be invaluable by acting as a unifying symbol and an umbrella which guarantees certain qualities and standards.

Numerous studies have shown that management place concern about their corporate image high on the scale of priorities. After all, a company's image can play a large role in becoming established in a new market by getting recognition with governments, local communities, potential employees, customers, and so on. And there is no mystery to corporate image, despite its intangible nature: it reflects the reality that permeates the entire organization. It can also be a powerful branding tool both for the corporation itself and to give added value to products and services.

In 1991 at Taylor Woodrow, director of corporate communications Mike Beard tried to ensure that the operating companies, which are involved in areas like construction, property, housing and trading, and can be quite autonomous, had a clear understanding of the corporate brand. He said:

> 'The operating companies obviously have far closer day-to-day contact with customers. However, it is the responsibility of the group to make sure of the environment in which Taylor Woodrow is well understood and regarded. Whereas, for example, in a housing company they have a marketing department that sells houses to consumers, it is the plc, the group, that has the trust of the Taylor Woodrow name and has to ensure that name adds value to those businesses. There is often a difference in emphasis between the role of the group and the role of the operating companies, a continual thesis and antithesis. The group is only the sum of its parts, which is one side of the coin, and means nothing without them. The other side of it is that the parts are enhanced by the added value that comes from the group's reputation.'

Too many companies, however, have made rods for their corporate backs by rushing headlong into communicating what they see as their core values in a superficial manner – as many companies did during the 1980s when faced with restructuring or takeovers – without making sure that reality and image are synchronized. As John Brace, of John Brace & Associates, said, if his clients tell him that they want a certain type of corporate image he replies: 'Well, you already have a corporate image. You may not be aware of what it is, and it may not be very favourable but you have it and are stuck with it and if you try to change it arbitrarily you are in danger of making things worse rather than better.'

Take the car maker Ford. In the early 1960s in the UK it decided to move upmarket and launched a range of what it called executive cars. But it confused the market because it already had an established reputation for selling good cars cheaply and few self-respecting senior executives wanted to be seen in a Ford. The company took a long time to bring its image and reality back into line, though it did so eventually very successfully.

The link between brand and corporate image is also crucial to establish. There will be cases where one can be used to bolster the other, or where corporate image is incompatible with brands because of alliances and/or takeovers.

Lack of a favourable corporate image has prevented more than one company from penetrating the market with a controversial product. For example, despite highly expensive public relations and legal counsel, a gross miscalculation of EU priorities and needs – not to mention an appalling lack of knowledge of recent EU history – prevented a US-based *Fortune* 500 company from launching an agriculture-related product in the EU.

Once the decision was made to allocate substantial resources to develop and market the company's product in a series of EU member states but without taking European realities into consideration it was too late to begin building a credible image for the company name.

'We don't even know them, so how can we believe them when they claim their product is revolutionary but safe?' summed up reaction from consumer advocates and regulatory authorities when the company sought to communicate the advantages of its product. 'It's not needed, so why take a risk?' European media asked.

After years of investment in product development and nearly three years of trying to introduce the product in the EU the company still had not earned a penny from European sales.

Case 7.4   *Reed, 1992*

Publisher Reed International (now Reed Elsevier) had changed substantially by 1992. About 50% of its business was in the UK, 32% in the USA, and smaller percentages in the predominantly English-

continues

continued

speaking worlds of Australia and Canada, while developments were taking place in Europe (which resulted in the eventual merger with Netherlands publisher Elsevier).

But when Jan Shawe, director of corporate relations, had joined five years ago, Reed was principally a manufacturing company. It made cardboard cartons, paper, it had printing works, it had paint interests. The ethos was very much that of a manufacturing company; it had sold the *Daily Mirror* group in 1984.

Now it was the very embodiment of a modern publishing company, consisting of a lean centre, overseeing very individual and powerful business magazines like *Flight International*, a whole clutch of women's magazines including *Marie Claire*, and other well-known titles such as *New Scientist*, *Country Life* and, in the USA, *Variety*, among others. But the branding was triply complicated, with powerful operating companies IPC Magazines, Cahners in the USA and Reed Business Publishing at the intermediate level managing groups of publications.

Both the publications and the operating companies could speak up on relevant matters. But there was coordination: 'Anything that has an impact on the share price has to go through my department. Otherwise there are many spokespeople in the company who have the freedom to speak and do so well,' said Shawe.

And the leash was not always that loose, of course. Shawe noted:

'There is a line in the manual which says you are not allowed to talk about profits or prices paid for acquisitions. This has been particularly sensitive in the last few years when we have made a lot of acquisitions and disposals. A lot of those were either implemented or initiated by the operating companies, and they are not allowed to make that announcement by themselves because of the share price impact.'

Shawe's department at the centre consisted of four executives, including herself, and four support staff. She reported directly to the chairman, and handled areas like investor relations (though very much as support to the main board directors), media relations, government relations and legislation, corporate charitable work, and corporate printed matter. But a lot of these areas were handled by the operating companies as well. Legislation, for example:

'Basically what we say is there are 10 issues facing us at this point in time, five of them we think are being handled very well by the operating groups, two of them where we think the operating companies will need help, and three of them no one is picking up on so we will keep a watching brief.'

The operating companies had their own public relations people as well. At IPC, for example, there was a department of six to seven people who were mainly concerned with product support. Many Reed

continues

continued

International companies also had their own in-house magazines for what could be a quite diverse staff. Shawe's relationship with the senior executives in the companies was based on 'goodwill and mutual respect', she explained. There was a dotted line to her from the divisional public relations people unless there was anything which might have an impact on Reed's positioning.

Reed had to think through its devolved, multilayered branding very carefully, said Shawe.

'When I came here, we had a different logo. Now I know logos are not corporate identity, but they are symbolic of it. We changed it because the old logo was associated with the manu-facturing groups which we had sold, so we devised a new logo and new corporate guidelines. Part of my thinking about our corporate logo was that it should be able to stand alone as Reed International and it should be a sign-off, a backdrop for powerful brands like IPC. I think it would be very wrong for us to wade into the forefront of all that.

'After all, the reader of *Woman's Own* has a strong relationship with that magazine, while the retailers care a lot about IPC because that's how they get paid. We are the sum of the parts, so the better thought of the parts are, it shines back on us. But then some brands have to be left in isolation: if you know that we are the same people who publish *New Musical Express* you might not have quite as much belief in the *Laws of England*.'

Sponsorship

Sponsorship can be an effective communications tool for reaching across borders. Some companies import sponsorship opportunities from outside the target market or markets: travelling art exhibits, for example. Others build a cumulative image by sponsoring a series of related national events and 'working' the sponsorship via national and international employee, customer and media relations. Clever companies create their own spon-sorship opportunities for maximum cross-border impact.

Sponsorship that provides cross-border exposure underlines the importance and value of being an international company. The European Community Youth Orchestra, for example, could not travel outside Europe if it were not for its sponsorship. Thus part of the benefits of contributing to Europe's 'cultural balance of trade' accrue to the sponsor's image.

Another valuable benefit of the right sponsorship can be image-building among potential employees. Good employees are hard to find. The pay-off may be longer term, but it is real for companies willing to invest in sponsorships that enhance their image as a good employer and support their efforts to recruit the right people.

It is also a fact that sponsorship can be highly cost-effective – provided certain guidelines are followed (see checklist below). But as an image-building tool, sponsorship has been much misused in Europe, where the US notion of 'good corporate citizenship' still is viewed with some cynicism. Influenced by the cupidity of the sponsored as much as of sponsors, corporate support of cultural institutions often is used as a substitute for advertising.

But companies that use sponsorship successfully make sure that their support goes beyond the signing of a cheque or the entertaining of customers. In Spain, where the concept is still new, some strange permutations pass for sponsorship, and there is talk of creating a code to govern the conduct of sponsors, as well as the obligations of the sponsored. This is echoed at the EU level where attempts are being made to create a coherent European policy towards communications as a whole, including sponsorship.

Using sponsorship across Europe – a checklist

(1) *Can the proposed sponsorship carry the company image across borders in Europe?* If the sponsored event itself cannot travel, the sponsorship might have to be 'worked' through European media spill-over, or invitations to target groups or comparable events in other countries, under the umbrella of a pan-European rationale that builds company image.

(2) *Does the proposed sponsorship communicate or reinforce the image that your company wants to project?* This is called 'fit' and, often, is not immediately obvious. A rationale may have to be created. Organizations looking for sponsorship are notoriously bad at this, but may be convinced to make appropriate modifications, for example in venues or travel.

(3) *Does the sponsorship proposal spell out a realistic budget?* If not, and depending on the publicity resources of the sponsorship seeker, additional resources will have to be allocated by the sponsor to make the project pay off. As a rule of thumb, budget 35% of the total amount required upfront to work an exclusive sponsorship (publicity, entertainment, gifts, ancillary events, travel, etc.).

(4) *Will the sponsorship seeker give full and visible credit to the sponsor on all printed material (catalogues, posters, programmes, press kits, invitations, etc.) and in verbal communications (at openings, press conferences, etc.)?* Do not take credit for granted. In countries where sponsorship is new or subject to political controversy full credit may have to be negotiated and spelled out in a contract before any corporate money is paid. Even then, sponsored organizations may have to be forced to live up to their obligations.

(5) *Can the image-building impact of the sponsorship be multiplied beyond the actual event(s)?* Records of concerts, catalogues with messages from senior management, books or portfolios of exhibited photographs all can be used as corporate gifts in and outside Europe. So can video cassettes of films, with appropriate language voice-overs. Films of sponsored events can be placed on European television, with media coverage that gives credit to the sponsor.

(6) *Is the sponsorship seeker willing to give exclusive credit to the sponsor?* Many companies will not touch a sponsorship that does not give them exclusive credit. Others will use the opportunity to link up for image-building purposes with other companies (customers, for example, or other major employers in a region), academia and/or government organisms.

(7) *Does the sponsorship provide an opportunity to enhance the company's image with employees?* Some companies will tour a sponsorship to often culturally isolated plant communities in Europe. Or they will transport employees to the nearest city where corporate sponsorship is making an event possible. Even when employees do not directly benefit (for example, a VIP reception after a museum opening), they should be informed (and, if possible, be involved in the planning) before they read or hear about it in the media. When times are tough, employee involvement helps head off complaints about company spending on sponsorship instead of wage increases. Employee newspapers and other in-house communications should cover and reinforce the image conveyed by company sponsorships.

(8) *Can some of the expense connected with the sponsorship be offset by company services in kind, in exchange for credit?* Can the sponsorship seeker give back to the company in some way, so that a true partnership is created? Amsterdam's municipal Stedelijk Museum helped to pioneer this concept in the 1970s. Works from the museum were loaned to office and factory installations of at least two multinational companies that sponsored major exhibitions at the museum.

(9) *Can the relationship between sponsor and sponsored be sustained over time?* The 'one-shot' sponsorship is relatively useless to all concerned and should be avoided. So should a situation where survival of the sponsored depends exclusively on support from the sponsor. Five years is usually considered the optimum duration for a sponsorship. This gives the sponsor time to build benefits and the sponsored time to find its feet and, eventually, another sponsor.

(10)   *Does corporate sponsorship fulfil a real need and help to build bridges between the company and other sectors of society?* If answers to any of these questions are definitely negative, in relation to a particular sponsorship, do not go ahead with it.

There are two more points:

(1)   *Resist the temptation to spell out sponsorship policy.* The vaguer you keep it, the easier it is to turn away supplicants for sponsorship funds. The way a company says 'No' can affect its image as much as, if not more than, the way sponsorship is selected and implemented.

(2)   *Be prepared to hire outside help on a project basis.* Working a sponsorship cost-effectively requires specialist knowledge and intense dedication of time in concentrated doses. For these reasons, many companies with limited headcounts turn to consultants when it comes to finding and working image-building sponsorships. Check consultants' credentials carefully, and confirm results of their alleged experience.

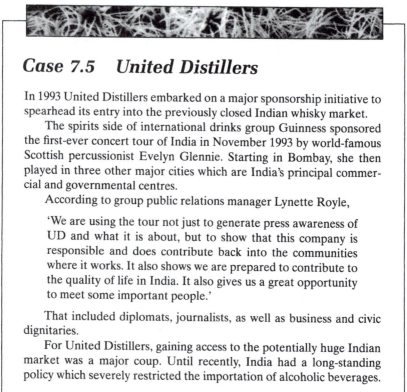

Case 7.5   United Distillers

In 1993 United Distillers embarked on a major sponsorship initiative to spearhead its entry into the previously closed Indian whisky market.

The spirits side of international drinks group Guinness sponsored the first-ever concert tour of India in November 1993 by world-famous Scottish percussionist Evelyn Glennie. Starting in Bombay, she then played in three other major cities which are India's principal commercial and governmental centres.

According to group public relations manager Lynette Royle,

'We are using the tour not just to generate press awareness of UD and what it is about, but to show that this company is responsible and does contribute back into the communities where it works. It also shows we are prepared to contribute to the quality of life in India. It also gives us a great opportunity to meet some important people.'

That included diplomats, journalists, as well as business and civic dignitaries.

For United Distillers, gaining access to the potentially huge Indian market was a major coup. Until recently, India had a long-standing policy which severely restricted the importation of alcoholic beverages.

continues

continued

In July 1991, however, a new economic policy introduced a more liberal approach which United Distillers capitalized on by setting up a joint venture with United Breweries which started bottling Scotch whisky in February 1994.

As Royle pointed out, the main objective of the programme was to heighten the corporate profile rather than raise brand awareness – although naturally guests were able to sample Scotland's most famous export. Because alcoholic drinks cannot be advertised in India, the sponsored tour helped underline United Distillers corporate values and social responsibility programmes, which are relatively new concepts for many Indian businesses, noted Royle. An accompanying exhibition at each concert was used to illustrate United Distillers other programmes around the world.

Deciding from the outset what a programme like the Indian event should achieve is a characteristic of the overall Guinness sponsorship strategy. It is part of what Royle called an increasingly more professional approach which the company takes towards the technique:

> 'When I came into the job five or six years ago sponsorship was far more driven by the heart and less by the head. Now we are much less emotional and more rational and I would say if it is characterized by one thing it is the development of sponsorship as a proper business tool. People are beginning to realize that if you use this tool properly – as in India – it can bring real business benefits.'

Case 7.6   Buckler

Pan-European sponsorship can be a powerful way to cut across cultural differences, as international brewer Heineken has found. Amsterdam-based Heineken has been using sponsorship as a central part of its marketing strategy for the last few years to boost the image of its non-alcohol brand Buckler across Europe.

Launched in 1988, Buckler was created to be pan-European from the start. While the company already had non-alcohol products in a few countries, several factors encouraged it to develop a new brand.

First, Heineken wanted to develop a product that tasted better and could exploit the focus on more healthy lifestyles around Europe. Another incentive was increasing government-produced campaigns throughout Europe against drink-driving.

continues

continued

Heineken did not want to position Buckler as a substitute for beer, but as a premium product beer drinkers can be happy with when they want to avoid alcohol. The resulting product had between 0.1% and 0.9% alcohol by volume (according to country-by-country legislation on labelling beer 'non-alcohol').

From the start the strategy for Buckler had been different from and far more centralized than that of other corporate beer brands like Heineken and Amstel. There were several reasons for this. First, because the company decided that non-alcohol beer was not determined as much by national cultural factors as regular beer is. People drink it for more or less the same reasons. Also, it was then a relatively new category. And, of course, there were the potential economies of scale from a centralized approach.

The pan-European promotional strategy had two main prongs: advertising and sponsorship. The advertisements for most European countries were and still are developed from the centre. The campaign has used television, radio and posters. They have had to take account of some local differences. For example, in France a French bar is shown, and in the Netherlands a Dutch one.

It is, though, the strategy towards sponsorship that highlights a creative cross-border approach. Sponsorship was chosen as the best way to be pan-European without diluting the message.

The first sponsorship was of a Dutch cycling team for three years. Cycling is the third most popular sport in Europe after football and tennis. What made the project attractive was that the team spent a substantial part of the year racing around Europe in what were seen as key Buckler markets.

It was also considered a sport with an active, dynamic and healthy image appropriate to Buckler's positioning.

After three years' successful sponsorship of cycling, the company started a major new project for pan-European promotion: the Buckler Challenge. It began in June 1993, bringing together top US college basketball players and Europe's best to play a series of 'All Star' games.

The company chose basketball because it saw the game as a global sport, not just one associated with the USA. It is also considered to be one of the fastest growing team sports in the world, with interest growing particularly in Spain, Greece, France and Italy.

For example, during the 1992 Olympics in Barcelona there was worldwide fascination with the US team's progress towards the Gold Medal, particularly since it included famous stars like Magic Johnson and Michael Jordan in the so-called 'Dream Team'. Basketball was thus considered a perfect vehicle to boost the brand's exposure.

The strategy for the Buckler Challenge was carefully thought through. It featured matches during 1993 between All-Star American

continues

continued

college teams and the national All-Star teams of France, Spain and Greece, with a slightly different programme mounted for Italy because of reorganization of the Italian basketball association.

Each event was televised in the host market, on a national level, with more coverage in the other countries and some in the USA. It culminated in July in the Buckler European Challenge, with a match between the best players from the four main countries. This was followed by the USA Challenge, with four of the top Divisions in US college teams playing each other in a knockout tournament in Paris at the end of the year.

There were spin-off activities, like the '3 on 3' competitions for consumers in major cities in Spain and Italy. '3 on 3' is a form of basketball created in the USA for playing in limited spaces. And the winners of those competitions were to meet and compete to go to the European Challenge in July 1993. There were promotional activities associated with all the events. The sponsorship generated massive amounts of television and print coverage for Buckler in Europe. Heineken continued with the programme though 1994.

Buckler is now available in more than 50 countries. By 1991 Buckler ranked second on the world list of non-alcohol beers, selling 100 million litres in a year. According to Heineken, Buckler has brought additional volume to the beer market rather than being seen as a substitute.

Summary

(1) The relationship between marketing and public relations/communications is often confused. One reason has been the lack of understanding about what marketing itself is, with the use of the term often synonymous with sales or advertising. And because marketing is reckoned merely to be about selling or creating images, then public relations becomes an even tackier part of the mix. It is rated as a relatively inexpensive way of acquiring publicity for a product, but as an add-on, not major, technique.

(2) That is changing as marketing itself moves up the strategic scale and is considered to be more of a framework in which the company should operate. This, in turn, shifts the perception of public relations, transforming it into more of a management service.

(3) When the brand publicity is well thought out and integrated, its payback can be multifold. But there has to be tight coordination among different groups for a more integrated approach to be effective and be consistent with the communications policy as a whole.

(4) Clients are increasingly seeking ways to make established brands stand out in the midst of cluttered and competitive markets where grabbing consumer attention for new products is never assured. The premium is on the unconventional, creative approach – but one that actually works.

(5) The techniques chosen can depend on whether the brand is established, has something new to say, or is a new product altogether. The more competitors in a field, the more the onus is on a high degree of creativity. And although new products might not have this problem, they need to be explained, which can be an uphill task unless it is from an established brand with a heritage.

(6) The corporate brand reflects the reality that permeates the entire organization. It can also be a powerful branding tool both for the corporation itself and to give added value to products and services.

(7) Sponsorship can be an effective communications tool for reaching across borders. Some companies import sponsorship opportunities from outside the target market or markets: travelling art exhibits, for example. Others build a cumulative image by sponsoring a series of related national events and 'working' the sponsorship via national and international employee, customer and media relations.

Note

(1) *Report on the Teenagers of The World.* London: Research International Observer, January 1994.

8

Internal communications

The value of communication

Factors which make for better, rather than poorer communication, include an appreciation by senior management and throughout the organization of the contribution that communication can make. Communication must be understood as a two-way process, and will be more likely to be valued, and be of value, in those companies which are flexible in their structure, and are less rather than more hierarchical. It is also rated highly by companies committed to making full use of their human resources, in particular providing equal opportunities.

Evidence for the contribution of communication to industrial competitiveness falls broadly into three categories:

(1) In the first, there are a limited number of studies which demonstrate strong correlations of good communication practices and employee satisfaction and commitment, and of communication, employee reaction to communication practices and industrial and corporate performance.

(2) In the second category, evidence for the value of communication is built up through case studies.

(3) In the final category, the value of good communication is asserted as a matter of faith.

A number of studies establish a correlation between communication and employee satisfaction. Two studies, in General Electric and Hewlett Packard in the USA, found that responses to five survey questions dealing with face-to-face communication between employees and their immediate managers on the companies' internal employee attitude surveys enabled prediction of employees' satisfaction.[1] One, carried out by the International Association of Business Communicators (IABC) concluded: 'The better the managers' communication, the more satisfied employees are with all aspects of their work life' and that 'most managers, when shown these results, are willing to allow that a more satisfied employee is a more productive employee'. Effective face-to-face communication programmes can thus be seen as a means to competitive advantage.

A study which establishes a strong correlation between approaches to communication and corporate performance is a longitudinal study[2] carried out by the communication consultancy, Towers Perrin. The consultancy's studies of higher performing companies track links over time, through employee attitude surveys and measures of company performance, between employee perceptions, on-the-job performance, product quality and customer service, and company performance.

The study tracks attitudes in 135 successful but otherwise quite different companies involved in nine industries, profitable over three years, facing competition and maintaining their independence. Despite their differences the high performing companies share a number of important characteristics:

(1) they are fast paced and ambitious – they have high goals
(2) they are market driven
(3) product/service quality is everything
(4) employees closest to the customer are valued
(5) contribution and innovation are rewarded
(6) improvements are constantly sought.

These companies constantly seek suggestions from frontline employees, they delegate and maintain two-way communication. As a result, 74% of employees in top performing companies feel their manager or supervisor asks for ideas to improve efficiency. In poorer performing companies, only 41% feel this to be true. Over 90% of employees in top and poorer performing companies feel that they know of ways that efficiency could be improved.

Strong correlations between good communication practices and corporate performance are problematic, however. As Marchington and his associates pointed out in their 1992 study[3] of employee involvement it may be that better corporate performance encourages employee involvement, rather than the other way around. Their own study was of 25 organizations which introduced a variety of employee involvement programmes – initiatives taken to improve communication with employees – during the economic upturn in Britain during the mid- to late-1980s.

They felt that employee involvement is essentially an article of faith, and that few managers would claim that employee involvement would be singled out as a key contributor to corporate performance.

Case studies do suggest a strong link between improved communication with employees and corporate performance. These are used heavily by communication management consultants, and by others, for example, in government, to support arguments for the introduction of improved internal communication. In the UK, the Employment Department's Investors in People programme argued the case for investment in people with a collection of 20 case studies[4]. That approach stressed employee involvement and communication.

Box 8.1   The Federal Express approach

Figure 8.1 is a communication quality methodology developed by Ed Robertson, manager of measurement and quality at Federal Express, to measure the results of messages targeted to employees. The approach utilizes 11 criteria arranged in a four-level hierarchy ranging from logistics to the impact of the message on audience attitudes, commitment and behaviour.

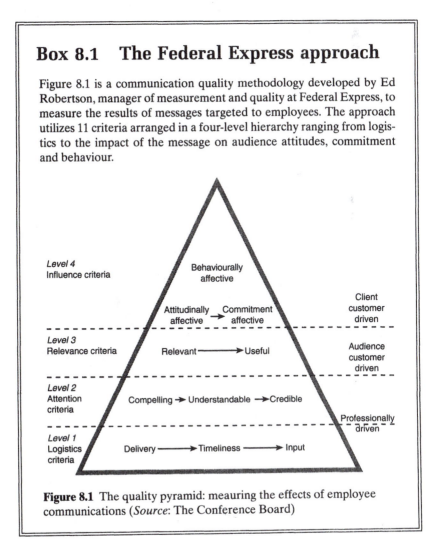

Figure 8.1 The quality pyramid: meauring the effects of employee communications (*Source*: The Conference Board)

Box 8.2   Royal Mail

In April 1992 the Royal Mail, part of the UK Post office, embarked on a 'change programme' entitled 'Delivering for you'. The purpose of the programme was to get closer to customers by focusing on total quality. As part of the implementation process it produced a large number of internal and external communications materials to prepare both the public and its employees for the restructuring.

For example, a video was developed so that top management could explain the process and its implications. It also broadcast a message to both employees and customers using television, telling the employees ahead of time when it would be broadcast. Briefings were prepared for the sales force to use with customers.

For the last few years the organization has been sending out annual attitude surveys to most of its employees. The intention is to repeat this exercise twice a year to improve internal communications. The Royal Mail also carried out *ad hoc* surveys on particular issues like sponsorship, often using the employee newsletter. In addition, it researches what its employees think of its public broadcasts both before and after transmission.

Hotpoint, one of the companies providing case study material, aimed to develop a workforce who were participants, not spectators, by briefing them thoroughly. The company prepared a training programme to encourage individual managers to develop their skills in communication and staff development. Hotpoint is a joint venture, owned in equal shares by GEC and General Electric in the USA. The company believes that its business performance has been improved, and has been able to save nearly £2 million at one of its factories by employee factory team working.

Other case studies, presented over recent years, detail the experience of Japanese companies in setting up in the UK. An example is provided by Komatsu, which took over a construction equipment manufacturing plant in County Durham in 1985. An examination of the company's experience[5] showed that the company 'by consciously involving each and every employee on an equal basis... has created a unity of purpose and working atmosphere too often missing in British-owned companies.' The company's approach to communication made it clear to employees that it wanted to hear from them. Employees interviewed for the article said that they knew that their ideas would be listened to, and that they were involved in decision-making.

Marchington and his associates suggested that carrying out cost-benefit analyses of employee involvement programmes could jeopardize their intangible but arguably real contribution to corporate performance.

They emphasized that use of techniques of employee involvement is an act involving faith in the value of the techniques. Faith is the keynote in a UK Department of Employment[6] publication, which suggests that 'employee involvement is important for companies because it increases their prosperity and productivity'.

The UK's employment minister, writing in the introduction to the publication, suggested that 'many of our leading companies... many of our top managers... believe that encouraging employees to be involved in the work of their organizations, and committed to their success, is a key factor in improving productivity and performance.'

The publication also includes case studies, which provide illustrations of best practice. One is Nissan, which is committed to continuous improvement in working practices. Employee involvement in the company means that everyone knows what is going on, and all communication is face-to-face, through daily team meetings. Employee involvement is 'simply the best way of running a business'. Another company included is Peugeot Talbot, which makes extensive use of team briefing to involve employees. Managers and supervisors in the briefing chain are thoroughly trained in the briefing philosophy and technique.

Case 8.1   BT's internal communications programme

By March 1991, BT (formerly British Telecom) had completed 'Project Sovereign', a radical, market-driven reshaping of the company with the aim of putting customers first. For a number of reasons, this stage was a milestone in the company's development.

Previously part of the Post Office, with a monopoly of domestic communications and virtually no international interests, BT had been

continues

continued

subject to increasing competition over the last decade, and in the private sector since 1984. The company needed to change as a strategic response to rapid and dramatic changes in the telecommunications marketplace. New competition at home demanded a fresh approach to customer relations. Deregulation overseas offered a tremendous opportunity for international expansion.

BT's 24-million customer base in the UK spanned the individual payphone-only user to the multimillion pound corporation with a sophisticated communications network. 'Project Sovereign' brought coherence and focus to BT's approach to these audiences, creating separate business and residential customer divisions to serve particular market segments. With the change of identity and name from British Telecom to BT, the company was signalling its determination to become a major player in the fast-growing international telecommunications market.

Employee understanding and endorsement of this new approach to the customer was vital to long-term success. The credibility of BT's corporate reputation, embodied in the new visual identity from consultants Wolff Olins, depended heavily on employees' active participation in delivering first-class service and quality products. BT briefed UK-based Imagination to communicate to the employees their central role in delivering BT's promise to customers by giving an inspirational, honest assessment of the reasons behind the reorganization.

It was vital to demonstrate senior management commitment to the reorganization and relaunch. BT agreed with Imagination that its own headquarters should be the venue so that employees could experience the changes within the company at first hand, and so that senior management were seen to 'own' the presentation.

Imagination created a temporary high-tech auditorium, raised 60 feet to fourth floor level. Steel chairs and linking bridges led the audience up to seating around a central presentation area which consisted of a revolving stage in-the-round set as if for an informal television interview.

Television monitors spanned four sides of the presentation area, while others were suspended above the space for maximum visibility. There were also audiovisual projection screens presenting a continuous series of slides.

The set was designed to generate excitement and suspense among the employees showing BT as an emerging global telecommunications force in a rapidly expanding market. The tone was measured, however, emphasizing a considered strategic approach and underlining the fact that the new identity was a necessary culmination of 10 years of controlled change. There was an accompanying exhibition to show how the identity would work across products, uniforms and so on.

A professional anchorman took the audience through the change, using film and video, recorded 'vox pop' and formal and informal

continues

continued

interviews to build up a picture of BT's present and future. There was an advance preview of both the new visual identity and the television advertising campaign for the new branding.

Satellite link-ups between a number of key locations enabled a live discussion about the impact of the change on different aspects of BT operations. The event was also transmitted to various other sites around the country.

Videos of the first event were dispatched the same night, and seen by further numbers of overseas employees over the following days and weeks. Imagination designed a range of corporate literature to support the event, placing the culture change and new visual identity within a more detailed context.

The BT presentation exemplified Imagination's belief that 'being there' is one of the most powerful means of internal and external communication. Immersing an audience in first-hand, real-time experience brings a brand, a corporate identity or an internal change programme to life. Blending information with entertainment helps an audience absorb a lot of complex material in a short space of time.

Integration with other elements in the communication mix was essential. Imagination ensured that the presentation was consistent with Wolff Olins' identity development work, Saatchi & Saatchi's creative proposals, Imagination's strategic design development of the BT 'public face' and BT's own public relations and marketing campaign.

It was also considered vital that the presentation was part of a larger process of internal communication. It had a direct impact on the 4900 employees who attended the event, while the key messages were communicated through a 'cascade' dissemination of the live event video and literature to everyone in the company.

BT research revealed that the event had unprecedented initial and subsequent impact on employee perception of the changes, and on the management team itself.

Recognition of requirements

The Memorandum on Competitiveness from the Department of Trade and Industry in 1993 pointed out that improved management practice depends on managers acknowledging a need to improve, as well as on their knowledge of techniques. British managers in particular need to reconsider their communication skills and the contribution effective communication could make to the performance and competitiveness of the organizations they lead. There is some evidence that British managers overestimate their capabilities or are complacent about their communication skills. A 3i/Cranfield European Enterprise Centre study,[7] for example, found that British managers rated themselves as the best in Europe, but that managers in other European countries believed British managers lacked compassion and ability to get on with people.

New ideas to provide solutions to management problems surface regularly and need to be integrated into current practice. Communication, however, is a fundamental process in management and needs to be approached with more commitment and a willingness to recognize its requirements. A number of studies have established that employees prefer to receive information about their role, their work and the organization they are part of from their immediate supervisor or manager.

Managers, as a number of companies cited in case studies here have recognized, need training for this direct communication with employees and with other communication tasks required in their roles. This needs to prepare managers for the emotional aspects of their communication tasks. After all, communication is not just a matter of making an effective presentation. It is also a matter of creating trust, developing a climate in which open communication can take place, of listening, and of acting in a way consistent with spoken and written communication, since actions themselves will communicate.

Managers also need help to develop the confidence needed for open communication. Guidelines from the UK's Confederation of British Industry (CBI) in 1979 on action for employee involvement suggested that an open style of communication requires strong managers, who have confidence, knowledge and skills. A barrier to effective communication is managers' fear of appearing not to have all the answers.

Training

Present programmes of management education and training deal with communication as an aspect of organization or group behaviour, or as a matter of learning presentation techniques, listening or writing skills. But communication requires imagination, emotional content, commitment, and a willingness to listen and respond to others. Current approaches to management in the British setting, for instance, would probably find the last comment naive or soft. In Danish or Dutch settings, however, it might be more acceptable, and these are countries ranked rather higher than the UK in the world competitiveness list.

Training for communication presents those involved with management education and training with the challenges of finding new ways of training and of adapting existing programmes, such as the standard MBA programme, to meet new requirements. A first step towards developing new approaches and programme elements will be to recognize that the need for them exists.

Experiments in communication

Some US examples of companies which have made effective use of communication to restore company performance demonstrate the range of techniques that can be used. The examples[8] include a chief executive officer with the toy company Mattel, who believes that employees should have fun and communicates accordingly. The article suggests that enlightened chief executive officers are recognizing that their first constituency is made up of their own employees and are working harder at communicating with employees while trying different techniques.

In the UK, there are examples provided in reports from the Department of Trade and Industry (DTI) and the CBI of company communication practices that appear to work, in fostering innovation or improving competitiveness, but British managers need to be more willing to experiment with these practices.

Research

Until recently, research into organizational communication was conducted to find out how managers could use communication to influence and secure cooperation from employees, rather than to contribute to organizational change or the quality of life of those working within organizations.[9] There is a need for more research into the contribution that communication can make to employee involvement, and to the achievement of organizational objectives, in the interests of everyone in the company.

Until now, much of this research has been carried out by research organizations, such as MORI in the UK, or by communication consultancies. Interest in research in organizational communication in British universities is growing slowly, with the appointment of senior academics to chairs in subjects such as corporate communications. But it will be some time before the attention of these researchers is focused on these questions.

Internal customers

Calling employees internal customers has become a central tenet of modern corporate jargon. But it is questionable whether executives who use it really understand and have put into practice the principles for which it stands. It is the result of a growing awareness of the need both for overall consistency and to be more 'marketing led' or, in other words, to listen to all the markets, both external and internal, in order to provide the goods and services that people want and will buy. It means that everyone in the company is seen as an essential part of the process, whether they deal with the outside world or not. It is also about treating employees as precious and crucial elements of the organization.

This concept shelters under a variety of phrases, from internal marketing to corporate culture. And most companies will argue that they carry out extensive employee communications programmes: in-house newsletters, videos and group meetings have been around a long time. Making this process far more two-way, and less top-down, meets more resistance and fear from senior managers schooled in the hierarchical way of dealing with those 'beneath' them. But it is an idea whose time has come and which has been fuelled by several trends:

(1) the growing spread of the principles of total quality management with their focus on delivering total customer satisfaction;
(2) as a consequence of that, the need to 'empower' employees at all levels to take the initiative;
(3) expansion into new countries and cultures, which puts the onus on companies to introduce themselves into the market effectively and sensitively;
(4) skills shortages, which demand that companies try not only to retain people, but also to attract new ones in a much more competitive recruitment environment;
(5) the push to harmonize working conditions across Europe underpinned by the Social Charter.

What those few, more forward-looking companies are doing is to marry all the communication activities together, so that the senior public relations person handles both external and internal communications in a consistent fashion. An example is Abbey National, which converted itself from a building society to a plc in the mid-1980s. Before it took what for it was a momentous step it had decided that it first needed to begin to create a 'plc' culture. A key plank of that strategy was to set up a function which would deal with both internal and external communications. 'Abbey decided that its image to both the outside and the staff had to be indivisible,' recalls Stewart Gowans, former corporate affairs manager, who came to Abbey to oversee that role five years ago. He noted:

'Their decision reflected the fact that communication is as much a part of their business as anything else and they wanted me to provide communications solutions to business problems wherever possible. Abbey had done a lot of thinking about what its core message was. And they recognized that how a decision is communicated, or the communication element that influences a decision, as well as consistency, are absolutely vital.'

Another example is Cargill, one of the largest privately owned companies in the world, with interests in trading, processing and financial management. Although it has been in Europe for a long time and now has 13,000 people there, it is only within the last few years that it has hired its first European corporate communications manager, Joan Wasylik, to oversee total communication activities, from media relations to trade shows to employee relations. And it is the latter that has been a priority with Wasylik since Cargill places great emphasis on its employee relations, she pointed out:

> 'Our goal is to double our size every five to seven years. So we want to continue to recruit people who will sign on at 21 and stay for life. So my job is to ask what do we need to do; how can I help that process. If it means that I have to focus my initial attention on improving our internal communications so that people recruited stay with us, or see that our recruiting material is right, that's part of my job.'

Case 8.2   American Airlines, 1992

Being number one in the home market, even one as big as the USA, is not a guarantee of instant success in other markets. Take American Airlines: number one on most counts in the USA, its tempo in Europe sharply accelerated when it picked up slots at Heathrow in the early 1990s from the ailing Pan Am. American Airlines had been in Europe, flying from Gatwick, in 1982. But the flights from Heathrow really focused its attention on Europe.

That explained the brief that Lizann Peppard, regional public relations manager for Europe followed: heighten the awareness of American Airlines both externally and internally, particularly since its very name made it seem as more of a regional player. This can be likened to BA's efforts over the past few years to rid itself of its British flavour by using its initials alone.

Peppard joined the airline in January 1990, although she had already been working on the account in an external public relations consultancy. There were 133 flights a week when she first joined the company: there were over 200 by 1991. 'I came here to raise awareness of the American name but also to establish ourselves as the quality US carrier,' she explained. But that was not all:

continues

continued

'My internal brief was also to raise the awareness of Europe among the US employees. We need to make them aware that we are an international airline, not just domestic. If you are working in a little airport in a place like Idaho Falls, Europe seems miles and miles away.'

American had over 100,000 employees, 2000 of whom were in Europe. Communications, aided by a heavy use of information technology, had a prominent role. At the corporate communications centre in its headquarters in Dallas, for example, there were almost 100 people, half of whom dealt with flight magazines with the other half split into internal and external communications. American was a highly centralized company – television advertisements for Europe were devised in the USA, for example – so Peppard reported directly into Dallas, with a strong dotted line to the vice president, Europe.

'Being an American company, but also being the company we are, means that communications in all its facets is supremely important. We spend more time communicating with our employees and the outside world than most British companies,' believed Peppard, who is herself British. She reckoned as much as a third or even a bit more of her time was spent on internal matters.

Her strategy was to try and blend long-term goals of raising American's profile with the need to be able move fast. During the acquisition of the TWA routes, for example, American Airlines had to wait for government approval which could come at any time. At the same time, its big US competitor, United, was also doing deals with Pan Am for its European slots. Said Peppard:

'We didn't know when we were going to get approval but our chairman said that within two days of approval we had to have a whole series of employee briefs set up for the 400 TWA employees at Heathrow, to introduce them to AA, explain the background of the company, have all the individual contracts ready.'

The awareness of the strong role that public relations has to play in the company came from the chairman, Robert Crandall, who was noted for taking journalists aback with his openness at interviews. 'I haven't got to do battle every time I want to do an interview,' said Peppard. 'The whole company is good at communicating. Also, if we have any bad news, it is a very, very strong edict that employees must know before anyone else.'

New techniques

Business television has been successfully established as a communications technique for both employees and customers in the USA since the 1980s, and has moved on from being a substitute for the corporate newsletter to become a vehicle for training, conveying marketing information, product launches and a range of other applications. Companies like it because everyone can watch it at once, unlike anything else. It eliminates problems like rumours because one lot of people gets one set of information. And secondly, it is totally timely in that it can be live. It also cuts down the time and money associated with travel since it can be used selectively to replace events like conferences and road shows.

The key to cost-effectiveness is regular use. At Ford in the UK, for example, programmes are broadcast weekly to 250 sites for half an hour, with slots covering different aspects and departments. It brings relatively high production values but lower costs in terms of time scales and putting magazine features together.

Box 8.3   Ford

The car industry has been going through a prolonged period of transition, Ian Slater, director of corporate affairs and internal communications for Ford of Europe, told a conference in November 1993. For example, in Europe in 1993 there was a year-on-year plunge in car industry volume demand of 17%, equivalent to the capacity of up to eight manufacturing plants.

Even though a partial recovery was expected in 1994, the forecast was that the industry would operate below trend for the next several years. And this would be exacerbated by the increase in production capacity as the Japanese transplants in Europe came fully on stream. That excess capacity meant, said Slater, 'the industry will experience severe structural problems. It is an environment in which effective communications assumes great importance.'

continues

continued

Slater compared the challenge to that faced by Ford in the early 1980s, when it developed the internal communications policy upon which its current policy is based: 'Some now-familiar concepts were embraced, such as participative management, teamwork, employee involvement and open communication.' And in order to set leadership standards, Ford wanted to augment its existing internal communications with the latest in electronic communications technology.

Ford in North America thus became one of the first companies to develop an in-house television network. The Ford Communications Network (FCN) today transmits a daily television news programme live by satellite to more than 300 locations in the USA, Canada and Mexico.

In Europe, where there are 24 major factories in seven European countries, Ford's communications challenge was even more complex and demanding, noted Slater, because of both the fierce competition and the need to take into account cultural differences. Thus Ford Communications Network, Europe was set up, which provides regular television programming as well as a continuous teletext service, including both locally and nationally generated news.

Programming covers everything from explanations of corporate strategy to stories about individual employees. Employees are encouraged to take the time to watch FCN on television monitors.

'Employees particularly welcome the speed and accuracy of the information received from FCN, meaning that they are no longer likely to hear of significant developments first through external media or the grapevine', said Slater.

FCN programmes are now produced in four languages in the UK, France, Spain and Belgium. Editorial coordination has also been improved between the various national Ford employee newspapers and magazines. A communications audit has produced wide-ranging recommendations for change which will be implemented over the next few years, particularly improving communications within the European management team.

Slater predicts that the future will see more global satellite link-ups, probably with an integration of some of the individual technologies in use now. This could include making FCN increasingly available on people's desks. Slater said, 'Like many other large organizations, Ford is going through a period of positive and far-reaching cultural change. The change process is being fostered by a completely re-engineered communications effort, based on continuous improvement.'

While car companies are among the original users, others are coming onstream. For example, less than 24 hours after the UK Budget speech in 1993 Norwich Union put out an interactive programme with a panel of financial experts and broadcast it to 42 different branches. ICI Pharmaceuticals has used its network to broadcast to 14 different countries, with almost 300 staff taking part in discussions about product development and marketing issues.

Retail and financial services could also benefit, notes Kevin Gavaghan, formerly marketing and communications director of Midland Bank and now a director at Visage, a major UK and European producer of business television.

> 'It depends very much at the moment on the perceived value of the product and the customer being sold to. Essentially business TV so far has been considered appropriate to the sale of high value products. People look at a car and say it is worth communicating with the sales force on this expensive item. But if you are looking at the much more important topic of the lifetime value of the customer, it is worth using business TV for many more industries. A bank, for example, will make as much out of a customer over a lifetime as a car company out of a single customer, although the nature and frequency of the transactions will be much greater.'

And the attraction of business television is that it can cut down on the need to produce reams of the written word. At the Midland, said Gavaghan, it was calculated that any one branch received up to 40,000 minutes of reading material a year, before doing anything else with it: 'Those minutes might have been spent talking to customers or answering the phone.' More importantly, the quality of the message received over the network will be higher: 'While business television is not intended to replace all paper-based or face-to-face communication, it provides key themes and messages which recur and are repeated consistently to audiences whose preferred method of learning anything these days is visual.'

At the heart of all this, of course, is communications, from informing and motivating to training. Companies are slowly coming to terms with the fact that not only do they need a clarity of corporate vision, but they also need to communicate it consistently to all its audiences. The pace of change and the fact that few products and services remain differentiated for long means that communications has to be accurate and swift and that there is a premium for good service. It is making visual communications a growth industry.

As Stuart Appleton, group marketing director of Metro-Video and formerly head of the International Visual Communications Association (IVCA), said,

> 'I think it is about effective business communication. It is about having a strategy for communications which helps you decide what to choose. And because pictures can be 35% more

effective, you have a tactical decision to make about delivery. It can range from acetate on an overhead projector to a good corporate video to state-of-the-art desk-top delivery systems. Or it could be a face-to-face event, from a small meeting to an annual general meeting for 5000. In between are things like product launches.'

That strategy should cover both internal and external communications.

'There is still a tension at the moment because external communications has received a lot more money. But now internal communications is getting more attention: middle managers are disappearing, so senior management needs more sophisticated communications techniques. Also, there is a recognition that to be successful organizations have to have improved customer care, and the best way to impart specialized knowledge is to show people how it could be and shouldn't be with pictures.'

Case 8.3 Chevron

Chevron UK is part of the international petroleum giant Chevron Corporation and employs 2,000 staff and contractors. After rapid expansion in the UK the company began to settle down in the mid-1980s, paying less attention to communications, downsizing the public affairs function and merging it with human resources.[10]

In 1987, perceiving that there was a lack of clarity with both their internal and external communications, public affairs was re-established as a stand-alone function reporting to the managing director. It was charged with establishing traditional communications mechanisms, which included the introduction of an in-house staff newspaper and the drawing up of an emergency communications plan – particularly vital for a company involved in North Sea oil exploration and production.

After about two and a half years the government and public affairs manager, Cedric Lavington, felt that the next step was to integrate the function into the business so that it could help develop and shape policy. To achieve this, it was critical to review the company's communications, determine what role government and public affairs had to play, and develop an understanding among managers of their roles and responsibilities. The company decided to use an outside consultancy,

continues

continued

Smythe Dorward Lambert, to carry out research into the perception among staff of the company's profile.

The results, based on a seminar with 25 senior managers and supervisors, laid the foundation for a sea-change in the way the company valued communications, since they showed that the messages managers passed to staff and the outside world could be contradictory, something that could obviously have an impact on the business overall.

A series of practical measures were developed to improve communications, including:

- a communication plan as part of the business plan;
- new approaches to presenting the business plan to staff;
- communications training for managers and supervisors;
- meetings between the managing director and senior supervisors twice a year;
- 'brown bag' sessions, where a department explains to other employees over lunch what it does;
- an issues planning group of nine senior UK managers to look ahead to issues inside and outside the company which may or will need a response now or in the future.

Interestingly, a quality improvement initiative was taking place at the same time and managers found that the two cultural 'shifts' fed off each other. The entire process allowed the company to define six issue areas vital for measuring progress towards its vision, together with achievable targets for each one.

Summary

(1) Communication must be understood as a two-way process, and will be more likely to be valued, and of value, in those companies which are flexible in their structure, and are less rather than more hierarchical. It is also rated highly by companies committed to making full use of their human resources, in particular providing equal opportunities.

(2) Evidence for the contribution of communication to industrial competitiveness falls broadly into three categories.
   - In the first, there are a limited number of studies which demonstrate strong correlations of good communication practices and employee satisfaction and commitment, and of communication, employee reaction to communication practices and industrial and corporate performance.

- In the second category, evidence for the value of communication is built up through case studies.
- In the final category, the value of good communication is asserted as a matter of faith.

(3) British managers need to reconsider their communication skills and the contribution effective communication could make to the performance and competitiveness of the organizations they lead. There is some evidence that British managers overestimate their capabilities or are complacent about their communication skills.

(4) Communication, however, is a fundamental process in management and needs to be approached with more commitment and a willingness to recognize its requirements.

(5) Present programmes of management education and training deal with communication as an aspect of organization or group behaviour, or as a matter of learning presentation techniques, listening or writing skills. But communication requires imagination, emotional content, commitment, and a willingness to listen and respond to others.

(6) There is a need for more research into the contribution that communication can make to employee involvement, and to the achievement of organizational objectives, in the interests of everyone in the company.

(7) Business television has been successfully established as a communications technique for both employees and customers in the USA since the 1980s, and has moved on from being a substitute for the corporate newsletter to become a vehicle for training, conveying marketing information, product launches and a range of other applications.

(8) External communications has usually received a lot more money. But now internal communications is getting more attention: middle managers are disappearing, so senior management needs more sophisticated communications techniques.

Notes

(1) Foehrenbach J., and Goldfarb, S., Employee communication in the '90s: greater expectations, *IABC Communication World*, International Association of Business Communicators, May–June 1990.

(2) Towers Perrin, *Improving Business Performance Through People*, 1993 (a continuing study supervised from Towers Perrin's San Francisco head office.)

(3) Marchington, M., Goodman, J., Wilkinson, A., Ackers, P. *New Directions in Employee Involvement*. Manchester: Manchester School of Management, UMIST and Department of Employment, 1992.

(4) *Investing in People: the Benefits of being an Investor in People*. London: Department of Employment, 1993.

(5) Gabb, Anabella, Komatsu makes the Earth move, *Management Today*, April 1988.

(6) *People and Companies: Employee Involvement in Britain*. London: Department of Employment, 1989.

(7) *The Euro-manager Survey, Special Survey* 6: *Attitudes to Managers and Companies in Europe*. London: 3i/Cranfield Enterprise Centre, 1983.

(8) Champions of communication, *Fortune*, 3 June 1991.

(9) Grunig, J. (ed.), *Excellence in Public Relations and Communications management*. Hillsdale, New Jersey: L. Erlbaum 1992.

(10) Review: July–December 1992, Smythe Doward Lambert.

9

Public affairs

Defining public affairs

Dealing with governments and other regulatory bodies at a local, regional and supra-national level has become a major focus of public relations. Within public relations, public affairs is a specialized practice that focuses on relationships which will have a bearing on the development of public policy. Public affairs is especially concerned with issues management, attempting to identify issues and matters of public concern which, if acted upon by significant groups, are likely to have an impact on business activities and other organizational interests.

Another major focus of public affairs practice is the management of relationships with government. This is unsurprising: governments try to balance the creation of an environment where business can flourish with a regulatory framework that prohibits bad practices and promotes certain standards of behaviour.

In practice, public affairs may be used as a term to describe the work of a public relations department. Public relations activities are referred to in a number of ways. One organization may describe its public relations activities as 'corporate affairs', another may use 'corporate communications' and others may use the term 'public affairs'. Practitioners themselves may be more comfortable describing themselves as 'public affairs' rather than as 'public relations' professionals.

Some public affairs practitioners will argue that their practice is superior to public relations, which they will view as mainly concerned with media relations and publicity. They will suggest that public affairs is more intellectually demanding, requiring more qualified staff and a more sophisticated approach to companies, their management, problems and opportunities. Their view is often supported in practice, by organizations and senior management groups who give public affairs activities a higher status.

Despite this, the argument about public affairs versus public relations is essentially an argument about a specialization within a broad area of management practice. The specialization does need in-depth knowledge, but it is not in the end different from the general practice of which it is part. It is a practice focused on specific relationships, and specific issues.

Public affairs is, in some ways, a defensive political practice. While public relations is concerned overall with the management of important relationships, public affairs focuses on relationships which are involved in the development of public policy which may affect a company's ability to operate and succeed. The practice is defensive, because it sets out to protect the organization's interests in public debate and the discussions which contribute to the formulation of regulations and legislation.

Many practitioners will say that public affairs, far from being defensive and reactive, is proactive. It seeks to anticipate events, issues and trends which, as they become a matter of public concern, may have an impact on the development of public policy, and ultimately on the organization's interests. More than this, public affairs practice may serve to bring issues to the surface of public debate, taking the initiative to shape debate and its consequences.

A 1984 study[1] carried out by Keith MacMillan, of Henley Management College, on the practice of public affairs in British industry found that certain activities were most commonly labelled as 'public affairs' while others were thought of as 'public relations'. This is illustrated in Table 9.1.

MacMillan concludes from examining respondents' groupings of these activities that public affairs is seen as 'political affairs' or 'government relations', while public relations is more concerned with orthodox or mainstream commercial activities. The 1984 study suggested that a fully developed public affairs function existed, at that time, in less than a score of the UK's largest industrial companies.

Table 9.1   (a) Activities labelled as 'public affairs'; (b) Activities labelled as 'public relations'.

(a) Activity	Target group
Monitoring policy Representation to ministers Representation to civil servants	Central government
Monitoring Lobbying Monitoring regulations/ directives/policies Lobbying European Parliament	Party political (including parliament, MPs' parties, etc.) EU
Monitoring	International organizations (OECD, UN, ICC, ILO, etc.)

(b) Activity	Target group
Corporate identity (logos, etc.) Corporate advertising	General public
Sponsorship Media relations Corporate literature Exhibitions Receptions	Customers (and general public)
Media relations Advertising	Financial

The European Centre for Public Affairs study

The European Centre for Public Affairs (ECPA), located at Templeton College, Oxford University, has – while Keith MacMillan was acting as director of research – researched the practice of public affairs in Europe. It sees the purpose of public affairs as:

> 'to enable business and government to meet their objectives to the mutual benefit of their stakeholders, hence in the long term optimizing a corporation's relations with the processes of government. To achieve this, the practice of public affairs must play its full role in the development of business strategy.'

A recent ECPA study[2] of European public affairs practice involved interviews with staff in 16 multinational companies headquartered in Europe or elsewhere. The companies included IBM, Nestlé, Siemens, Guinness and Ford.

The study established that public affairs as a term is not used by all companies to describe their activities in the public affairs area. Other terms used include corporate affairs, communications or external affairs.

The study suggested that in a wholly integrated function the following activities would be included under the public affairs heading:

- government relations
- issues management
- press and media relations
- publications
- community relations
- corporate advertising
- investor relations
- employee communications.

The list provides further evidence of the confusion of terms which still marks discussions of public relations practice and special areas of practice.

The IABC study of excellence in public relations and communications management (see Chapter 2) also makes clear that public relations and communications activities are best managed from an integrated function or department. In such a department, government relations and issues management will often be found grouped together.

None of the heads of public affairs activities in the ECPA study were members of the main boards of their companies, but they were found to report, either directly or indirectly, to a main board member who had additional responsibilities, for personnel or for a geographic region for example.

The ECPA study was carried out partly to find out about the characteristics of European public affairs practice. The researchers found that there has not been a shift of public affairs activity towards Brussels. It is still more important for senior public affairs staff to be close to their own senior management group and to try to influence developments in Brussels through national governments.

US companies provided an exception to this pattern, tending to locate their public affairs representatives in Brussels, in the same way that they would locate their public affairs staff in Washington, within the USA.

A problem for public affairs staff identified in the ECPA report is that of maintaining close contact with managers in the organization they work for, when most of their contacts are outside the organization in Brussels. The ECPA research indicates the need for public affairs staff to network within the firm, to be effective in the public affairs role. This requires close contact within senior management, but also depends on alliances built among middle management.

Public affairs management will be influenced by the structure and geographic spread of the corporation. An organization large enough to have significant subsidiaries in a number of countries will probably have public affairs staff in place to support subsidiaries. These staff may report to senior management in the countries in which they work, but also have a reporting relationship to central or head office public affairs staff.

There is a need to coordinate public affairs activities in several countries: this may be achieved through regular meetings of public affairs staff, for example on a Europe or worldwide basis. At these meetings, issues facing the organization can be reviewed and priorities attached to them.

In companies making sophisticated use of public affairs practice, the results of these meetings can be fed into planning activities, and significant issues facing the organization can be incorporated into strategy development. Companies such as IBM will go so far as to appoint staff to champion certain issues, to become familiar with all aspects of an issue so as to be able to brief senior management on it and advise on courses of action.

The ECPA study found that the degree of planning within the companies studied varied. Some companies had plans in place, phrased in terms of broadly stated objectives, while others had very detailed plans which were developed from a highly formalized planning process.

Case 9.1   SmithKline Beecham, 1991

One of the world's leading health-care companies, SmithKline Beecham was created from the merger of SmithKline Beckman (USA) and Beecham Group (UK) in July 1989. That year, SmithKline Beecham reported total sales of £4.9 billion, nearly 27% from continental Europe and 13% from the UK (separated out from the rest of the EC for historical reasons).

Continental Europe contributed nearly 33% of the Anglo-American health-care group's total pretax profit in 1989, with another 10% coming in from the UK. In 1990, the company boosted profit on total sales of £4.7 billion: 31% of sales came from continental Europe and 30% of profit, while the UK contributed 13% of sales and 10% of profit.

Sitting in Brussels, where he had kept an eye on the EC (now the EU) for his company for the last 13 years, Michel V. Philippe admitted that it helped to 'belong to an Anglo-American multinational headquartered in an EC member state'. It was not always thus, but it is fair to say that SmithKline Beckman (headquartered in Philadelphia in the USA) had seen One Market coming for a long time and, over the years, had given Philippe the senior management support he needed to communicate the company's point of view in Brussels and Strasbourg.

continues

continued

Prior to the merger, Philippe used to write a regular 'Letter from Europe' for SmithKline International's internal publication. The letter used humour to raise the consciousness of SmithKline people about Europe.

If anything, SmithKline's merger with Beecham strengthened the group's image-building function at government affairs level in the EU. Philippe's new title became vice president and director, government and public affairs, Europe (SmithKline Beecham). Reflecting due concern for national sensibilities in Europe, the business card that Philippe used with MEPs and Eurocrats, as well as in the UK, read: director and vice president, government and public affairs, Europe. The difference was subtle, but it took national realities into consideration and it works.

A new government and public affairs team took its place for SmithKline Beecham in Brussels. Philippe and a colleague, who spent 80% of her time on issues related to the company's significant animal health business, biotechnology and the environment, were joined by a lawyer (with the company for 20 years) who backed up Philippe on pharmaceutical issues and those related to intellectual property rights. An administrative assistant handled contacts with the European Parliament, screened proposed legislation and monitored developments important to the company. The team reported through Philippe to SmithKline Beecham's head of corporate affairs, who in turn reported to the chairman.

On the same level as Philippe were a vice president and director, government/industrial affairs, international, and a US government/public affairs counterpart, both based in the USA. A director, corporate information, was also based in the USA. The SmithKline Beecham corporate affairs organization covered corporate communications and investor relations out of the UK, via directors for both functions.

The overall brief of the Brussels government and public affairs office was to support SmithKline Beecham management with information and intelligence, as well as with a road map to the inner workings of EU institutions and with direct communication when necessary. When the company's Belgian subsidiary came under investigation by the European Commission's Directorate General IV (Competition) for receiving regional aid from the Belgian government, for example, the subsidiary's senior management contacted Philippe. Familiar with the EC people concerned, and well informed on the official (and unofficial) issues at stake, SmithKline Beecham government and public affairs was able to help select an appropriate legal consultant, expeditiously assemble and distill the information needed, and, most important, help to write 'from a public affairs and strategic marketing point of view' the final document submitted to the Commission on the company's behalf.

Only about 30% of Philippe's lobbying time was spent on the Commission, however. Significantly, he and his colleagues 'actually,

continues

continued

physically, go over there only four or five times in one year'. But there were business meetings with Commission officials elsewhere in Brussels, and in Strasbourg with the European Parliament. This way, SmithKline Beecham's people always knew what was going on and knew what to do with the information.

Another 20% of the SmithKline Beecham government affairs team's time was given, at EC Council level, to Coreper (the EC's Committee of Permanent Representatives from member states), communicating the company's point of view on national issues in the context of the Community. This activity was bound to become more important after 1992, when playing the EC card in the right way at the right time would become critically important to political and regulatory developments at national level.

The European Parliament was by far the most important EC institution 'at the present time' as far as Philippe was concerned. He spent about 50% of his lobbying time on the institution that gave its opinion on all proposals for EC legislation that the Commission forwarded to the Council. It helped that he was a card-carrying journalist accredited to the European Parliament, but now he was also a familiar auditor of meetings of parliamentary committees and multi-party groups dealing with specific issues in Brussels, as well as of the Parliament's plenary sessions in Strasbourg, where he spent about three days every other month. Because of his track record, internationalism, knowledge and humour, Philippe was welcomed by parliamentarians of all nationalities and political stripe when he came to communicate the point of view of his company or industry.

SmithKline Beecham's image was a great support. 'We are known for our heavy research commitment in Europe, as well as for the quality of our products and the integrity of our marketing behaviour,' Philippe said. SmithKline Beecham Pharmaceuticals deployed 2700 sales representatives throughout Europe. A major vaccine production plant just outside Brussels supplied 40% of the world's requirement for oral polio vaccines, as well as other well-used vaccines. And it was at this site that the world's first commercially available genetically engineered vaccine for the prevention of hepatitis B was developed.

The image of SmithKline Beecham in Europe was that of a research-based, innovative, transnational company, able to contribute positively to the EC's trade balance with the rest of the world, as well as to a better quality of life for EC consumers. SmithKline Beecham had a presence in every EC member state. Still, 'a UK numberplate doesn't make a Cadillac a British car,' Philippe pointed out. 'SmithKline Beecham is a true transnational.' So he worked closely not only with the European Pharmaceutical Industry Federation (EFPIA), but also with the UK's pharmaceutical association (ABPI) and the US Pharmaceutical Manufacturers Association (PMA). He believed in and

continues

continued

worked actively with the EC Committee of the American Chamber of Commerce in Belgium. 'In government and public affairs work, you often have more clout if you downplay your company identity and work with others who have an interest in the same issue,' Philippe said.

At SmithKline Beecham, a major issue was defined as 'one which could significantly affect the company's operations and performance in more than one major market'. In this respect, a major issue could be a critical national phenomenon that could conceivably spread to other markets, or an international issue like EC harmonization (of pharmaceutical product registration procedures, for example). In this context, SmithKline Beecham's Brussels office also monitored developments at United Nations agencies in Geneva and Vienna, as well as those of non-government organizations accredited to the United Nations and active in Europe.

Philippe's EC/UN watching function had evolved over the years. What began as a 'passive' monitoring operation moved through a phase that relied on spotting 'threats and opportunities' to a genuinely 'proactive and participative' operation that was helping to build SmithKline Beecham's image at the highest level of decision-making in Europe.

As recently as 10 years ago, most national governments and their elected representatives claimed to operate completely independently of 'those bureaucrats in Brussels'. Today that is not possible. The 'long toes' of the EU reach into every national government and elected assembly in the EU, and the provisions of the Treaty of Rome are taken seriously by even the most provincial member of an EU country's national parliament. The interdependence of Brussels and national governments works both ways, and is a critically important feature of the communications landscape of the EU.

The prominence of public affairs

Public affairs practice has come to prominence over the past 15 years for a number of reasons:

(1) Multinational companies, operating across national borders, have had to take national political and social environments into account in doing business. US- and now Japan-based multinationals have, for example, had to demonstrate their 'European credentials' in their activities in the European Union.

(2) In national contexts, businesses have had to defend themselves against increasing government intervention in their activities, and hostile interest from pressure groups, concerned, for example, with environmental conservation.

(3) The role of business in wealth creation and national prosperity is not sympathetically understood and needs to be constantly defended and explained. This happened in the 1980s in the UK, but a recently reported set of studies of British social attitudes from Social and Community Planning Research[3] showed how the British public is still prepared to look to government rather than business for the protection of social interests.

(4) An increasingly competitive world marketplace means that businesses have to pursue advantages in arenas hitherto left unattended. Marketing writers such as Philip Kotler have suggested that marketing – mega-marketing – now has to make allowance for social and political trends in marketing activities. MacMillan, in his 1984 study of public affairs in UK companies (see page 183), concluded that more investment in the professional competence and resources of the public affairs role in more companies might help to create an environment more conducive to business success.

Skilled public affairs practitioners need a familiarity with the workings of government, at political and administrative levels, and need to know how politicians and civil servants work together to respond to public issues and interests, social needs and political imperatives. They also have to understand how issues – matters of concern to the public or to special interest groups – emerge and come to provide a focus for public debate, and political and legislative action.

Public affairs practitioners also need to be familiar with interest groups involved in issues of concern – who are their leaders, how are they structured, what is their ideology, where does their support come from and how are they effective? It is important to know the personalities involved and the extent to which the interest groups are willing to use conflict and confrontation as means of pursuing their goals. This information forms the basis of intelligence about interest groups, and can be used to work with, against, or in spite of them. Public affairs, because of information gathered in the course of scanning and monitoring activities, and because of its potential to gather useful information about the intentions of government and special interest groups, is an important source of intelligence. This should be fed into strategic planning and senior management decision-making.

Public affairs – proactive or reactive?

The Niagara Institute, a management and leadership training institute in Canada which offers programmes in public affairs for senior managers, has argued that public affairs can be distinguished from public relations as a proactive practice. The institute sees public relations as reactive.

The word 'proactive' has entered the language of public relations practice to signify anticipation and action to influence the course of events, rather than simply to respond to them. In public affairs practice, the term suggests that action can be taken before an issue develops and emerges into public debate. It is important to recognize that even action taken in this way is reactive: it is action taken in response to events perceived as taking place, or likely to take place, inside or outside the company.

Public affairs can be defensive and offensive in practice – reactive and proactive – but its ultimate objective is the defence of the organization's interests. The practice is more effective if it is proactive, based on anticipation and allowing the organization to take the initiative in social action.

Some examples of public affairs practice illustrate defensive, offensive, reactive and proactive approaches.

Defensive

In 1983, a takeover bid was made for the British fine arts auction house Sotheby's. The company, in a widely reported move which brought public affairs practitioners to prominence in the UK, used lobbying effectively to have the bid referred to the Monopolies and Mergers Commission. This had the effect of killing the bid, and protecting the company's interests.

Offensive

In an award winning public affairs programme, D. J. Edelman worked with the Tobacco Alliance, a grouping of tobacco companies and others with an interest in the viability of the tobacco industry, to take the offensive against any likely increase in taxation on tobacco in the 1987 budget. The offensive involved systematic lobbying of members of parliament by, among others, tobacco retailers whose interests would be damaged by any fall in the sale of tobacco products. The campaign was successful: no increase in tobacco tax was made in that year, and sympathetic coverage of the issue was achieved in the national media.

Reactive

Lord Young, then minister responsible for the Department of Trade and Industry, was 'minded' to accept the recommendations of the Monopolies and Mergers Commission (MMC) regarding a reorganization of the British brewing industry to introduce more competition and to break the link between brewers and tied public houses obliged to sell their products. A well-managed campaign by the Brewers Society brought so much pressure to bear on the government, partly through an appeal to the public that the traditional public house would be threatened, that Lord Young had to change his mind and lessen the effects of the MMC recommendations.

Proactive

Kerry Tucker and Bill Trumpfheller of the San Diego-based issues management firm Smith, Tucker Inc. have developed a five-step plan for setting up an issues management system[4].

(1)   Anticipate issues and establish priorities

This can range from a very basic set of assumptions through to a very elaborate issue anticipation system. The authors suggest setting up internal cross-departmental task forces to exploit different areas of expertise and help track information from a variety of sources on potential concerns.

Alternatively, brainstorming sessions can be run which focus on questions like:

- What changes do we project in each category in the next three to five years?
- What trends are likely to affect the organization?
- What special events are likely to take place and have an impact on the organization?

Once these issues are identified, the organization can set priorities and decide how much time and resources to devote to them. The authors suggest that no more than three or four issues be tackled at a time.

(2)   Analyse issues

Develop a formal brief or analysis of the issue, looking at the opportunities and threats. It should cover what could happen if the issue is ignored, and an assessment of how stakeholders are likely to be affected by the issue. There should also be a summary of the direction in which the issue is heading. This should give management a broad view of the issue and its affect on a number of areas such as the bottom line and legislation.

(3)   Recommend an organizational position on the issue

While the ideal position should be one that 'mutually benefits the organization, others affected, and the greater public good', write the authors, this is not always possible. The analysis from the previous step, however, provides a database to develop a position designed to create support from the greatest majority affected.

The database is built from answers to the following questions:

- Who is affected?
- How do the affected publics perceive the issues?
- What are their likely positions and behavioural inclinations?

(4)   Identify publics/opinion leaders who can help advance your position

Publics should emerge from the following questions:

- Who makes decisions on the issue?
- Who is likely to support the organization's position?
- Who is likely not to?
- Who can we target successfully to make the biggest difference in advancing the organization's position?

The authors recommend carrying out formal research to validate assumptions about groups made during the analysis stage.

Opinion leaders can be powerful allies in dealing with publics. Criteria for selecting them include:

- Who do members of your public look to for advice on the issue?
- Who will the public trust on the issue?
- Who has the credibility to best advance your position on the issue?
- Who is likely to be open to your position on the issue?

(5)   Identify desired behaviours of publics/opinion leaders

This is too easy to overlook, say the authors. 'Advancing specific behaviour relating to your organization's position drives development of the rest of the planning process: behavioural goals, objectives, strategies, messages, tactics and budgets. Managing issues often requires action plans which expand beyond the scope of communication.'

Finally, the authors recommend that evaluation of progress is incorporated into plans so that adjustments can be made if necessary.

Public affairs in the European arena

The European Single Market is throwing up all sorts of issues in public affairs. For example, historically, the private and the public sectors in Europe have lived together in an atmosphere of mutual distrust. Business rarely made the effort to communicate its point of view in a rational or credible manner. 'We have always had the feeling that if we put our heads up out of the trenches, we'd get shot at,' a French executive said.

In the past, management in Europe concentrated on finding the best way to work with the operating environment as it existed. The idea that business can shape legislation and operating conditions is new. It is a reflection of the fact that so much public policy and legislation needs to be formulated, or adapted, in the process of creating a single market in Europe.

Even in France, where '*le lobbying*' still is not clearly understood, companies are working much more effectively to communicate their point of view and arrive at a consensus that meets the needs of all concerned. What is more, companies are learning that they must communicate in advance of crises or issues. The days of resisting and reacting are over.

In the absence of communication from the private sector, governments in the past have turned to other sources for information and direction: United Nations agencies, consumer groups, environmentalists, academia.

But communication, in and of itself, does not solve the problem. The experience of a well-meaning Dutch pharmaceuticals company is informative in this regard. The company organized a briefing session on the pharmaceuticals industry for middle-level officials from the Ministry of Economic Affairs. The report that came back from the ministry showed that the government officials had not understood the company's presentation at all. 'From their ages, they all must have been at university in the 1960s,' a bemused company source said. 'This generation now has come to power in the public sector in Europe, and they have no idea what you're talking about when you try to explain the way the private sector works. You need a whole new vocabulary to communicate with them.'

The key to participating in the political process in Europe today is finding this common vocabulary, finding a way to construct alliances with people who share common goals. Sometimes the commonality of these goals is not obvious and relationships have to be built to create a common ground.

Personal ties on the public side of the European economic ledger are very strong. Similar ties are being built between representatives of the public and private sector, as the political process evolves across national borders. In the new Europe, ideological divisions are blurred by economic pressures, financial constraints, and the need for the public and private sector to work together if the job is going to get done.

As Larry Snoddon, president of Burson-Marsteller Europe, told a Conference Board seminar on 'Communications Strategies for a United Europe' in 1991, the challenge facing portable telephone manufacturers illustrates how the public policy process works:

> 'Pocket phone manufacturers need a special frequency in all participating countries to make these telephones operable across Europe. If countries harmonize these frequencies, it is first a political issue. Second, and only second, it is a regulatory, technical issue.

> 'To create their market, companies must become part of the political process. They must first help shape the dialogue, at the national and the EC level. They must demonstrate how this move will further the creation of Europe, benefit each country and many other business interests, even if it may impinge on national prerogatives. And they must enhance their credibility and extend their reach by building strong relationships with allies and activists, particularly those who will benefit from the change.'

Having well-defined connections to the appropriate people, from a local mayor to the prime minister, can often make the difference to a company if it is confronted with what it considers an ill-thought-out piece of legislation.

Case 9.2   Time Warner, 1991

Time Inc. and Warner Communications Inc., the two corporations that merged in January 1990, together had a presence in every country in the EU and employed nearly 5000 people in the Union. In addition, substantial numbers of people were employed whenever a corporate unit took on a specific project in the EU. *Batman*, the movie, was made at Pinewood Studios outside London, for example, and, apart from the principals, the entire payroll was European. Altogether, Warner invested over $25 million in Europe to make *Batman*, but the end result generally is considered a US product.

Time Warner was strong and active in the EU, and its potential contribution to the technology of Europe's nascent pan-European

continues

continued

audiovisual sector was enormous. Yet Time Warner was essentially, and deliberately, a US media and entertainment group with an American image that was part of its working capital in the global marketplace.

For Time Warner, there was no question of spending time and money to try to become European. Yet functioning effectively in the European public affairs arena was essential to the company's success.

This was objective number one for Louise Dembeck, vice president, Time Warner Europe, head of the corporation's brand new Brussels office. A lawyer, Dembeck specialized in intellectual property protection – especially copyright, the underpinning of nearly all the company's core assets throughout the world.

She worked out of corporate headquarters in New York. But after she had flown back and forth across the Atlantic for nine months to look after the interests of what was then Warner Communications in the EC, it became apparent to senior management that the corporation needed to pay more attention to the Community in the run-up to the single market.

What Dembeck called 'the jolt' came in October 1989, when the EC passed the 'broadcast directive', otherwise known as Television Without Frontiers. 'We didn't expect it,' Dembeck admitted. 'We knew then that we had to be on the spot.' The Time Warner merger occupied senior management attention in the last months of 1989 and in early 1990, but finally Dembeck received the mandate and moved to Brussels in September 1990.

War in the Gulf intervened and it took time before Time Warner senior management felt able to travel to Europe again. Yet communication with New York (and Los Angeles) was no problem, and there had been constant 'support from the highest level', Dembeck said. 'This support is essential if a company wants more than just a monitoring function in the EC.' The importance that Time Warner accorded to EC government affairs was clear from the fact that Dembeck reported directly to the vice chairman. Her successor would report to 'senior management' in New York.

Based on Dembeck's experience, analysis and first-year results, the decision to build up the Brussels office had been made, and the search was on for a permanent head. Time Warner wanted to have a three-person office in Brussels, headed by a European, with its lawyer and a third person who knew the company and its businesses. Dembeck would act as a bridge between Brussels and the expectations of senior management in New York.

Time Warner was very decentralized. There was no head of European operations. Business units operating on both sides of the Atlantic were manifestly 'delighted' with the service that the corporation's Brussels office provided. 'There are issues here that we didn't even know existed,' Dembeck said, 'and the pace will intensify in the months leading up to the deadline for One Market.' Looking ahead, a principal objective was to anticipate and influence legislation, not just react to it.

In 1991, for example, drinks group Guinness was faced with a Customs and Excise decision that all European countries should raise their duties on spirits to the UK level to solve the problem of Scotch whisky being sent to another European country with a lower spirits tax and then sent right back to the UK, avoiding the high tax rate. Guinness heard about it at the last minute, just before a meeting by the appropriate EC committee to discuss it. It swung into action by getting in touch with the UK chancellor and explaining the harmful effects on the company's markets; the chancellor then lobbied successfully for a rethink. But it has not ended there: now the MEPs in Brussels are fighting to introduce minimum excise duty rates on wines, beers and spirits.

Guinness not only maintains close contact with the UK government, it has also set up a Brussels office to be at the heart of Europe: 'The work we are doing with the EU has grown enormously,' said Chris Davidson, director of public affairs.

> 'Although we are British-based we have a huge commitment to the global marketplace and increasingly the way we can put pressure on international problem areas for us like Korea and Taiwan is not simply by using the UK government but the EU. Those countries will listen more readily to the EU than any single government, though we always start with the UK.'

But many other companies have yet to figure out how the process works. According to Sir Bernard Ingham, formerly press secretary to Margaret Thatcher and now a consultant in his own right, too many British companies have had no idea of how government is organized: 'When a company has a problem, how does it go about communicating with government? The frequent answer is that it probably doesn't have a clue.' He recalled meeting the chairman of a public company in heavy industry who asked Ingham how he should get through to government to deal with a foreign export problem:

> 'I said do you know the secretary of state? Ministers at the Department of Trade & Industry? The permanent secretary? The deputy or under secretaries? The MPs where the plants are located? He knew no one. Maybe this man was the exception that proves the rule but it shows that there is a problem. Industry doesn't often understand, and the EC is a complicating factor.'

The other side to this coin is the fact that governments have also grasped the fact that consistency is just as crucial for them as for a commercial organization. Although politicians have always relied on presentation to put policies across, governments of all nationalities and hues increasingly rely on trained communications professionals, while all sorts of marketing communication techniques have been imported from the USA, some admittedly less savoury than others. As the issues for governments and politicians have become more complex, so has the use of public relations proliferated to the often fierce criticism of the media, which can regard the increased reliance of politicians on public relations people for advice and help with contempt and dismiss it at its worst as 'PR hype'.

Box 9.1   Bernard Ingham

If anyone could be said to represent the central role the press secretary enjoys, it would be Sir Bernard Ingham, who worked closely with Margaret Thatcher throughout the 1980s and who attracted both respect and controversy for his robust views on how he should do his job. But, like any director of corporate affairs, his main concern was consistency. He said:

> 'I was criticized because I was doing it too well. Any company or even government is quick to attract criticism from showing a lack of consistency. I wouldn't have been attacked if I had been doing a lousy job. You might think this is undue arrogance but I think it is realistic to say they wouldn't have spent time attacking me if they thought I was no damn good.'

Ingham began his career as a journalist, but then moved into the Government Information Service and climbed to the highest possible rung. He fought shy of having the role of a Government Information Service (GIS) professional compared with that of a public relations officer:

> 'I tend to think of gin and tonic sodden people being full of bonhomie. Undoubtedly, if you consider that the object of public relations is to win friends and influence people then quite clearly politicians are in that game. So are government information people; but I do think that the government side in this country has to be considered separately because it operates by separate rules and is subject to parliamentary control. For instance, the prime minister could be called to account on the floor of the House of Commons for anything I did, as could ministers because of departmental information.'

Ingham reckoned that the GIS, which in 1991 numbered over 1200 people, probably received more 'weathering and battering' than a private public relations firm:

> 'A consultancy like Hill & Knowlton [where Ingham was now a non-executive director] has a parliamentary dimension

continues

continued

because they seek to motivate public opinion through the House of Commons. But they are less acutely attuned to it than the GIS because of this parliamentary dimension and the limitations within which it must work because of constraints of political propriety, parliamentary procedure and privilege and public finance. What you are doing is operating with the public through the media because that is what you are forced to do in government. Limitations on the use of taxpayers' money to communicate with the public are very severe.'

But there were more traditional elements of public relations in the GIS brief, like rehearsing ministers – in his case, the prime minister – for public appearances like speeches or interviews.

'Generally speaking whenever she was doing something like that I would write a brief and say these are the public relations demands – I would say requirements – of this occasion. For example, I might say: the important thing, prime minister, is to relax, be confident, don't admit doubts because once you doubt they go straight in and you will be completely undermined. And that advice can reinforce itself. Because you have to be pretty certain that your principal does know and mean what they say because if they don't stick with it they will look even worse.'

Ingham saw some similarities with someone like a director of corporate communications in a communication-conscious company.

'I don't go along with the idea that you decide a policy and then hand it over to the information people. This is rather what Mrs Thatcher first thought: all she had to do was decide policy and it will sell itself. That is slightly overstating it, I said.
    'The difference in private industry, I guess, is that unless you are very fortunate you are going to have to fight hard to get in on policy formulation whereas in government the civil service is trained to take account of presentation and what you have to do is make sure they take account of this, that and the other in policy formulation. What I wanted to do was to make sure the considerations I thought important were taken on board and considered.'

Ingham believed that the onus on communicators was to educate people – and to have a thick skin. He said:

'I always felt that my real difficulty was with officials. If that slightly contradicts what I said I am really talking more about emphasis. Politicians are all presentation in a sense – or are in danger of becoming so – whereas with civil servants the emphasis is more on substance. But you have to try and get the

continues

continued

emphasis right. My efforts were almost entirely deployed with civil servants rather than ministers, who have to be natural communicators. And of course a lot of officials deeply resent the interference of people like me as information people because you become so important to the person they feel you are usurping their position, their exclusivity, and if they are fairly small minded or insecure you will have difficulty with them.'

One constant challenge facing anyone in public relations is what to do with a policy or strategy with which he/she does not agree. Ingham believed that:

'You have just got to try. You may be extremely sceptical about the whole thing and feel it is totally misguided in which case I think you have to build in protection against the damage this misguided policy might do. What you have to do is be very careful and tell the minister about the consequences. There is a bargain there that is immediately struck. You say, look, I have real reservations about this – there are real dangers in this and in trying to do it you have to take account of these. You might not agree with everything you do – and it is very difficult to agree with everything you do in government since there are some loopy people in it – but on the whole either you accept you are doing a sensible and reasonable job or you don't and then you just get out.'

Summary

(1) Within public relations, public affairs is a specialized practice that focuses on relationships which will have a bearing on the development of public policy. Public affairs is especially concerned with issues management, attempting to identify issues, matters of public concern, which, if acted upon by significant groups, are likely to have an impact on business activities and other organizational interests.

(2) Another major focus of public affairs practice is the management of relationships with government. This is unsurprising: governments try to balance the creation of an environment where business can flourish with a regulatory framework that prohibits bad practices and promotes certain standards of behaviour.

(3)   The argument about public affairs versus public relations is essentially an argument about a specialization within a broad area of management practice. The specialization does need in-depth knowledge, but it is not in the end different from the general practice of which it is part. It is a practice focused on specific relationships, and specific issues.

(4)   Public affairs is, in some ways, a defensive political practice. While public relations is concerned overall with the management of important relationships, public affairs focuses on relationships which are involved in the development of public policy which may affect a company's ability to operate and succeed. The practice is defensive, because it sets out to protect the organization's interests in public debate and the discussions which contribute to the formulation of regulations and legislation.

(5)   But many practitioners will say that public affairs, far from being defensive and reactive, is proactive. It seeks to anticipate events, issues and trends which, as they become a matter of public concern, may have an impact on the development of public policy, and ultimately on the organization's interests. More than this, public affairs practice may serve to bring issues to the surface of public debate, taking the initiative to shape debate and its consequences.

(6)   Public affairs management will be influenced by the structure and geographic spread of the corporation. An organization large enough to have significant subsidiaries in a number of countries will probably have public affairs staff in place to support subsidiaries. These staff may report to senior management in the countries in which they work, but also have a reporting relationship to central or head office public affairs staff.

(7)   The European single market is throwing up all sorts of issues in public affairs. In the past, management in Europe concentrated on finding the best way to work with the operating environment as it existed. The idea that business can shape legislation – and operating conditions – is new. It is a reflection of the fact that so much public policy – and legislation – needs to be formulated, or adapted, in the process of creating a single market in Europe.

(8)   The key to participating in the political process in Europe today is finding a common vocabulary, finding a way to construct alliances with people who share common goals. Sometimes the commonality of these goals is not obvious and relationships have to be built to create a common ground.

Notes

(1) MacMillan, K., Managing public affairs in British Industry, *Journal of General Management*, **9**, (2), Winter 1983/4, 74–90.

(2) MacMillan, K., *The Management of European Public Affairs*. European Centre for Public Affairs, Occasional Paper 1, July 1991. Templeton College, Oxford: ECPA

(3) Social and Community Planning Research, 1991. *British Social Attitudes*. London: SCPR.

(4) Building an issues management system, *Public Relations Journal*, **49**(11), November 1993, 36–40.

10

Crisis management

Anticipating the worst

Public relations and public affairs are anticipatory practices, which attempt to foresee events, trends and issues which may develop to disrupt important relationships. Partly because these practices look to the future, practitioners have gained expertise in 'thinking the unthinkable' and in crisis management.

They are prominent in crisis management for other reasons. Crises place organizations experiencing them into the public spotlight and call management competence into question. They impose a need for companies to communicate quickly, accurately and skilfully with a number of important groups, such as employees, shareholders and the media. At the same time, they create conditions that will make it difficult for managers to make good decisions, and to communicate well. Public relations practitioners have the skills that should enable them to make a vital contribution to crisis management during its several stages.

Crisis management begins with crisis planning, imposes unique demands at times of crisis, and involves managing the aftermath of crisis. Crisis planning is generally neglected by many organizations until a crisis reveals the lack of planning. To be useful, it should involve thinking of the situations that might arise to create serious difficulty for the organization.

What can go wrong?

Otto Lerbinger, a professor in the College of Communication at Boston University, has outlined a number of broad categories of corporate crises:

(1) *Technological crises:* in a world increasingly dependent on technology, when technology fails the consequences may be catastrophic. Examples of these crises are Chernobyl, and the Bhopal industrial accident when gas released from a Union Carbide plant in Bhopal, India, caused many people to die or be permanently affected.

(2) *Confrontation crises:* caused when groups confront corporations and criticize their actions, or go to more extreme lengths to express their opposition. An example of this is provided by the consumer boycott of Nestlé products, as a result of the company's distribution of powdered milk in the developing world.

(3) *Crises of malevolence:* these are crises caused by the malevolent actions of individuals or groups, such as terrorist groups placing bombs in unlikely locations to provide maximum disruption to business and everyday life. Recent examples have been provided by IRA bombs placed in the City of London.

(4) *Crises of management failure:* these are crises caused by management groups within the organization failing to carry out their responsibilities. A recent example in the UK was caused in the London Ambulance Service when management introduced a new computer system for directing ambulances to emergencies without adequately checking the system. When the system failed soon after its introduction, the Ambulance Service was unable to provide essential services.

(5) *Crises involving other threats to the organization:* examples include unexpected takeover bids.

A crisis concentrates the corporate mind like almost nothing else. Suddenly the need for public relations/communications becomes wonderfully clear. Within these broad categories, so many things can go wrong:

- defective product recall
- factory fires, explosions, and so on
- accidents
- strikes
- sudden resignations
- takeover threat
- discovery of fraudulent activities.

Crisis planning

The sheer number of events that can give a company instant and unwanted headlines can be overwhelming and unpredictable. It is feasible, however, to devise a system which outlines personnel, procedures and policies that should go into action. Because events are unexpected this by no means precludes planning: it would be the naive consumer goods company, for example, that did not have a tried and tested policy for product recall, from physically removing defective or tainted products from shelves to having pre-agreed channels for publicity.

One of the problems is that companies are too reactive when it comes to 'crises', as Peter Walker, chairman and chief executive of the UK consultancy Pielle, argued at the 1991 world congress of the International Public Relations Association:

- discrete events, crises, situations are being managed, not issues;
- organizations are trying to manage parts of an issue with little knowledge of where it came from or what trends they are connected to;
- companies equate issues to problems, not opportunities;
- issue management is defined in political terms and attempts are made to manage issues after they have become politicized and when management options and the likelihood of success are both limited and expensive – most of us are loathe to invest in 'anticipation'.

Crisis management pays good fees and is an exciting public relations product; contingency planning requires systematic, informed organized monitoring and analysis on a multinational basis. In Walker's words, 'action' manager has yet to evolve into 'listening' manager.

What the clever head of communications should do is try to think the 'unthinkable'. Take Vickers, for example: 'You sit here and suddenly think – what would they do in Newcastle in a defence factory if a tank suddenly ran amok and ran down a bus queue? Or if the Queen was touring the Rolls-Royce factory and the sprinklers went on? You need a plan of action,' declared Terrence Collis, former director of public affairs. But it can take a long time to get an acceptable format which will deal with what the risks are, who the key figures are, what they will do, relevant telephone numbers, where they keep a spare copy of the manual, and so on.

Sometimes it can be straightforward, such as making sure you have access to extra telephone lines: what happens if you start getting 1000 phone calls an hour? Or the answer may be to be constantly vigilant: according to Fiat director of external communications Cesare Annibaldi, the group, which over the years has had to face a range of problems from an oil crisis to social unrest, has one single concept: restructuring is permanent. 'We are permanently restructuring plans, policies, and so on so we do not restructure as a crisis arises. It is a continual process. A crisis, though, may accelerate or strengthen something that is going on.'

A carefully devised action plan can make the difference between survival and defeat during a takeover battle. When Lord Hanson's group made its surprise move on ICI, it probably assumed, with its wealth of experience on the takeover scene, that ICI was little match for it; that the chemicals company's campaign would be sluggish and ungainly. Instead, Hanson was confronted with a well-orchestrated attack on his management style and the quality of his company's profits. And what the newspapers called a 'phoney' communications war was nevertheless fought in deadly earnest.

Crisis management is not just about having a manual for action, but about having enough forethought to face the unexpected with fast but effective responses. In fact, having a rigid manual could be a dead hand. But there should be at least some sort of guidelines on who can talk to the media, what needs central clearance, who will speak for the company depending on what problem it faces, and so on. Often an effective communications system is one based on trust and delegation as much as on pre-planning.

Corporate image in a crisis

In a crisis, corporate image – built up over time and across frontiers – can indeed make a difference. A venerated example in public relations annals is Tylenol and the way that Johnson & Johnson acted to restore public confidence in its products and company name.

In 1982, Tylenol was the leading pain relief medicine sold over the counter in the USA, with 35% market share. Then seven people died in the Chicago area. The cause of death was traced to Tylenol capsules to which cyanide had been added. It is still not known who tampered with the two-part capsules. But even before Johnson & Johnson's consumer products subsidiary had been cleared officially of all responsibility, the corporation took steps that drew upon and reinforced Johnson & Johnson's credible corporate image.

Within a week of the deaths, and with no prompting from others, Johnson & Johnson issued a market-wide recall of all Tylenol capsules, whether in stores or consumers' hands. Advertising was suspended. Management involvement began at the top. The corporation's board chairman and chief executive officer communicated with the victims' families, the media and the public. A key tool was Johnson & Johnson's corporate 'credo', written nearly 50 years ago, which states the company's obligations to consumers, employees, plant communities, environmental protection and stockholders. A seven-member strategy committee took charge from the start. Composed of top management, the committee met twice every day to handle developments and make decisions to help rebuild consumer acceptance of Tylenol.

Open communications prevailed. Every bit of information that could be gathered was given in response to literally thousands of inquiries. A satellite news conference exposed Johnson & Johnson senior management to the media and reached across the USA. Consumers were warned not to take Tylenol capsules in their possession. More than two million messages were sent to health-care professionals, wholesalers and retailers.

Consumer and trade reaction was monitored. Surveys showed that 90% of respondents believed that Johnson & Johnson was not to blame for the product tampering. And 41% of regular Tylenol users said that they 'definitely' would buy the product again and 35% said they 'probably' would buy it. Results were communicated to the trade and the public via the satellite news conference. So was the information that Tylenol packaging would immediately be redesigned to prevent tampering.

The corporation did not hesitate to spend money commensurate with the value of credibility in its corporate image and confidence in its products. The cost of recalling, testing and destroying Tylenol capsules has been calculated at about US$100 million. Free coupons worth US$2.50 towards any Tylenol product were widely distributed. These costs represent only the tip of the iceberg.

Apart from the fact that it stands today as a classic example of successful crisis management, the Tylenol case comes down to one basic fact that applies across borders whether in Europe or the USA: corporate image counts in a crisis. Carefully and professionally tended over the years, Johnson & Johnson's corporate image came through when the company and its products needed it most.

The steps that Johnson & Johnson followed in the USA can be adapted for use anywhere in the world. But in the context of the EU, a Dutch example is revealing. Akzo is an major transnational with interests in chemicals, fibres, polymers, coatings and pharmaceuticals. Based on his experience and the advice of specialized consultants, Akzo's director of corporate communications, R.A.Q. van Min, listed five elements of Akzo's crisis management plan:

(1)   A top-level multidisciplinary crisis committee 'must include legal, technical, marketing, PR and any other expert needed for the job at hand'. The purpose of a crisis committee is to provide access to the expertise of a broad range of specialists, to centralize all sources of information, incoming and outgoing, and to act upon it. The committee must have full authority to make decisions and the ability to develop plans and messages under fire.

(2)   Centralized and controlled information 'should flow through a communications center... that can provide consistent information based on facts... when conflicting rumors are spreading'. It is consistent, for example, to say 'We don't know at this moment' at the same time that an investigation is announced. 'Speculation should be avoided at all costs.'

(3)   Continuity of information and contact, particularly with the media, can be maintained through a carefully selected spokesperson with full authority from management. 'It is of paramount importance to maintain the same spokesperson since continuity creates, over time, a sense of familiarity among reporters covering the story and reduces the possibility of the company contradicting itself.'

(4)   Direct communications tools should be used to reach audiences that are very important for the company. These include 'employees directly affected by the crisis, their families, corporate executives not on the crisis committee, plant and divisional managers and supervisors, the sales force, work council, union representatives, and medical and security personnel'.

Outside the company,

'audiences that need to hear the story directly include community residents and their leaders; local, provincial and national authorities; the financial community; technical experts; and, above all, the company's suppliers, customers and distributors... The media are the most uncontrollable tool available to reach these audiences during a crisis. It is therefore essential to organize direct communication systems such as hot lines, letters, teleconferences, personal visits, advertisements and sales force calls to make sure that the corporation's message is being conveyed.'

(5)   Allies in industry, the community and the media

'should be identified and kept informed every step of the way. These are the people who can help create a positive attitude toward the company during the difficult days of the crisis itself and long after the crisis has passed. Outside experts, scientists, government officials, customers, community leaders and public interest groups all are people of standing and respect whose support is vital at a time when a company's judgment, goodwill or competence may be called into question... The real challenge is not to focus on yesterday's headline but to decide what should be said today, and to make sure that the message is delivered to the right audiences.'

Three principles underly Akzo's five steps to effective crisis management:

(1) A positive public consensus is needed in times of crisis, but a crisis is no time to manage by consensus.
(2) Crisis management is an art, not a science.
(3) There is life after a crisis and corporate image must be preserved at all costs.

It is also important to remember that corporate image in Europe may be adversely affected by developments that management (particularly non-Europe-based management) may consider ordinary hazards of business life. Events that may require crisis management in the EU include:

- environmental conflict
- centralization of production
- job losses (or reduced working time)
- strikes
- rumours that affect sales
- any other development that affects the credibility of the company and its products or services.

Like many of his counterparts in other companies in Europe, Akzo's van Min is a firm believer in opinion research. It is important to remember, he says, that there is life after a crisis. A company must be able to continue to operate successfully. Consequently, 'Nothing is more important than the distinction between what the media says about you and what key audiences believe.'

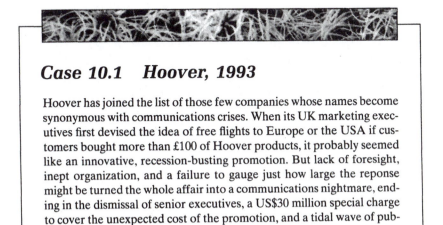

Case 10.1 Hoover, 1993

Hoover has joined the list of those few companies whose names become synonymous with communications crises. When its UK marketing executives first devised the idea of free flights to Europe or the USA if customers bought more than £100 of Hoover products, it probably seemed like an innovative, recession-busting promotion. But lack of foresight, inept organization, and a failure to gauge just how large the reponse might be turned the whole affair into a communications nightmare, ending in the dismissal of senior executives, a US$30 million special charge to cover the unexpected cost of the promotion, and a tidal wave of publicity which castigated the company for its treatment of its customers.

continues

continued

Hoover had not done its sums properly for the offer, nor had it taken out insurance. Perhaps the worst error was offering too good a bargain: the chance to acquire air tickets worth as much as £400 by buying an appliance for only £119. Many consumers bought the equipment just to qualify for the free flights.

However, Hoover did not make clear that the flights were limited to certain dates and destinations, never imagining the take-up would be so enormous. Even those who did qualify – and who had read the 'small print' – had to wait because the travel agents carrying out the scheme were overwhelmed.

What exacerbated the problem was the company's sluggish responses and secretive approaches to questions about, for example, exactly how many people had applied for the offer.

Crisis management

While crisis planning involves trying to think the unthinkable and planning for all foreseeable events, a crisis is by definition unexpected, an event for which no accurate planning is possible. A crisis is defined by aspects of the situation. It involves:

(1) a high degree of threat, to life, safety, or to the existence of the organization;
(2) time pressure, which means that decision-makers have to work quickly to deal with the situation;
(3) stress for those people who are responsible for managing the situation.

A situation which has been anticipated, for which management already have a detailed and rehearsed plan of action, is not a crisis, serious though it may be. A recent example was the crash of a cargo plane in a suburb of Amsterdam shortly after takeoff from the city's Schipol airport. Although the crash was serious, and involved significant loss of life in the buildings destroyed by the crashing plane, it was not a crisis because the emergency services had rehearsed for just such an incident a few days before the crash.

A crisis takes organizations by surprise, and previously formulated plans may be an obstacle to dealing effectively with it. It may, in its earliest moments, give rise to panic and confusion among organization members, and to responses which, with hindsight, are shown to be quite inappropriate.

Crisis management, at the time of crisis, involves making arrangements to take pressure off decision-makers, so that they can concentrate on the immediate tasks involved in managing the crisis – taking steps to preserve life, care for the injured, restore essential services, minimize further danger and so on. Public relations practitioners who have developed special expertise in crisis management, such as the UK's Michael Regester, advocate establishment of special facilities to manage crises effectively. These, for large organizations, such as oil companies and airlines, may involve suites of rooms, with abundant communications links, for decision-makers, information and operations staff, who will be acting to deal with the crisis. Public relations staff, in these arrangements, act as advisers to decision-makers, and as a buffer between them and outside pressures.

An immediate pressure may come from the media, seeking information about the crisis. A task for public relations practitioners at this time is to manage requests for information, and to attend to the need to communicate with the media and other important groups.

Well-managed public relations activities at the time of crisis show that the organization is coping with the crisis and deserves public understanding and support.

Managing the aftermath of crisis

How a company manages public relations at times of crisis may also have consequences in the aftermath of the crisis. The behaviour at the time of crisis will be remembered and may be held against it. When the immediate crisis is over, the organization is faced with the task of rebuilding. This may involve earning public trust which has been lost, and rebuilding the reputation.

The public relations activities required to rebuild position, reputation and credibility will need to be planned on the basis of accurate information about the damage that has been done. They will need to be planned over a long-term period, and measures of progress towards restoring the organization's position will also be needed.

Summary

(1) Public relations and public affairs are anticipatory practices, which attempt to foresee events, trends and issues which may develop to disrupt important relationships. Partly because these practices look to the future, practitioners have gained expertise in 'thinking the unthinkable' and in crisis management.

(2) Crises place organizations experiencing them into the public spotlight and call management competence into question. They impose a need for companies to communicate quickly, accurately and skilfully with a number of important groups, such as employees, shareholders and the media. At the same time, they create conditions that will make it difficult for managers to make good decisions, and to communicate well. Public relations practitioners have the skills that should enable them to make a vital contribution to crisis management, during its several stages.

(3) Crisis management begins with crisis planning, imposes unique demands at times of crisis, and involves managing the aftermath of crisis. Crisis planning is generally neglected by many organizations until a crisis reveals the lack of planning. To be useful, it should involve thinking of the situations that might arise to create serious difficulty for the organization.

(4) There are a number of broad categories of corporate crises:
- technological crises
- confrontation crises
- crises of malevolence
- crises of management failure
- crises involving other threats to the organization like takeover bids.

(5) Crisis management is not just about having a manual for action, but about having enough forethought to face the unexpected with a fast but effective response.

(6) While the sheer number of events that can give a company instant, unwanted headlines can be overwhelming and unpredictable, it is feasible to devise a system which outlines personnel, procedures and policies that should go into action. And because events are unexpected by no means precludes planning.

(7) In a crisis, corporate image – built up over time and across frontiers – can make a difference.

(8)   A crisis takes organizations by surprise, and previously formulated plans may be an obstacle to dealing effectively with it. Crisis management, at the time of crisis, involves making arrangements to take pressure off decision-makers, so that they can concentrate on the immediate tasks involved in managing the crisis -- taking steps to preserve life, care for the injured, restore essential services, minimize further danger and so on.

(9)   How a company manages public relations at the time of crisis may also have consequences in the aftermath of the crisis. The behaviour at the time of crisis will be remembered and may be held against it. When the immediate crisis is over, the organization is faced with the task of rebuilding. This may involve earning public trust which has been lost, and rebuilding the reputation.

PART THREE

Managing relationships

11

Customers and suppliers, investor relations, the community, pressure and interest groups

Managing public relations activities can involve dividing the work according to groups or publics of interest. The large in-house department, or the well-resourced consultancy, will have groups responsible for relations with areas like government, the media, the community and investors. In some cases, responsibilities for working with these groups, particularly investors, employees, customers and suppliers, may be shared, with other departments or specialists in finance and human resource management, for instance.

Media and government relations have been discussed in other chapters. This chapter looks at some of the features of relations with customers and suppliers, investors, the community and pressure groups.

Customer and supplier relations

The drive towards total quality, and recent recognition of the need to satisfy or 'delight' customers have focused management attention on relations with customers. Marketing practitioners have begun to talk of relationship marketing, which carries with it the suggestion that organizations now offer not only goods and services which meet customer requirements, but also relationships which will meet customer needs. These relationships have to be built over time to support the organization's marketing efforts.

217

Responsibility for building relations with customers could be seen as belonging to marketing staff, but public relations practitioners are also involved in a number of ways. They may provide support, by developing communications for use with customers, such as sales literature, or company audiovisual presentations. More comprehensively, they may be involved with marketing staff in planning to develop the relationship with customers to achieve marketing and other objectives.

An example of this is ICI Polyurethanes. The company is involved in the manufacture and sale of polyurethane worldwide. Polyurethane is the versatile product of a simple chemical reaction between two components. It can be used for insulation, construction, furniture and clothing. In conjunction with gases like chlorofluorocarbons (CFCs), for instance, it has excellent insulating properties and is widely used in refrigerators and food storage. Recent international regulations, however, are forcing the elimination of CFCs from manufacturing processes, so ICI Polyurethanes is phasing their use out. But products made with alternatives are not as good as those using CFCs. The company is thus faced with the task of explaining this to its customers, and with winning their support in discussions with government regarding future regulation of production processes.

In this case, communication with customers is not solely concerned with marketing objectives or customer requirements but is carried on to win customer understanding and support.

What this means is that as more emphasis is placed on relationship marketing and the need to involve customers in the strategic objectives of the organization, the division of labour between marketing and public relations staff in customer relations will need to be examined.

The relationship with suppliers is also one where good communications plays an increasingly important role. It might seem to be the sole concern of those within the company receiving goods and services from them. However, a recent study from the Royal Society of Arts in the UK[1] has suggested that the relationship with suppliers needs to be re-examined to produce greater collaboration. This will depend partly on better communication, which can be developed by drawing on the resources of public relations staff.

Investor relations

'You could say that if the institutional investors didn't like us we would all be out of a job.' That succinct statement from a group manager of investor relations and planning at telecommunications group Cable & Wireless, sums up what can be one of the toughest areas of communications for a public company. While maintaining a steady flow of consistent information to all target audiences, particularly customers and employees, is of equal importance, investor relations demands special skills: investors read the press and watch the financial programmes, journalists talk to analysts and investors, and round it goes in a circular process which can break apart with the slightest whiff of inconsistency.

Investors are not always as vigilant as they might be, of course. They can be supine, or overwhelmed by the 'We know best' attitude of management or simply taken for a ride. But they are becoming more vocal and more demanding, a trend moving to the UK from the USA and underpinned by increasing interest in corporate governance.

How investor relations is handled is a subject of continuous debate. The chairman should always be involved. The question is often under whose aegis should it sit, whether the finance director, the company secretary or the director of corporate communications.

A lot of companies put investor relations under the finance director/ company secretary, with the head of communications playing a strong role in presentation. While the investor relations manager will often have a depth of expertise in complicated matters like tax, general matters can be handled in a coordinated fashion by his/her communications colleague.

Others will place it in communications but with the finance director assuming overall responsibility. In 1992 at publisher Reed International, director of corporate relations Jan Shawe dealt with investor relations but called herself more of a background and support person, helping to answer the question of to whom Reed should be speaking, and what it should be saying to them. She said:

> 'I think it is wrong for any public relations person to pretend to do investor relations in its entirety because even if they help with it, it has got to come from the chairman, finance director or a board member. If I were an institution I wouldn't want to be seeing the corporate communicator; I would want to speak with the chairman or finance director. But also, as a main board director there are things you are in a better perspective to say, that I don't feel I should whether I have the information or not.'

Good investor relations have to be built up over time, not hurriedly cultivated because of the appearance of a predator, for example. The fact that Vickers had a close relationship with the financial institutions made the difference when it was being stalked by the Australian Sir Ron Brierly in 1988. The opposite was true at drugs and scientific company Fisons. A letter to the *Financial Times* from one of its shareholders complaining about its investor relations was the start of much critical comment about the company's relationships with the investment community and its tradition of secrecy and sensitivity. That meant that there were few supporters when Fisons faced potentially profit-harming problems with the US Food and Drug Administration. Finally, the chairman/chief executive resigned on health grounds.

Box 11.1 BAT

Investor relations is a notably difficult area to define, wrote Martin Broughton, chief executive of BAT Industries, in the *Financial Times*.[2]

> 'Is it an art or a science? The dictionary defines the former as "skill as the result of knowledge and practice", while the latter is "often opposite to art" or, more usefully, "a branch of study concerned with a demonstrated body of connected truths". Given that no less an expert than Lex in the FT once wrote that Wellcome's shares "might either double or halve", the field seems to be a little short on science.'

BAT's objective, he noted, was not to promote the company directly as an investment but to explain it:

> 'The syndicated tracking research which we do every year through Mori is a useful starting point because it helps us to understand what sources of information are important to our audience.'

BAT started reporting quarterly in 1987, which gives the company twice the number of formal occasions on which to talk to the City. It also makes the information flow more frequent. Apart from results days, which consist of a press conference and video conference with US analysts, as well as other UK analysts' briefing, the other face-to-face elements in the BAT programme include facility visits to the operations and small group meetings with investors.

As Broughton noted, 'The typical six-month gap between preliminary and interim results can allow uncertainties to develop or can lead to a company that is "out of sight" also being "out of mind".'

What did Broughton think shareholders were looking for? He commented:

> 'Again, the Mori research tells us that the two most important factors are the quality and strength of management and the company's financial status. Given the first of these, it is not surprising that leading investors should want to meet the management face-to-face.'

Finally, Broughton stressed that investor relations does not exist in isolation. It is supported 'by a range of corporate information and even some corporate hospitality. The annual and quarterly reports are another essential part, while advertising our results on the financial pages of national newspapers enables us to explain the company's performance, in a controlled way.'

One of the least savoury aspects of investor relations has been seen in the UK with the notorious 'Friday night drop', whereby financial public relations firms hawk stories around to the UK Sunday newspapers. It took off during the privatization campaigns of the 1980s, and was underpinned by the pressure on the Sundays to compete for stories. The practice meant that the public relations consultants would offer exclusives on other stories in exchange for an upbeat piece on their clients. Although it still goes on, it has become increasingly devalued and the fact that price-sensitive information can be involved means that it is beginning to attract closer scrutiny from City regulators.

On a more international scale, investor relations is coming to the fore as companies both engage in cross-border takeovers, which means persuading shareholders of the benefits of a bid, and look for new sources of capital.

Although the takeover and merger scene in Continental Europe has been nowhere as active as in the UK and USA, the signs are there, even though harmonization of the rules will take a much longer time. A recent example was Italian tyre-maker Pirelli's abortive bid for its German counterpart Continental. As David Wynne Morgan, head of Europe for public relations consultancy Hill & Knowlton and chairman of the executive board for the international group, pointed out in 1992,

> 'The big takeover battles are beginning to happen on the continent but it is absolutely against their culture. They hate and loathe it. They don't like the expense, or the disruption of their business. After all, many of the companies are controlled by comparatively few industrial families and they have been used to sitting down behind closed doors and sorting it out themselves. Now they are finding that is not always the best way and there have been a few contested takeovers but quite often they have petered out like Continental and Pirelli.'

What he saw was a growth of work in controlled auctions, where a merchant bank goes to a company, the founder of which might have died or be retiring, and offers to help sell its business. While the successful purchaser has to be prepared to pay the price, there are all sorts of public relations activities that can help a potential bidder to be looked on with favour.

Companies are also hunting fresh sources of capital which demands a much higher and better understood profile. As Charles Cook, managing director of the Saatchi-owned Grandfield Rork Collins said, continental companies in particular are approaching this with a considerable degree of caution:

'It is not suspicion, it is caution. If you are talking about communication to capital markets which is often what it is about as far as London is concerned, what they want is to be better understood in this market and then in the other key European markets. One of the first things one has to say to them is that the demand for information is going to be much greater than they are used to and they have to come to grips with that. Some of them don't even have professional advisers; they may have a London branch office, or branch office of their home bank which, with the best will in the world, is not going to be the appropriate one.'

A notorious example of how a relationship with investors can go wrong came with Gerald Ratner. As chairman of jewellers Ratners, he was considered one of the high flyers of the 1980s. Not only had he transformed what was a tiny family company into a transatlantic retailer with profits to April 1991 of £112 million, but he had changed the face of jewellery selling itself, by demystifying it and making it an integral part of the High Street retail scene.

The company's share price was consistently healthy, reflecting the esteem in which Gerald Ratner was held. But it all changed very rapidly when remarks he made at an Institute of Directors' function were picked up by the tabloid newspapers and created a furore. Ratner had made disparaging remarks about some of his products, calling a sherry decanter, for example, 'total crap'. In the resulting public relations fiasco, his comments were interpreted by the papers as an insult to his customers, and his company's share price started its downward slide, plunging from a high of 184p.

What had worried the City was not so much his remarks (which he had apparently been making at private functions for some time) but his error of judgement in allowing them to reach a wider audience. Coupled with his generally flamboyant, publicity-seeking personality, the episode prompted renewed fears that the man in charge of Ratners' race for growth (fuelled by a series of rights issues) might not be acting with a proper concern for the underlying stability and long-term strategic direction of the company.

Ratners' plight was made much worse by a recession-hit Christmas period. As profits plummetted Ratner stepped down as chairman and appointed the former deputy chairman of Coats Viyella in his place, although he kept his position as chief executive. Even that was not enough: the company now has not only new management but a new name as well.

Box 11.2   Dragon report

City audiences are looking beyond the traditional indicators of success when assessing company performance, according to a 1993 research study, 'Views from the City', from UK marketing/communications consultancy Dragon International.

A series of 70 in-depth interviews were carried out among brokers' analysts, fund managers, venture capitalists and financial journalists to assess the key factors which are influencing a change in attitudes and the implications for companies.

There were a number of findings:

(1) Trust is now a major issue. The City felt badly misled during the late 1980s and early 1990s, according to the report. The City will now analyse companies far more rigorously.
(2) Management is being scrutinized with a new level of intensity. The aggressive management style of the last decade will no longer be a source of admiration. Instead, corporate ethics will increasingly be viewed as a critical part of the assessment of management. Honesty and openness are seen as vital to a company's City profile – the emphasis is on quality as well as quantity of information.
(3) Brand performance is becoming more important as the City recognizes consumer purchasing power as a measure of company success.
(4) Communication is of major importance and an area where City views were surprisingly negative. 60% of those interviewed felt that the level and quality of information supplied by companies was inadequate.

The study concluded that many companies have not recognized the City's changing requirements within a new business environment. Failing to take account of this, and communicating ineffectively with City audiences, could have serious implications in the long term, it argues.

The community

All companies can reap communications benefits from joining charitable initiatives. In the USA, there is the One Per Cent Club of corporations that pledge to give a minimum of 1% of their pre-tax profits to charity.

The trend towards charitable giving in the UK is not so pronounced and leaders of the business community had to settle for the Per Cent Club – 1% was not seen as an attainable target. Half a per cent is the charity contribution target set by sponsors, but average levels are less.

Taking a high profile on community and charitable issues tends to raise expectations about a company's activities across the board, and donating money to charity does not solve tough issues like plant closures. Sir Hector Laing of United Biscuits in the UK was one of the founder members of Business in the Community in 1980, which has as its slogan: 'Making involvement in the community a natural part of successful business practice.' However, the high profile that the company took on the issue of private-sector responsibilities to regenerate inner cities only served to focus attention on the company's own programme of closures.

There is also an issue of plain scepticism. Some would argue that business has different interests (see Box 11.3) which are often in conflict with those of the community and employees and these dictate its actions.

A key influence in the debate on corporate responsibility is the shift from private ownership of industry to institutional shareholder control. No longer do the personal moral views of the founding philanthropic businessmen set the high watermarks for corporate responsibility. Actions have to be justified to shareholders. Quaker-influenced firms are still at the cutting edge of corporate social responsibility: Rowntree (when independent and now part of Nestlé) and Cadbury Schweppes.

Paternalism in business, or religious influence in commerce have provided a seed bed of ideas for the new debate on corporate responsibility. Particularly among Quakers and Methodists, social values and morals were an important part of business conduct. Companies with founding directors with personal moral beliefs have been distinctively organized. Sir Adrian Cadbury reflected on the origins of his company's modern commitment to social responsibility:

> 'My grandfather was able to resolve the conflict between the decisions best for his business and his personal code of ethics because he and his family owned the firm which bore their name... The possibility that ethical and commercial considerations will conflict has always faced those who run companies. It is not a new problem. The difference now is that a more widespread and critical interest is being taken in our decisions and in the ethical judgements which lie behind them.'[4]

Sir Adrian doubted whether the principled stand his grandfather took on issues such as investing in gambling and supplying the UK government's Boer War effort at the end of the nineteenth century would hold sway in a modern context. 'His dilemma would have been more acute if he had to take into account the interests of outside shareholders, many of whom would no doubt have been in favour of both the [Boer] War and profiting from it.' The difference now is that social responsibility is expected from corporations, regardless of their origins or purpose.

Box 11.3   Business in the Community

When Samuel Brittan, a respected senior newspaper columnist on the *Financial Times*, wrote that there was a 'systematic ambiguity' in the arguments for corporate responsibility, and that business and the community should keep their distance, he attracted a number of letters rebutting his points. One of these[3] was from senior industrialists associated with Business in the Community, an organization which includes 470 member companies. The letter was signed by Neil Shaw, executive chairman, Tate & Lyle, Eric Nicoli, United Biscuits group chief executive, IBM (UK)'s chairman Sir Anthony Cleaver, Grand Metropolitan's Sir Allen Sheppard, Peter Davis of Reed Elsevier, and the chairmen of the Post Office and Wessex Water.

They argued that Brittan missed a vital point:

'Business in the Community has always agreed that the primary role of business is to create sustainable wealth by meeting customers' needs. We differ from Brittan in our belief that, by working in the wider community, business can help to build the social environment it needs for long-term wealth creation.'

They also argued that business needs well-educated and highly skilled people to succeed in more competitive global markets: 'That is why companies are playing a more active role in education and training by, for example, training teachers in skills like financial management and marketing and by giving young people quality work experience placements.'

They disputed Brittan's contention that corporate responsibility attempts to achieve public policy objectives 'on the cheap':

'Our view is simply that business has legitimate interests in public policy matters. Social priorities like protecting the environment, raising the quality of education and regenerating local communities call for participation by all partners in society... This is not about business replacing government, but "adding value" by bringing its own skills, attitudes and resources to the public policy table.'

Shell Oil has taken a high profile through advertising and sponsorship of educational and arts projects, pushing a socially responsible image. Market research showed the company to be high in the public's esteem on environmental issues at a time when it was facing prosecution in the USA for cleaning up notorious toxic waste sites through its liabilities under US legislation on liability for toxic waste. When it was fined £1 million in 1989 by a UK court for an oil spillage in the Mersey River estuary, the judge said that if the company did not have an exemplary record on donations to charity, the fine would have been much higher.

Box 11.4 The Body Shop

What is good for an ethical stance is also in the long-run going to be good for business if The Body Shop is anything to go by. It has even managed to overcome a spate of critical articles in mid-1994. Its strong stand on a number of issues and its involvement in the communities where it operates has been accompanied by a solid financial performance.

Each shop, for instance, has a public relations officer who is responsible for forging links with the local community and encouraging the staff to get involved with local projects. Another element in The Body Shop's marketing approach is its strong corporate identity and distinct design. The shop windows themselves are also used effectively both for campaigning issues and products.

While the philosophy, design and many of the products are driven from the centre, the local markets have to take into account particular market needs. For example, The Body Shop as a rule encourages customers to bring back bottles for refilling. That, however, is not allowed in Spain so the head franchisee has to adjust the core message of refill and reuse to reuse by recycling, where customers are encouraged to bring back bottles and other products for recycling.

But its own evaluation of success stretches beyond its figures. It has to be profitable because it would not exist if it were not. But it also measures what it calls second bottom line values which is how effective it is in the community. It includes issues like environmentalism, community action projects, labelling – what information are its shops giving customers about products? The first and second bottom line is effectively the measure.

Sir Allen Sheppard, chairman and group chief executive of international consumer products group Grand Metropolitan, made a strong case for the need for companies to be involved in the community in a newspaper article:[5] 'Of all the aspects of corporate life which influence employees' attitudes and motivation, none is more important than the active contribution made by the company to the communities where it operates.'

This is something those already committed to corporate community involvement know well from experience, he wrote. But the results of a new Mori poll commissioned by the UK's *Evening Standard* backed that up even more solidly. The poll consisted of interviews with 800 full-time workers throughout the country. Almost 60% said they would work for a company that was active in the community where it operated. More than half of those would strongly prefer such a company, while two-thirds agreed that senior management set an example in doing voluntary work.

As Sir Allen commented:

'These findings underscore an important point that is all too often misunderstood. Corporate community involvement is not simply "charity", it is good business. It is also arguably the most powerful tool available to management in getting the most from its workforce.'

Sir Allen cited some examples:

(1)   The employees at ICI's Grangemouth plant were demotivated by outside perceptions that typecast them as people too little concerned with the environment because of their work. Management responded by developing a project with the Scottish Wildlife Trust that involved employees and local communities working together on conservation projects to protect wildlife in the region. The reported results included improved employee motivation and greater retention of skilled staff.

(2)   When the management development team of the Halifax Building Society were looking for an effective way of developing creative and communications skills in the workforce, they chose a community involvement project. Through the creation of 'Community Development Circles', 350 staff planned and carried out a variety of projects, including fund raising for a local children's play group. Management reported that the programme met all of its goals for enhancing employee performance while making a major contribution to the community.

As Sir Allen concluded:

'The Mori findings demonstrate in a very compelling way the great potential of community involvement as a management tool for businesses of every size, in every industry, to attract and retain employees – the "inner market". But as in any other market, a dialogue is essential if communication is to be effective.'

Box 11.5   Grand Metropolitan

Sir Allen Sheppard, chairman and group chief executive of Grand Metropolitan, has played a major role in spreading the view that community involvement now represents a core element of corporate responsibility in what he has described as the new age of 'consumer-driven capitalism'.[6] According to Sir Allen, 'Customers are increasingly looking through the front door of the companies they buy from. If they do not like what they see in terms of social responsibility, community involvement, equality of opportunity, they won't go in.'

Grand Metropolitan is now one of the UK's largest providers of training and job counselling for the unemployed, allocating between 1.5% and 2% of profits before tax. In 1992, for example, more than 20,000 people received help from company schemes. There is help through a number of inner city initiatives, along with a range of educational and training projects and sponsorship programmes. Company employees are also encouraged to be volunteers.

The following are just two of its initiatives:

(1)   Burger King employees from the UK headquarters work with students at the West London Institute of Higher Education providing advice in the areas of marketing and finance.

(2)   Drinks subsidiary International Distillers and Vintners has set up a pilot tutoring scheme with Cities in Schools in Tower hamlets.

Grand Metropolitan has gone through a thorough reappraisal of its 10-year-old community programme to make it more consistent and targeted. It takes a long-term approach, developing three-year plans which are reviewed annually. As Sir Allen pointed out, it can be risky: 'The worst thing you can do is flash a chequebook around, especially as it's not your money. If you go upfront and make a big song and dance about helping out and are then forced to retract, your reputation can fall a long way.' However, he concluded, 'Businesses which don't recognize their obligations in this respect face a stark choice – they will fail either rapidly or progressively.'

Drinks group Guinness is another company active in the communities where it has operations, where a local plant or office gets involved with local groups. While expenditure is left to the plant manager's discretion, the centre gives them strong guidelines on using sponsorship: "Whereas we wouldn't tell them what to do, we give them guidance based on experiences from other parts of the group. We discuss aspects like identifying the audience they might reach, and projects to which that audience could relate," according to group public relations manager Lynette Royle.

Guidelines for both social and community sponsorship are relatively consistent, according to Royle:

> 'But you have to recognise that we are operating in 170 countries around the world, and the situation in developing countries can be very different from ones like the US and UK, so we try not to be too prescriptive. We try to give common sense guidelines that allow local managers to use their own knowledge to develop a sensible strategy within the broad overall framework.'

Education takes a major chunk of the entire Guinness spend: 'We are a major employer and so are very conscious of the need to forge closer links with education to encourage talented people to consider industry as a career.' Arts also attracts a substantial portion of the expenditure, while a third area is employee projects.

Box 11.6   Philip Morris and J.P. Morgan

The following case studies show how companies can marry involvement in cultural activities as good corporate citizens with business objectives.

Philip Morris

The consumer goods company had been underwriting a series of early Rossini operas by the small, independent but respected classical recording label Claves of Switzerland. In 1993 Philip Morris hired Paris-based consultancy Broad Romero International to create a culture project and special events to promote the launch of the recording of the series. The objective was to enhance the reputation of Philip Morris as a responsible corporate citizen, contributing through its support of the arts to the enjoyment and moral well-being of the communities its various companies served in Europe and elsewhere. This message had to be conveyed to an audience of business and political leaders, mainstream media, and the general public.

The consultancy came up with 'Rossini at the Ritz', a musical and gastronomic gala evening at the Hotel Ritz in Paris, to commemorate the 200th anniversary of Rossini's birth. The dishes at the five course dinner were inspired by the composer, while recording artists performed excerpts from the material in the collected recordings. The event not only allowed the company to reach its target audience in a sophisticated

continues

continued

manner, but also increased awareness of the company's major food and beverage lines of business in the face of its better-known tobacco business.

In terms of media coverage, stories ran in major European and American publications, including the *Wall Street Journal* (Europe), and the *Wall Street Journal* in the USA, and *Time International*. And when some of the publications in France and Belgium reprinted recipes from the dinner, readers wrote in for all of them, giving the company added publicity.

J.P. Morgan

To celebrate its 125th year of operations in France, J.P. Morgan mounted an exhibition at the Louvre in Paris in 1993 of 125 fourteenth-to-nineteenth century French master drawings, selected from the collection at the Pierpont Morgan Library in New York.

Broad Romero was hired to publicise the event and promote J.P. Morgan as a financial services organization and patron of the arts. The goal was to cultivate among European business and political leaders an awareness of J.P. Morgan's historical and continuing relationship with France, especially in the light of the current privatization plans for major state-owned industries. It also wanted to draw attention to J.P. Morgan as a major financial concern with an enduring international commitment to the arts, and deliver these messages through elite European and international print publications.

The approach was to personalize the organization by focusing on three senior officials to be the 'face' of J.P. Morgan: the chairman, vice chairman and the director of the Pierpont Morgan Library, who carried out interviews during the exhibition. There was also a 30-second radio advertisement about the exhibition on the French classical radio station, and print ads in certain French and British publications.

The result was coverage in leading European publications, including the *Wall Street Journal* (Europe), *Le Monde*, *La Tribune* (a leading French financial daily) and the UK's *Financial Times*.

Relations with pressure and interest groups

There are many possible ways of enhancing corporate credibility. One is to set up a high-profile association with campaigners. One partnership that caused some wry comment is between an environmental consultancy and the convenience food giant McDonald's. The company had long been a favoured target of the healthy food lobby and haters of litter, and the subject of a persistent rumour – that has never been substantiated –

that the company was cutting down tropical rainforests in order to graze cattle for hamburgers.

The company took this image problem seriously. Criticisms of its labour relations policy in the UK were swiftly followed by threats of court action against a research group in London and a national newspaper that published the allegation. In the USA, the company introduced a high-profile recycling programme. To take the new philosophy to the heart of the company, it formed a relationship with an environmental consultancy.

Taking high-profile environmentalists or campaigners on board does not always work, however. The credibility of the radical campaigners evaporates rather rapidly once they have been taken to the inner enclave of business – credibility is all reputation, and reputation can be lost by being associated with what has been seen as the enemy. Rechem, a toxic waste incinerating company, did not deflect attention from its potential threats to health and safety by appointing an ex-staff member of Friends of the Earth. The appointment did not change the nature of Rechem's business, which in dealing with lethal substances made local residents nervous.

Some companies have managed to triumph over past misdemeanours and even profited from them. After Switzerland's second largest chemical company, Sandoz, attracted international publicity for the pollution of the Rhine in 1986, the company developed a new business opportunity – selling its environmental expertise gained in handling the clean-up. The company also discovered that there were financial benefits from improving the company's own internal affairs from a health and safety perspective by making a more efficient use of raw materials.

Companies that try to cash in on the opportunities afforded by past errors, however, run the risk of public ire. A number of conservation and environmental groups such as Friends of the Earth, Survival International and Justice for the Victims of Bhopal demonstrated outside a London hotel in November 1990 where Union Carbide was due to present a paper to other companies on its experience of handling the Bhopal disaster, although in the event the speaker withdrew. One of its themes was to be 'ensuring sensitivity to the environmental dimension to ensure "incidents" are seen in perspective' and 'taking the heat out of the environmental debate about business as a polluter'. With 3000 people killed and thousands more injured as a result of a gas leak at its Bhopal plant, and with victims still petitioning for additional compensation, the company's stance attracted criticism from environmentalists.

Sometimes companies are under competing pressures. Ford, for instance, was under pressure from anti-apartheid activists to sever all links with South Africa when it disinvested. But trade unionists in South Africa wanted the company to maintain some links to keep the company viable after Ford withdrew.

The larger the company, the bigger the target. DSM is the largest chemicals company in the Netherlands, and faces continuous pressure concerning its environmental performance: complaints from residents about odours and noise, enquiries from local authorities about investment plans, and questions in parliament. Joseph Geerards, corporate director for safety, health and the environment, estimated that responding to these concerns took 30–50% of his time. And there appeared to be little prospect of a reduction in public concern: despite significant cuts in some pollutants, the public is becoming increasingly sensitive. DSM believes that an open-door policy is the most effective way of handling the issue. According to Geerards, 'We now have a very open attitude with regard to the government, local authorities and the works council – if you close your books, it only causes trouble.' The public relations department also publishes a quarterly briefing on environmental issues that is distributed to every home around the huge Geelen plant.

In Finland, Neste has one of the highest profiles among industrial conglomerates. As a result it has frequently been exposed to tough scrutiny. In response, the company has developed an open-house policy designed to avoid public confrontation over its environmental performance through a sustained campaign of media, public (local community groups) and political briefings.

Neste's head of corporate information believed that there was no room for complacency. He said:

> 'It is not just the company image but our operations in the future that are at stake...We must provide more and faster information that the acts and statutes prescribe. We must remember that information passed on to the authorities does not simultaneously reach the media, not to mention the general public. Negative publicity usually derives from our own mistakes, and not from any ill will in the media.'

In the UK, the Royal Society of Arts' Interim Report on Tomorrow's Company emphasizes that consumer concerns can easily translate, through pressure groups, into calls for legislation. Pressure and interest groups – activist groups in US terms – may create difficulties for companies as regulation adds costs, constrains flexibility and obstructs the relationship between companies and their customers.

The task for any organization in relations with pressure groups, which should draw on the skills of competent public relations staff, is to identify which ones are to be taken seriously and which are likely to have an impact. Learning about pressure groups, and developing a response to them, is an exercise in intelligence gathering and interpretation:

(1) Given the organization's interests and objectives, which pressure groups are likely to show an interest in them (and which groups might come into existence to respond to the organization's intentions)?
(2) Once groups are identified, what can be learned about them – who are their leaders, on what are their public positions based, what are their methods, how effective are they, and do they have an impact?
(3) Can they be worked with, or will their arguments and opposition be fixed?
(4) Should the organization accommodate the arguments and opposition of pressure groups in any way (for example, by replicating their research, or by considering their arguments)?

If the organization is not going to accommodate pressure groups' arguments, and the pressure groups' opposition is fixed, how is conflict to be prepared for and managed?

Consideration of the role of pressure groups, and the company's response, takes the practitioner into an analysis of social and political reality, an analysis of how things really work in a particular society and who wields influence. Single issue pressure groups are able to present their arguments without acknowledging the complexities involved. A good example is provided by the smoking and health issue. Anti-smoking groups are able to present the powerful argument that smoking is harmful to health and that sale of tobacco products should be restricted and eventually banned. It is irrelevant to these groups that tobacco manufacture provides employment for many, and income to those countries that grow a substantial tobacco crop.

Taxation of tobacco products also provides a significant source of revenue to governments in all countries in which tobacco is sold. Many people still choose to smoke despite the increasing evidence regarding smoking and health. The 'smoking' issue involves a number of pressure and interest groups, a number of arguments, and substantial amounts of money. It is not going to be resolved easily, despite the arguments of the anti-smoking pressure groups.

Clear-sighted social and political analysis is needed to guide action towards pressure groups. Public relations and public affairs practitioners have the task of preparing this analysis and of clarifying the interests involved.

Summary

(1) The drive towards total quality, and recent recognition of the need to satisfy or 'delight' customers have focused management attention on relations with customers. Responsibility for building relations with customers could be seen as belonging to marketing staff, but public relations practitioners are also involved in a number of ways.

(2) As more emphasis is placed on relationship marketing and the need to involve customers in the strategic objectives of the organization, the division of labour between marketing and public relations staff in customer relations will need to be examined.

(3) While maintaining a steady flow of consistent information to all target audiences, particularly customers and employees, is of equal importance, investor relations demands special skills: investors read the press and watch the financial programmes, journalists talk to analysts and investors, and round it goes in a circular process which can break apart with the slightest whiff of inconsistency.

(4) How investor relations is handled is a subject of continuous debate. Many companies put investor relations under the finance director/company secretary, with the head of communications playing a strong role in presentation. Others will place it in communications, but with the finance director assuming overall responsibility.

(5) On a more international scale, investor relations is coming to the fore as companies both engage in cross-border takeovers, which means persuading shareholders of the benefits of a bid, and look for new sources of capital.

(6) All companies can reap communications benefits from joining charitable initiatives. But taking a high profile on community and charitable issues tends to raise expectations about a company's activities across the board, and donating money to charity does not solve tough issues like plant closures.

(7) Corporate community involvement is not simply 'charity', it is good business. It is also arguably the most powerful tool available to management in getting the most from its workforce.

(8) One way of enhancing corporate credibility is to set up a high-profile association with campaigners. But taking high-profile environmentalists or campaigners on board does not always work.

(9) Pressure and interest groups, activist groups in US terms, may create difficulties for companies as regulation adds costs, constrains flexibility and obstructs the relationship between companies and their customers.

(10) The task for any organization in relations with pressure groups, which should draw on the skills of competent public relations staff, is to identify which ones are to be taken seriously and which are likely to have an impact. Learning about pressure groups, and developing a response to them, is an exercise in intelligence gathering and interpretation.

Notes

(1) *Tomorrow's Company: The Role of Business in a Changing World. Interim Report. The Case for the Inclusive Approach.* London: Royal Society for the Encouragement of Arts, Manufactures and Commerce, 1994.
(2) Broughton, Martin, 'An art that deserves a high priority', *Financial Times*, 15 November 1993.
(3) *Financial Times*, 14 September 1993.
(4) Cadbury, Sir Adrian, Ethics in Business prize article, *Harvard Business Review*, 1986.
(5) Sheppard, Sir Allen, Giving the community a helping hand, *Evening Standard*, 9 June 1993.
(6) Cassell, Michael, GrandMet's life on the streets, *Financial Times*, 2 July 1993.

PART FOUR

Issues in the practice

12

Ethical and legal issues

Taking a more ethical approach

Environmental concern is the latest in a wave of social issues that have swept across industry: civil rights, equal opportunities for women, armaments, nuclear power have all been leading issues in their time. Environmental pressures take social concerns to a new height. Single issues are no longer enough. A reorientation of purpose for business seems inevitable – not just the targeting of individual companies over single issues, but a reappraisal of industrial processes, undermining some of the time-honoured systems. New targets, new performance standards and even new definitions of growth abound: sustainable development is the new buzzword taking over from 'bigger is better'.

A major influence is the effect of the liberal-minded middle classes from the late 1960s and 1970s who now have money to invest. The impact of demographics has been important as a socially conscious generation ascends the corporate ladder and brings its financial influence to bear on the market through pensions, mortgages, life insurance and equity plans. Market research has identified this new consumer of investment products. The translation of social activism into legislation, new consumer patterns and attitudes among opinion formers has created a powerful new force for change in companies.

Behaving ethically makes increasingly good business sense. In the USA, for example, there are a growing number of specialized investment houses which deal exclusively with ethical and social investment. For example, Franklin Research and Development has developed a highly detailed rating system for the companies it researches on corporate citizenship, employee relations, energy, the environment, the product (considered from a perspective of social use) and arms. It then produces its judgement or rating on whether the company is average, outstandingly good or unsatisfactory in the area being focused upon.

Box 12.1 A sample of Franklin's screening questionnaire

Employee relations

This assessment looks for such specifics as inclusiveness and equality in employment, concern for the health and creative development of workers, and employees sharing in ownership, decision-making and profits.

Questions

(1) Is the workforce (including management and board) representative of the surrounding population? Does the company have programmes inclusive of those with special needs such as the handicapped?

(2) How does the company's cash compensation compare with the industry average? Does the company provide equal pay for equal work? What is the employee turnover rate? Does the company open its employment records for public inspection?

(3) Is the company's workforce unionized? Have there been labour disputes resulting in strikes? Has the company been actively anti-union?

(4) How does the company communicate to its workforce? Does the company involve its employees in decision-making? Does the company solicit ideas and suggestions from its people? Are workers stakeholders in the financial success of the company (stock ownership plans, profit sharing)?

(5) Does the company go beyond traditional benefits to offer programmes such as day care, tuition reimbursement, subsidized meals or recreation facilities, maternity/paternity leave, sabbaticals, and so on?

(6) What is the company's policy on reductions in the workforce? Are job retraining and employment counselling offered when a worksite is closed?

Ratings

(1) The company is a unique leader in its employment practices as made evident by innovative employee participation, competitive compensation (including employee stock ownership and profit sharing programmes), a representation of women and minorities in its professional ranks equal to that in surrounding communities.

continues

continued

(2) The company has strong commitment to workers, maintains healthy work areas and generally positive management/worker communication.
(3) The company has average employee relations with no reports of strikes, employment discrimination or employee safety violations.
(4) The company's employee relations are below acceptable standards in one major area (labour disputes, employee safety, discrimination).
(5) The company has serious ongoing employee relations problems as made evident by strikes, current national labour boycotts, safety violation, or fair labour judgements against the company.

In the UK, the mid-1980s saw a broadening of interest in ethical investment – not just as a moral issue involving the churches, but as something that involved other sections of society too. The debate on corporate responsibility was picked up by other groups who defined the issue in different ways. 1984 saw a number of new initiatives that reflected the growing interest in ethical investment.

For example, in that year the British Medical Association commissioned a study of medical charity holdings and tobacco stocks, researched and published by a group called Social Audit. The report hit the headlines and was swiftly followed by the announcement from a number of medical funds that they would be selling their shares in tobacco manufacturers like BAT and Rothmans. The Royal College of Nursing decided to dispose of its shares in tobacco companies and the British Heart Foundation promptly sold its shares in a number of tobacco stocks, claiming to be 'deeply shocked at the relevation'. The embarrassment value to campaigning groups of pointing to the contradiction in their investment portfolios was considerable.

In May 1985, the London listings magazine *Time Out* published details of the Royal Society for the Protection of Cruelty to Animals (RSPCA) investments in companies conducting animal experimentation – including two which the RSPCA itself had criticized in a report to the Home Office. The accounts were rejected at the RSPCA AGM as a protest against the society's investment policy. More recently, the Worldwide Fund for Nature's shareholdings in companies against which it was running campaigns were exposed by staff leaking details of the investment portfolio to the press.

Ethics has taken root as a discipline in universities and business schools across the USA, the UK and elsewhere. There has been a growing interest in the issue of business ethics among companies: almost one-third of large UK companies and four-fifths of their US counterparts – an example is Levi Strauss (see Figure 12.1) – have codes of ethics. These can be both guiding principles, and can set specific policies about purchasing, environmental behaviour, and so on.

An international survey[1] by The Conference Board found that corporate ethics codes 'once regarded as a reactive phenomenon to deflect cyclical outbursts of public distrust of business institutions... now enjoy a broad base of support within individual companies' (see Figure 12.2).

Harvard Business School was forced to ponder what is still more a theoretical than a practical subject when it was endowed with a US$20 million dollar gift for the teaching of ethics. The electrical retailer Dixons has endowed £1 million for a chair of business ethics at London Business School.

Courses on business ethics are not short of material. Past case studies include Nestlé selling powdered milk to developing countries which it was alleged resulted in babies' deaths – and this shows how long the taint can linger around a company name – to the more recent ones like the Guinness scandal, Robert Maxwell, and the 'dirty tricks' campaign by British Airways against Virgin Airlines.

Case 12.1   BA/Virgin

British Airways, the 'world's favourite airline', according to its advertising, was shaken to its foundations when small but nimble competitor Richard Branson accused it of 'dirty tricks' in wooing Virgin passengers to transfer to BA. This included tapping into Virgin's database, and offering all sorts of inducements to people to switch.

What made it worse was that the executive directors denied all knowledge, eventually putting the blame on the head of public affairs and an outside consultant. Not only did BA have to pay a High Court settlement and apologise to Branson, but the effect on staff morale was sapped by the Virgin affair, while damage was done to a carefully built up corporate reputation.

The pressures on business are mounting, and increasingly social investors wield big money. The ethical consumer is an established marketing concept. The legal framework is also tightening through initiatives like the Superfund Law in the USA and the Social Contract Directive in the EU. Even bankers are beginning to mutter about 'hidden liabilities' in companies that do not conform to standards – in the EU, in fact, banks are likely to be held liable for companies they have lent money to and which face multi-million pound costs for cleaning industrial sites they have polluted.

LEVI STRAUSS & CO.

Mission Statement

The mission of Levi Strauss & Co. is to sustain responsible commercial success as a global marketing company of branded casual apparel. We must balance goals of superior profitability and return on investment, leadership market positions, and superior products and service. We will conduct our business ethically and demonstrate leadership in satisfying our responsibilities to our communities and to society. Our work environment will be safe and productive and characterized by fair treatment, teamwork, open communications, personal accountability and opportunities for growth and development.

Aspiration Statement

We all want a Company that our people are proud of and committed to, where all employees have an opportunity to contribute, learn, grow and advance based on merit, not politics or background.

We want our people to feel respected, treated fairly, listened to and involved.

Above all, we want satisfaction from accomplishments and friendships, balanced personal and professional lives, and to have fun in our endeavors.

When we describe the kind of LS&Co. we want in the future what we are talking about is building on the foundation we have inherited: affirming the best of our Company's traditions, closing gaps that may exist between principles and practices and updating some of our values to reflect contemporary circumstances.

What type of leadership is necessary to make our Aspirations a reality?

New Behaviors

Leadership that exemplifies directness, openness to influence, commitment to the success of others, willingness to acknowledge our own contributions to problems, personal accountability, teamwork and trust.

Not only must we model these behaviors but we must coach others to adopt them.

Diversity

Leadership that values a diverse work force (age, sex, ethnic group, etc) at all levels of the organization, diversity in experience, and a diversity in perspectives. We have committed to taking full advantage of the rich backgrounds and abilities of all our people and to promote a greater diversity in positions of influence.

Differing points of view will be sought: diversity will be valued and honesty rewarded, not suppressed.

Recognition

Leadership that provides greater recognition – both financial and psychic – for individuals and teams that contribute to our success.

Recognition must be given to all who contribute: those who create and innovate and also those who continually support the day-to-day business requirements.

Ethical Management Practices

Leadership that epitomizes the stated standards of ethical behavior.

We must provide clarity about our expectations and must enforce these standards throughout the corporation.

Communications

Leadership that is clear about Company, unit, and individual goals and performance.

People must know what is expected of them and receive timely, honest feedback on their performance and career aspirations.

Empowerment

Leadership that increases the authority and responsibility of those closest to our products and customers.

By actively pushing responsibility, trust and recognition into the organization we can harness and release the capabilities of all our people.

Figure 12.1 Levis Strauss & Co.'s code of ethics (*Source*: The Conference Board)

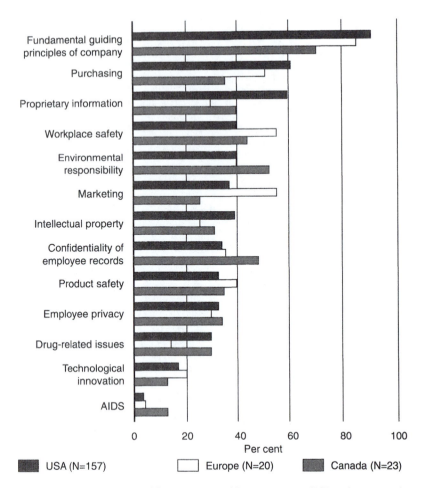

Figure 12.2 Issues addressed by company ethics statements (200 code companies responding). (*Source*: The Conference Board)

Environmental issues

Environmental regulations are rapidly becoming a major issue for corporations around the world. In Europe, environmental rules have traditionally been regarded as a technical matter, compared with the more highly articulated US approach. And, until relatively recently, rules in Europe were set by the individual countries.

Now, however, the EU is becoming more involved in setting a wider range of environmental regulations and standards. The net result is a complex web of regulations at the local, national and EU level which could ultimately produce a more stringent regime than that of the USA.

Whatever the rights and wrongs of a position, companies, particularly those in vulnerable areas deemed major polluters like chemicals or oil, have to have a carefully thought out and implemented 'proactive' communications policy, one where messages are received and understood, about their environmental stance. A few years ago, for example, chemicals concern Albright & Wilson received a lot of unwelcome publicity when a group of Greenpeace campaigners 'plugged' a pipe spewing 8 million gallons a day of discharge from the company's detergents and phosphates factory into the Irish Sea. The company was breaking no rules. It had scientific and business arguments on its side. But it had not made sure that its position on the environment was well enough understood so that its defences proved surprisingly ineffective weapons against the simple and emotional Greenpeace message about the effect of the pollution.

John Elkington[2] tells the tale of W.R. Grace and Co., the US chemical company:

'A senior vice-president wanted to hang an aerial photograph of their Curtis Bay plant in his office. The plane duly flew low over the plant and photographed the operations. When the prints were blown up, they showed a two square mile red stain from pollutants leaking into nearby Chesapeake Bay. "Do something about that," barked the vice president. The public relations department had it dealt with immediately. They airbrushed the spillage from the photo.'

Companies which already face more stringent national legislation, both in the USA and Europe, and/or those that already deal across borders and have made the toughest standards their corporate norm, understand that the environment is either at the top, or close to it, of the list of big issues they face. While they might squirm slightly under the growing avalanche of restrictions, they realize that reaction to events is no longer an option – they have to get their environmental policies translated into reality, and be seen to do so. They also have to form a close relationship with those that make the rules, at both local and regional level.

As director of external relations, Cesare Annibaldi, explained, the environmental question at Italian car-maker Fiat is a broad one and covers the processes, the products, and the wider issue of perception.

'Traditionally in the past we have concentrated on the processes, making sure that Fiat plants would not affect the environment with waste products, emissions and so on. Being mostly a mechanical group we historically didn't have the impact on the environment that a chemical plant might have.

'In the last five or six years the sensitivity related to the use of the products has increased. So we want to demonstrate and prove that our interest doesn't stop when the vehicle rolls out of the factory, but goes well beyond that. We have taken specific steps, many of them very tangible and others related to communications, in those areas we believe are most important and where public opinion sees it as a priority like emissions. Then there are areas like recycling of products.'

But Fiat also has wanted to demonstrate its environmental policy in a less direct way by working with city councils in Italy to try to improve traffic mobility and alleviate jams. For example, it has been sponsoring emissions testing in Rome and Milan.

Thus integrating environmental criteria into the heart of corporate practice will be one of the key competitive challenges for the 1990s. For instance, there is a growth of whole new markets for both products and services relating to the socially responsible company – such as waste disposal, emissions monitoring, design consultants, environmental auditors and energy conservation consultants. Ecotec, a UK-based waste sector consultancy, estimates that the European market for waste management alone in 1989 was £23 billion.

Far-sighted companies see their new concerns leading to a transformation of their business and recognize the need to make both a short- and a long-term response. Volvo, for instance, has evolved a strategy which says that in the long term car-makers cannot survive. Environmental pressures and the rising price of fossil fuels as shortages emerge will mean that public transport will come to dominate the economy, as private transport does now. Hence the company has been diversifying into other areas like traffic planning. Short-term changes of strategy include major breakthroughs in paint spraying which remove the need for solvents through a shift to water-based paints and innovatory work in developing three-way catalytic convertors. As the company has stated in a brochure, 'Our products create pollution, noise and waste.' Hype is not intended as a new by-product from the greening of the company. One of the key components of the Volvo strategy, in fact, is an internal and external information plan emphasizing the responsibility of the president for managing the information issue.

Box 12.2 3M

Some companies have made a feature of good behaviour. It is written into their corporate strategy and seen as fundamental to their success. One such favourite among environmentalists is the Minnesota Mining & Manufacturing Company, more commonly known as 3M. Founded in 1902 as a sandpaper manufacturer, it is now involved in industrial and consumer products and information technology.

As one of the largest coating companies (it makes Scotchguard and Scotchbrand adhesive tape) it has traditionally used solvents to dissolve its adhesives. The solvents evaporate and pollute the air. It was a concern for profits rather than the environment that originally motivated the company to reduce pollutants in the mid-1970s. In 1975, when anti-pollution legislation was being passed at state and federal level, the US economy was in recession. The management decided then that to meet new anti-pollution standards, it should find ways to prevent pollution rather than rely on the installation of costly anti-pollution equipment. The result was a programme to encourage employees to prevent pollution at source in the products and manufacturing processes rather than just removing it after the fact.

In the mid-1980s, the company decided that it should not only meet government anti-pollution standards, but also stay one step ahead, reasoning that exceeding standards would alleviate worry about problems down the road and allow it to keep its eye on business matters. The long-term goal is to eliminate or reduce all releases to the environment by 90% – including air, land and water – by 2000.

The company argues that its policies on the environment have paid off financially. For example, in the 15 years since its programme, 2700 new projects have been developed which have resulted in total savings of US$600 million from materials recovered or not lost, and pollution control equipment that did not have to be installed. It also represents business saved by having a new process, since the company has in some cases kept customers by changing formulations to solvent-less ones which met their needs better.

The company's plant managers are trained to educate employees and the local communities about the chemical processes and accident prevention mechanisms in place at each plant. They communicate regularly with local legislators, people who live near the plants and the media, inviting them to tour the plants. That has made it easier for the firm to gain zoning variances, as well as environmental and construction permits.

It also has helped raise employee morale and the stature of the company in the local community. 3M has a strong employee and community relations record on an international level as well. It is committed to hiring locals rather than US citizens and invests in local plants and equipment wherever possible.

Decisions about enviromental purity when it comes to products are currently hampered because of variations in what 'green' means. It has come to embody a wide range of opinions about the environment. This has led to discussions about setting up an eco-label for Europe as a whole, following the introduction of standards at national level, most notably Germany's Blue Angel scheme. The EU Eco-Label Award Scheme, adopted in March 1992, can be applied to products that 'have reduced environmental impact during their entire life cycle'. It does not apply, however, to food, drinks, pharmaceuticals or dangerous substances; nor does it displace or preclude national initiatives.

Environmental communications is thus not a passing fad but a serious business which is here to stay. That case was put by William J. Koch, director of corporate communications at US-based waste management company Laidlaw, to the 1993 meeting of the Public Relations Society of America conference. But from his observations, most environmental communications fail for the following three reasons:

(1) they are either rooted in 'technicalese' or over-simplified to the point of triviality;
(2) they are more often than not shrouded by concerns of legal liability;
(3) they are largely reactive, not proactive.

Activist groups, as he pointed out, rarely suffer from any of these problems. So Koch suggested getting back to basics.

(1) Know who your audience is and where they are coming from. Too many environmental communicators talk jargon. As Koch said: 'No wonder the emotional appeals of the environmentalists have a better chance of changing behaviour – at least the listeners know what they're talking about.'
(2) Throw away risk communication theories. Koch commented: 'All you can communicate is trust and credibility. And to do that, you have got to build genuine, lasting relationships with your stake-holders. This is an ongoing process that requires constant attention and a consistency of interaction.'
(3) The environmental communicator has to sensitize the rest of the organization, or the client, to the process. As Koch said 'Managers at all levels need to understand the context in which they operate – how the public views their actions.'

Summary

(1) Environmental concern is the latest in a wave of social issues that have swept across industry: civil rights, equal opportunities for women, armaments, nuclear power have all been leading issues in their time. Environmental pressures take social concerns to a new height. Single issues are no longer enough. A reorientation of purpose for business seems inevitable – not just the targeting of individual companies over single issues, but a reappraisal of industrial processes, undermining some of the time-honoured systems.

(2) Behaving ethically makes increasingly good business sense. In the USA, for example, there are a growing number of specialized investment houses which deal exclusively with ethical and social investment.

(3) In the UK, the mid-1980s saw a broadening of interest in ethical investment – not just as a moral issue involving the churches, but as something that involved other sections of society too. The debate on corporate responsibility was picked up by other groups who defined the issue in different ways.

(4) There has been a growing interest in the issue of business ethics among companies: almost one-third of large UK companies and four-fifths of their US counterparts have codes of ethics. These can be both guiding principles, and can set specific policies about purchasing, environmental behaviour, and so on.

(5) The pressures on business are mounting, and increasingly social investors wield big money. The ethical consumer is an established marketing concept. The legal framework is also tightening through initiatives like the Superfund Law in the USA and the Social Contract Directive in the EU.

(7) Environmental regulations are rapidly becoming a major issue for corporations around the world. The EU is becoming more involved in setting a wider range of environmental regulations and standards. The net result is a complex web of regulations at the local, national and EU level which could ultimately produce a more stringent regime than that of the USA.

(8) Whatever the rights and wrongs of a position, companies, particularly those in vulnerable areas deemed major polluters like chemicals or oil, have to have a carefully thought out and implemented 'proactive' communications policy, one where messages are received and understood, about their environmental stance.

(9) Environmental communications is thus not a passing fad but serious business which is here to stay.

Notes

(1) *Corporate Ethics Practices*. New York: The Conference Board, Report No 986, 1992.
(2) Elkington, John, *The Green Capitalists*. London: Victor Gollancz, 1989.

13

The future of public relations

A key management task

The leading US academic writer on public relations and communication management, Professor James Grunig, suggested in his book, *Managing Public Relations*,[1] that the future for the practice looked bright, but not for many current practitioners. His argument was that the tasks involved in public relations are increasingly important in management, but practitioners are not, as a group, sufficiently qualified, skilled, or credible to be able to provide senior management with the advice and service they need. There are, of course, many exceptions to this point, but it does indicate some features of the future of public relations practice.

In future, public relations, involving skilful management of important relationships and communication with groups of people on whose support any organization depends, will come to be regarded as a key task for senior management. Sir John Harvey-Jones, a former chairman of ICI, has gone on record to suggest that the chairman of any major company has two principal tasks: strategic planning and public relations. A question for the future is how will this task of senior management be carried out, and by whom?

Public relations practitioners will need to develop their qualifications and skills, or will find that their role will be usurped by others, possibly management consultants, or advisers from other areas such as marketing or law.

There is a pressure to force public relations into a marketing framework. In this, public relations is seen as marketing support, or as part of promotional activity within the marketing mix. As such, the practice is seen as a collection of communication techniques, carried out by staff working as communication technicians.

One view of the future of the practice sees public relations practitioners joining the ranks of management consultants, providing advice in the area of management in which they now claim expertise. Some consultancies questioned for this book have already redefined themselves as communication management consultants, to position themselves to take advantage of this development.

The reputation of consultants

Public relations consultants generally have a much less secure reputation than other categories of consultants. One of the main reasons is that clients have both misunderstood and devalued public relations as a management function. On the other hand, consultancies can be their own worst enemies by behaving in ways that can verge on the unprofessional or incompetent.

In an informal survey of companies around Europe carried out in conjunction with this book, senior in-house communications managers were asked what problems they had encountered with consultancies. The following answers are listed in order of number of mentions:

- don't understand the company/products
- overrunning budgets
- ineffective contacts
- too many junior staff
- poor communication with clients
- not international enough
- not proactive enough
- too many changes in the account team in a short period of time.

One company, however, was honest enough to admit that the blame lay with its inadequate briefing and lack of clarity about its corporate identity.

The somewhat shaky reputation of consultancies seems belied, however, by the sheer growth in their numbers. For a profession more scorned than saluted, there is an awful lot of lucrative work around. But the nature of that work is changing as clients are becoming more sophisticated in their understanding and use of public relations and are demanding a higher level of service, including a more strategic under-standing of the company and its markets. This has been fuelled by the rise in both stature and power of the in-house communications experts who have a much clearer idea of what their companies need. This desire for more control and for more measurable results has seen a shift away from retainer work to one-off projects, with the consequent effect on the way consultancies have to operate.

Issues

There are some substantive issues consultants have to face over the next few years as the client–consultant relationship comes under much more critical review. These include:

(1) demonstrating that they can have the ability to offer more added-value service by having a better understanding of strategic implications of what their clients do and a tactical grasp of the work needed – in other words, to be true 'consultants' as opposed to 'agents';

(2) improving both their specialist skills and their understanding of their clients' markets;

(3) making quality a major preoccupation. This will affect not only the skills offered and the ability to measure their effectiveness, but also the way they run their businesses. This will entail more of an emphasis on the principles of total quality management as their clients become more TQM-focused;

(4) spreading the message of self-regulation throughout the industry, particularly in the sensitive areas like financial public relations and lobbying, before regulations are imposed on them;

(5) coming to terms with growth. As consultancies polarize between big international firms and more local niche players, middle-sized con-sultancies will have to rethink how they operate.

While being seen as offering a more 'strategic' service is, of course, the Holy Grail pursued by all consultants, there are signs that the top rank of public relations is moving slowly to the higher ground. In the USA the buzzword is 'counselling'. Sue Bohle, for instance, runs a 16-strong public relations consultancy in Los Angeles: 'In my firm I feel strongly that our role is counselling. That means giving advice about our business to clients and telling them if we don't agree.' Over half of Bohle's work comes from high technology companies, however, which have long embraced public relations as a strategic tool, considering it vital to positioning and success: 'Venture capital firms in the US insist that new firms that they finance have PR firms from day one. It is nothing for a company of under $5 million to spend $100,000 on public relations,' noted Bohle.

But the view that public relations is moving several notches up the strategic scale is also echoed in Europe. Guido Bellodi, managing director of consultancy GCI Chiappe Bellodi Associates in Milan, believes that the modern consultancy will not survive with specialist skills in areas like lobbying, consumer affairs and so on alone: 'You need strategists. You need someone who is perhaps not a specialist and who knows a bit about it all, but who has a very philosophical brain and can put a strategy together.' Added to that is the demand for efficient management: 'It is an entirely different job to service clients and serve the company,' he says.

Being a niche player by no means precludes a consultancy from being involved in top-level strategy. Brunswick Public Relations, a small London firm, has won attention in the field of financial public relations for its success in campaigns like ICI against Hanson and the BTR bid for Hawker Siddeley. Managing director Alan Parker founded the firm with a specific vision:

'Consultancies went through almost exactly what the securities industry went through in the mid-1980s when they all decided they could go integrated, go public, go global, go everything. They found new partners, took capital out of the business and ended with a lot of people who had expanded well past their ability to manage or deliver consistent and progressive quality of service.

'The opportunity for Brunswick was to look at a much more stable base to attract and hold the best quality people in town who were interested in practising in a framework almost exactly like the best brokers, bankers, lawyers and accountants. Our view was that the models were not those of ad agencies, which public relations companies have followed for so long, but very much based on the partnership structure.'

According to Parker, corporate and financial work is characterized like public relations in general by extremes:

'At the top end of this business you are advising very important people in very important organizations about highly sophisticated problems. The bottom end is utterly ratty and is basically a charlatan's game. It is a very interesting business because it is an invented industry for a start – high growth, but no rule book. No traditions except poor ones. So you can have the fun and challenge of creating best practice and quality of service not there now.'

Two seemingly conflicting trends can be seen in public relations consultancy work: on the one hand, more work is being put on a project basis instead of retainers. On the other, consultants are being used for top level strategic advice. According to James Arnold, of US-based James E. Arnold Consultants, the former is probably a function of the increased sophistication and capability of in-house communications people and of clients generally becoming more results-driven:

'There has been an interesting development in the US. Many public relations consultancies are beginning to resemble the in-house capability of the corporate communications department. They are becoming the standby arms and legs, being brought in to augment the workforce. It is probably because the in-house manager wants more control.'

At the same time, the in-house department is 'downsizing', having to do more with less and becoming more strategic in its thinking. This is happening particularly at companies that are restructuring. Agencies will get involved strategically but, Arnold believed, it is a niche business: 'Only the very top do it at the highest level. There may be four or five of them and they are very visible.'

What consultancies in Europe have to do is decide just how much of what happens in the USA will travel across the Atlantic – and how quickly. In 1991 David Wynne-Morgan, head of Hill & Knowlton Europe and chairman of the group's executive board, recalled that:

'Fifteen to twenty years ago public relations in the US slowly began to move from general to more specific skills like takeover work, public affairs and crisis management. That started to come to the UK about five years ago and what took 10 years to do in the US has taken five to do here. Exactly the same thing is happening in the rest of Europe, but it will be done in two or three years which puts tremendous pressure on the big agencies because the rewards for success will be immense but the penalties for failure will be just as big.'

Size and skills

In terms of size and sophistication in Europe, the UK consultancy sector far outstrips the rest of Europe. This is partly because so many US multinationals chose London as a base when they first moved to Europe, and partly because of the more advanced and diverse media.

A big consultancy in continental Europe is far more likely to have 20–25 staff, compared with the 150–200 in the UK. There is beginning to be more convergence, but the disparities have not been without their

Box 13.1 Arnold survey: the future for the public relations consultancy

Issues and Trends, by New York-based James E. Arnold Consultants, analysed in 1990 the top 50 US public relations firms in terms of growth during the 1980s. It also tried to examine what the future holds for them.

The report argued that it was no longer clear what a public relations firm was: while the vast bulk were still publicity-related, a raft of new businesses had come in under the aegis of public relations, which could now cover areas like lobbying, sports promotion, point-of-sale promotion, merger and acquisition support, design, speech training, product publicity, grassroots issues campaigns, environmental and other crisis communications and much more.

While collecting data for the 1990 survey, the authors also asked executives to define a public relations firm. Some of the answers they received are telling:

- 'Each [PR firm] has its own definition.'
- 'We sell influence, empowerment.'
- 'We are chameleons. We go where the client's need is.'
- 'PR was about getting media, advising clients on how to present themselves well to the media and doing it for them. Today it is all over the lot.'

The report wondered if public relations would be the first service industry to prove that the much-vaunted one-stop shopping in communications could work. It concluded it could not: 'When service firms expand their boundaries without limit, at some point they outrun their expertise and get into trouble.' The trouble comes in trying to define those boundaries, a process the report called 'almost insuperable'. However, it came up with a definition it considered more important than any other: 'The definition that comforts a prospect seeking to retain a public relations firm by accurately and usefully describing the services and value a particular firm provides.' Or, put more simply, one which resulted in a sale of services.

Skills which distinguished public relations firms from other service companies included writing, an understanding of how to relate to journalists and verbal ability to make a case for an idea, product or service. But client demand could create a need for new skills including:

- increased ability to simplify and translate complex topics into lay language;
- an ability to measure at least some, if not all, public relations activities;

continues

continued

- better understanding of the working of politics on the local, national and international level;
- better understanding of legal and courtroom procedures and pre-trial manoeuvring;
- efficient service delivery skills which could compete with in-house public relations delivery costs;
- broad strategic business understanding that could define corporate communications usage and redirect it for competitive advantage;
- multilingual and multicultural sensitivity to adapt local, national and international boundaries.

It concluded that not only will public relations have to offer more strategic skills, but the practice could also see the development of a new type of professional – what it called a 'private sector diplomat' who is 'heavily relationship-oriented'.

advantages: the very youth of the public relations industry in countries like Germany Italy and Switzerland, plus quite different and in some ways less demanding media, have meant that public relations has had a slightly better reputation and attracted entrants from backgrounds in economics, the law and languages. It is not surprising that some of the skills which Americans are learning from Europe include dealing with environmental issues and corporate positioning.

The skills offered, however, do vary substantially depending on what each market wants. Take Switzerland. As Dr Hans Balmer of Dr Hans Balmer AG, noted:

> 'Ten years ago public relations meant press and lobbying. Five years ago that spread to more multimedia services as private radio stations began. Large companies began to issue securities so financial PR has become more important, while non-profit organizations began to think about public relations.'

What seems inescapable is that consultancies will have to respond to the client drive towards integrated communications, towards sending out a consistent message across all horizontal and vertical divides. What this does not mean is that the client simply hands over all public relations to a multiservice consultancy. On the contrary, companies are beginning to 'cherry pick' consultants according to where they judge they have strategic or tactical 'holes'. A diversified company might have on its books a con-sultancy that handles brand work, one that covers business-to-business in a particular industrial sector, and one that monitors the media, all coordinated by the same manager.

Alternatively, there could be a number of consultancies working for different parts of the company around the world: it will be the responsibility of the more powerful in-house communications executives to ensure that they are all rowing in the same direction, even if the actual work is geared to local conditions. This will include a close liaison with managers of other service providers, like advertising and direct marketing.

Those consultancies that do offer a wide range of skills have to make sure they can put together teams of specialists with the right skills. One client, for example, might need strong corporate communications advice, crisis management, product marketing and lobbying in Brussels. Another could want takeover advice, employee relations, and a campaign aimed at a particular audience. And that matrix of skills offered by consultants has to be allied with a demonstrable grip on what are increasingly complex industrial sectors. Take health-care and high technology. Consultants have to prove that they can penetrate issues like EU directives on pharmaceuticals and the changes in the UK health service at both the strategic and the tactical level in order to be able to explain the long-term implications for their clients. In high technology, the advent of more open systems lessens the dependence of customers on particular technologies which means that high technology companies of all sorts will need help in rethinking how they position their products.

Another key to survival will be investing in skills before the client actually needs them. In financial public relations, for instance, PR consultancies that will really move ahead could be those that can provide a research-based investor relations service on databases to their clients. The shareholder base is as important a property for the company as is the product or the brand. It has to be managed and given attention. Also companies are increasingly making decisions about the sort of shareholders they want and the level of relationship they want with them. And, if the USA is anything to go by, the shareholder base is becoming more demanding of information, of understanding, and of having a say in terms of corporate governance.

The relationship with advertising

What this all means is that the shape of public relations consultancies could substantially change over the next decade, as they move out of the shade of the advertising agencies: during the 1980s, public relations firms were seen as one of the useful adjuncts to advertising's move into global one-stop shopping. For example, marketing services group WPP bought advertising agency J. Walter Thompson, which itself had snapped up Hill & Knowlton, along with Ogilvy & Mather, which had its own extensive public relations subsidiary. But the perception of advertising as a more sophisticated profession meant that agencies with public relations capability often treated it as a poor relation, thus decreasing the effectiveness of the practice.

Sir Tim Bell has seen both advertising and public relations at first hand. In advertising for 25 years, he now heads up Lowe Bell Communications. One of the high profile figures in communications because of his work with the former prime minister Margaret Thatcher, he believed that in the mid-1980s the public relations sector was not a happy mix with advertising. He said:

> 'The advertising industry doesn't like public relations – it thinks it is an inferior skill, if it is a skill at all. But ad agencies who hated and despised public relations bought public relations companies in the 1980s as they went public. It was hopeless for these companies to be run by people who despised them. They were starved of investment and starved of love.
>
> 'The definition of advertising is the use of paid-for media space to inform and persuade. The definition of public relations is the use of third party endorsement to inform and persuade. Clearly the use of paid for space means you have control over content, tone of voice, timing and so on. With third party endorsement you do not. The net result of that is that advertising thinks public relations is an inferior skill because it is so risky. And public relations thinks advertising is grossly inferior because it is so absolutely easy. What neither side faces up to is that the greatest skill is the ability to decide who you want to talk to, what you want to say, how and when – and that is communication strategy, and whether you are doing it to fill out an ad or put a story in the press is utterly irrelevant.'

Bell found that his move into this end of the business did not make much of a difference to the way he operated: 'My last 10 to 15 years in advertising was about management and strategy so it was not a very big jump. It has been about clients and business and creating communications strategies.' And while the advice changes as issues do, Bell reckoned the process was still the same:

> 'God used the Bible – a great publication that sold more copies than anything else. To this day publishing a book is an absolutely classic technique and a powerful means of communication. What

has happened is that other things have been added to it. But I don't think the validity of the process has changed: the truth works, dishonesty doesn't.'

One of the big problems public relations consultancies have faced in the past, he believed – and to some extent perhaps still does – is that they did not know how to value their services:

'So they would say to a client – "that will be xx thousand". And the client would say – "sorry, that is too much. I only want to spend x thousand". So the top man would give it to his assistant who would do an inadequate job and the client would say – "that doesn't work frightfully, well that PR stuff. I think we will have even less next year."'

Bell attributes this to three reasons:

(1) the client did not understand because public relations companies did not explain or even understand themselves;
(2) few consultants had found a method of keeping people in the company and growing it – the good people all left to start their own businesses;
(3) no one knew what 'good' meant. Was it the width of cuttings the next day? Was it getting name mentions?

Raising standards

The dramatic growth consultancies enjoyed in the 1980s has meant that some of these underlying problems have yet to be resolved – there was so much business around that there was little need to do any serious stocktaking. The recession has been a salutary shock for them: a number of weaker consultancies have either disappeared or been absorbed by others. No one doubts that there are still some questionable practitioners around, least of all the industry itself. But, both in the USA and Europe, leaders of the public relations field are now trying to get its house in order in several ways:

(1) putting great emphasis on education and training, both through the various professional bodies and with consultancies and companies;
(2) heightening the awareness of how total quality management will affect consultancy practice;
(3) trying to establish self-regulatory codes of practice covering both general behaviour and more particular areas like financial public relations and investor relations;

(4)   arguing the pros and cons of registration and licensing of public relations practitioners.

Consultants have usually been their own worst enemies when it comes to the state of their own image: fielding enthusiastic but unprepared junior staff, less-than-clear billing practices, lack of measurement – all these charges have been levelled at them by unsatisfied clients. Organizations like the UK's Institute of Public Relations (IPR) and the Public Relations Consultants Association (PRCA), along with their American and continental counterparts, are trying through education and training to begin to improve both the substance and thus the image of the profession.

It is commonplace to hear bodies like this – which count a relatively small percentage of all practitioners as members – derided by people who work in public relations, who call them ineffective. But, as Sue Bohle, in 1991 president-elect of the Counselors Academy, which is part of the Public Relations Society of America, argued: 'It is up to us in the profession to make them better and so improve the image of public relations itself.'

One of the most topical questions in Europe is: what should the educational basis for training for public relations be? Is it a general university/college degree? Is it a series of training courses in skills like writing or events management? Is it a spell working in a company in a line management role? Or is it learning on the job? There are as many opinions as there are consultants.

In the USA it is not uncommon for students to get either first or second degrees in public relations, or a more general marketing degree with public relations as part of it. Canadian-born Joan Wasylik, European corporate communications manager for Cargill, believed that:

'Having a degree in public relations doesn't make you better but it ensures that you have at least been exposed as a student to standard practices, codes of conduct, ethical techniques and so on. You have had a chance to look at case studies, see what works, what the current trends are, how it has changed, what the history of the profession is.'

What that gives, she felt, is a framework in which to operate:

'You also come out with skills that should make you able to go to work right away. Obviously those skills have to be honed through expertise, but the basic learning curve should have been accomplished: you can write, you can put together a budget, you know the elements that go into it. You can put together a strategic document: it may not be as good as someone with 10 years' experience, but you know at least the elements of it. You have also been trained to write in a journalistic format because if you look at it from a marketing standpoint, my customer is someone who is reading the material I have prepared and they expect a standard of writing.'

What this also means is that juniors enter a consultancy armed with at least some basic skills. As Wasylik said,

'The fact that you have to train these people to write in an agency is not a particularly effective way of doing things: that person is not producing while you are training them. And from the client side, I do not want somebody in here who can't write because I have better things to do than edit the person I am paying to do the copy.'

Many large consultancies solve the problem by running training schemes for graduates. What the Institute of Public Relations is trying to do in the UK is to go some way in emulating the USA by starting further back down the educational line. From 1992, for instance, the IPR changed its membership rules dramatically to try and raise standards among individual practitioners:

(1)   Applicants will need to have at least four years' substantial experience in public relations and have suitable academic qualifications approved by the IPR. This includes degree courses currently being set up in a number of higher educational institutions.

(2)   Alternatively, they can either have 10 years' public relations experience, some of it in a senior role, or be already highly qualified in other professions.

As John Lavelle, IPR executive director, said, 'We are not trying to say that this is an exclusive club. We are trying to raise standards. Public relations has seen a lot of second jobbers moving in – people like barristers, medical people, accountants – and it would be crazy to keep them out.' Lavelle's long-term goal is to push the IPR along the same road as what is now the UK Chartered Institute of Marketing, which has striven over the years to raise its profile by bringing a stronger awareness of marketing to business. 'But that won't come until we get the educational thing right and people are exposed to what public relations can and can't do, on the way up to the boardroom,' he said.

There are a lot of critics of the moves in both the USA and Europe of a more stringent approach to what has been such a maverick industry. However, as Sue Bohle argued,

'Public relations needs good PR. We continue to struggle with the image of our profession and the only way we can change it is to be professional people. I look at most of those people who won't take a test as being more afraid than honest with their comments.'

Consultancies could find a more professional approach being thrust upon them as they get swept up by the total quality movement. The emphasis on setting up accredited procedures and processes backed up by measurable results of customer satisfaction could have enormous implications for the public relations firm of the 1990s.

Allied to that is the question of licensing, or registration. This is another area of heated debate. On one side stand those who argue that some sort of licensing, registration, or whatever is important for public relations to rid itself of bad practices and hence improve its image. On the other are those who fiercely maintain it will kill the creativity essential to do it well, that it will make what should be an art into a science.

But those internal arguments could well become meaningless if rules are thrust upon them. The UK industry has been trying to pre-empt any move by bodies like the EU to consider regulation by promoting strict codes of practice, defining professionalism both in general terms and in specialized areas such as financial public relations and lobbying, the latter a practice already under scrutiny by the UK House of Commons.

Shandwick chairman and chief executive Peter Gummer was, in 1991, firmly in the pro-registration camp:

> 'At the moment, people can go out and put a shingle on the door and say they are a PR consultant, as I did. That is a dangerous situation, because public relations is immensely influential. You learn an immense amount of private and confidential information, particularly in City and takeover work. Unless there are certain codes of behaviour which everyone adheres to, that will be abused. At the moment there is no penalty but even worse, no commercial penalty.'

He would start with the obvious area of financial public relations, registering firms with the Stock Exchange:

> 'And once that happens, the rest will follow. I know we are an increasingly deregulated society, but you wouldn't want to de-register banks, stockbrokers, solicitors or accountants. I am 100% in favour of having a system which stops people from abusing what is an enormously powerful tool.'

Gummer worried that,

> 'Sooner or later someone will get caught doing something totally unacceptable. As a result they will find themselves at the centre of a major scandal and then the whole of public relations will be brought into disrepute. We have achieved hard won growth, and the last thing we need is for the whole damn thing to come falling around our ears because of some stupid behaviour. Then we would probably be faced with punitive legislation and regulation beyond anything we have ever dreamt.'

There is also the encroachment of the EU into communications in general. As Colin Thompson, director general of the PRCA and secretary of the ICO, said,

'We talk about the communications industry. One of the problems we have is that because we don't have a universal language within Europe, by the time you translate one word from one country into another language, the meaning chamfers or gets thinner. Communications is one. I am at the moment appealing – demanding would be a better word – for public relations to be identified as a separate discipline and to have no connection with the advertising industry at all.

'There is a lot of pressure on advertising on what may or may not be advertised on the screen. I don't want legislation to sweep in from Europe that says there will be no communication on this subject. I actually went to the appropriate directorate and said, this is what advertising is, and this is public relations, and there is no connection. I don't think they understand. But it is like anything else – you say it enough until they get sick and tired of you.'

Questions of growth

As if consultancies did not have enough to contend with, they have to think like any other business about growth. On the one hand, they need to tighten up on cost control, sharpen up management skills, exploit information technology and inculcate better business controls in general. On the other hand, they have to find ways to expand. That is one reason why public relations firms all over the world are eyeing the European market as a potential gold mine, full of public relations issues just waiting to be resolved. The big firms already have well-established European networks; now the middle-sized ones are scrambling to offer a more cohesive international service by forming themselves into networks, both formal and informal, or linking into existing ones. The problem for all of them is that although there is very little international business yet, they have to spend the money upfront to be in place when it does appear.

Peter Hehir, chairman of Countrywide Communications, which is linked into the international Omnicom network, believed that although there is a lot of myth about the actual amount of international business, consultancies have to demonstrate that the capacity to handle it is in place.

Shandwick chairman and chief executive Peter Gummer agreed: 'I think most clients now want the security of having a firm which has international capability. I think they say to themselves we will want that some-time in the future, if not tomorrow morning.' The media, as much as anything, is forcing clients, particularly in financial dealings, to tap into an internationally connected network in order to have access to people who understand the local markets:

> 'When I went public in 1985, the *Financial Times* had only just started appearing in the US. Now, in New York, it appears with my breakfast together with the *New York Times* and the *Wall Street Journal*. The same thing in Tokyo. So if there is a bid going in London, another one could easily come in from New York or Tokyo.'

Forming networks across Europe is a route for middle-sized firms which both allows them to expand and lets them keep their independence. The private UK consultancy Pielle, for example, has joined with similar sorts of medium-sized firms throughout Europe, with each taking an equity stake in the holding company, European Communication Partners. Pielle chairman and chief executive Peter Walker has a clear idea of how such networks should operate:

> 'It is very difficult to conceive of any network working other than on a very tightly defined basis because the problems of multi-national, multicultural coordination can become quite ridiculous. Any programme which is to stretch across all 12 to 14 countries and is to be centrally coordinated will probably be issue or brand driven and have a simple, single focus exercise because otherwise the nuances of communication become almost impossible.'

Other middle-sized consultancies are being bought up by large international groups. GCI Chiappe Bellodi Associates joined the GCI network – owned by the advertising group Grey – in 1987. Guido Bellodi saw it as inevitable: 'If we look at other industries the trend is globalization so that if big multinationals are growing through acquisition, and are present in many markets, they are our clients and we have to be able to service them in more than one market.'

One notable trend already mentioned that is bound to affect the service consultancies offer is the move by the public relations industry to acquire the quality standard which involves undergoing a rigorous examination of procedures and the establishment of accredited processes. Countrywide Communications was the first registered public relations consultancy in the UK to have reached part one of the standard. As Barry Leggetter, joint managing director, said, his firm put a lot of effort into becoming eligible because 'I became utterly convinced that in under five years unless a PR consultancy can demonstrate that it has this quality accreditation major clients won't shortlis it. It is as important now as showing that you have an international and regional network. The quality evolution is turning into a quality revolution.'

But it is not for the faint-hearted, he said. It took a year, and cost £15,000 in direct costs and a lot more indirectly in terms of time. 'It was the greatest spring clean the company could have had.'

Another trend that will affect the industry is the move towards integrated communications, where clients will want to see evidence that their various agencies are working towards the same goals.

The debate about how public relations will evolve and at how high a corporate level it works is set to continue. John Smythe of UK communications consultancy Smythe Dorward Lambert argues that too many public relations consultancies are still stuck in the 'agentry' world, while the client base wants more thoughtful, analytical advice about areas like corporate affairs and communications:

> 'There is a dichotomy of language there. I think the idea of corporate reputation has always had much greater currency in the US, where there are fewer divisions between marketing, corporate communications and employee relations. I think the box that British PR has got itself into is a marketing services box, one that is tactical, and consumer-driven as opposed to broader managerial disciplines. I think the new discipline of corporate communications will drive PR further into a tactical box, or the traditional industry will wake up and see that it needs to welcome new thinking and broaden its horizon.'

Possible futures for public relations

There are a number of possible futures for public relations. In the first scenario, it becomes a largely technical practice, using communications techniques to support marketing activities and is involved in work on product and corporate branding, corporate reputation, market penetration and development.

In the second, public relations will increasingly become a social practice, helping organizations fit into their social environments, and working on relationships between groups to help bring about social and economic development, and to help in completing social tasks.

These futures are not mutually exclusive. Public relations is a strategic and enabling practice. To progress, it will need to mark out its agenda, and to invest in a programme of research and development to do this.

Summary

(1)   In future, public relations, involving skilful management of important relationships and communication with groups of people on whose support any organization depends, will come to be regarded as a key task for senior management. A question for the future is how will this task of senior management be carried out, and by whom?

(2)   Public relations practitioners will need to develop their qualifications and skills, or will find that their role will be usurped by others, possibly management consultants, or advisers from other areas such as marketing or law.

(3)   Public relations consultants generally have a much less secure reputation than other categories of consultants. One of the main reasons is that clients have both misunderstood and devalued public relations as a management function. On the other hand, consultancies can be their own worst enemies by behaving in ways that can verge on the unprofessional or incompetent.

(4)   The somewhat shaky reputation of consultancies seems belied, however, by the sheer growth in their numbers. For a profession more scorned than saluted, there is an awful lot of lucrative work around. But the nature of that work is changing as clients are becoming more sophisticated in their understanding and use of public relations and are demanding a higher level of service, including a more strategic understanding of the company and its markets. This has been fuelled by the rise in both stature and power of the in-house communications experts who have a much clearer idea of what their companies need.

(5)   There are some substantive issues consultants have to face over the next few years as the client–consultant relationship comes under much more critical review. These include:

   (1)   demonstrating that they can have the ability to offer more added-value service by having a better understanding of the strategic implications of what their clients do and a tactical grasp of the work needed – in other words, to be true 'consultants' as opposed to 'agents';

   (2)   improving both their specialist skills and their understanding of their clients' markets;

   (3)   making quality a major preoccupation;

   (4)   spreading the message of self-regulation throughout the industry, particularly in the sensitive areas like financial public relations and lobbying, before regulations are imposed on them;

(5) coming to terms with growth. As consultancies polarize between big international firms and more local niche players, middle-sized consultancies will have to rethink how they operate.

(6) There are a number of possible futures for public relations. In the first scenario, it becomes a largely technical practice, using communications techniques to support marketing activities and is involved in work on product and corporate branding, corporate reputation, market penetration and development.

(7) In the second scenario, public relations will increasingly become a social practice, helping organizations fit into their social environments, and working on relationships between groups to help bring about social and economic development, and to help in completing social tasks.

Note

(1) Grunig, J. (ed.), *Excellence in Public Relations and Communications Management*. Hillsdale, New Jersey: L. Erlbaum 1992.

Bibliography

Barrows, D.S. and S. Morris (1989). Managing public policy issues, *Long Range Planning*, **22**(6), 66–73

Broom, G. and Dozier, D. (1990). *Using Research in Public Relations Practice: Applications to Program Management*. Englewood Cliffs, New Jersey: Prentice-Hall

Coates, J.F. (1986). *Issues Management*. Mt Airy, Maryland: Lomond Publications

Confederation of British Industry/KPMG (1990). *Employee Involvement – Shaping the Future for Business*. London: CBI/KPMG

Confederation of British Industry (1991). *Competing with the World's Best*. London: CBI Manufacturing Advisory Group

Confederation of British Industry (1993). *Innovation – the Best Practice*. London: CBI/Department of Trade and Industry

Coulson-Thomas, C. (1992). Communicating for Change, *Internal Communication Focus*. Feb./March

Crable, R.E. and Vibbert S. (1985). Managing issues and influencing public policy, *Public Relations Review,* **XI**(2), 3–16

Cutlip, S., Center A. and Broom, G. (1994). *Effective Public Relations* (7th edn). Englewood Cliffs, New Jersey: Prentice-Hall

Department of Employment (1993). *Investing in People: the Benefits of Being an Investor in People*. London: HMSO

Dilenschneider, R. (1991). *Power and Influence: Mastering the Art of Persuasion*, London: Business Books

Dunn, S.W., Cahill M.F. and Boddewyn J.J. (1979). *How Fifteen Transnational Corporations Manage Public Affairs*. Chicago, Illinois: Crain Books

Economist Intelligence Unit (1990). *Managing the Environment*, No. P025. London: EIU

Economist Intelligence Unit (1991a). *Building a Pan-European Image*, No. P501. London: EIU

Economist Intelligence Unit (1991b). *The Greening of Global Investment*, No. 2108. London: EIU

Economist Intelligence Unit (1991c). *Marketing 2000*, No. 2126. London: EIU

Economist Intelligence Unit (1992). *Why You Need Public Relations*, No. P654. London: EIU

European Centre for Public Affairs (1991). *Information Material.* Oxford: Templeton College

Foehrenbach, J. and Goldfarb S. (1990). Employee Communications in the 90s: Greater Expectations, *IABC Communications World,* May/June

Grunig, J. (ed.) (1992). *Excellence in Public Relations and Communications Management*, Hillsdale, New Jersey: L. Erlbaum

Grunig, J. and Hunt T. (1984). *Managing Public Relations.* New York: Holt, Rinehart and Winston

Innovation Advisory Board (1993). *Getting the Message Across: Improving Communication Between Companies and Investors.* London: Innovation Advisory Board, Department of Trade and Industry

House of Lords Select Committee on Science and Technology (1991). *Innovation in Manufacturing Industry.* London: HMSO

International Association of Business Communicators (1991). *Excellence in Public Relations and Communication Management, Data Report and Guide.* San Francisco: IABC

Jones, B.L. and Chase H. (1979). Managing public policy issues, *Public Relations Review*, (2), 3–23

Kotler, P. (1986). Megamarketing, *Harvard Business Review*, **64**(2).

Kotler, P. and Mindak W. (1978). Marketing and public relations, *Journal of Marketing*, October

Lesly, P. (1984). *Overcoming Opposition: a Survival Manual for Executives*, Englewood Cliffs, New Jersey: Prentice-Hall.

Marchington, M., Goodman, J., Wilkinson, A. and Ackers, P. (1992). *New Directions in Employee Involvement.* Manchester: Manchester School of Management UMIST and Department of Employment

MacMillan, K. (1983/4). Managing public affairs in British industry, *Journal of General Management*, **9**(2), Winter, 74 –90

MacMillan, K. (1991). *The Management of European Public Affairs.* European Centre for Public Affairs, Occasional Paper 1, July. Templeton College, Oxford: ECPA

Morita, Akio (1992). *The UK Innovation Lecture.* London: Department of Trade and Industry

Olasky, M. (1987). The development of corporate public relations, 1850–1930, *Journalism Monograph*, No. 102, April

Raucher, A.R. (1968). *Public Relations and Business, 1900–1929*, Baltimore, Maryland: Johns Hopkins University Press

Renfro, W.L. (1987). Issues management: the evolving corporate role, *Futures*, October

Research International (1985). *Working in Britain: A Survey of Working People's Attitudes, Market and Opinion.* London: Research International

Royal Society for The Encouragement of Arts, Manufactures and Commerce (1994). *Tomorrow's Company: The Role of Business in a Changing World. Interim Report. The Case for the Inclusing Approach.* London: RSEAMC

Social and Community Planning Research (1991). *British Social Attitudes.* London: SCPR

Sussman, L.A. (1948–9). The personnel and ideology of public relations, *Public Opinion Quarterly,* **12**(4), Winter, 697–708

Van Schendelen, M. and Jackson R.J. (eds) (1990). *The Politicisation of Business in Western Europe.* London: Routledge.

White, J. (1991). *How to Understand and Manage Public Relations.* London: Business Books

World Economic Forum and International Institute for Management Development (1993). *World Competitiveness Report.* Lausanne: IMD

Index